MIGRATION OF FINANCIAL RESOURCES TO DEVELOPING COUNTRIES

MIGRATION OF FINANCIAL RESOURCES TO DEVELOPING COUNTRIES

Dilip K. Das

St. Martin's Press   New York

All rights reserved. For information, write:
St. Martin's Press, Inc., 175 Fifth Avenue, New York, NY 10010
Printed in Hong Kong
Published in the United Kingdom by The Macmillan Press Ltd.
First published in the United States of America in 1986

ISBN 0–312–53217–2

Library of Congress Cataloging-in-Publication Data
Das, Dilip K., 1945–
Migration of financial resources to developing
countries.
Bibliography: p.
Includes index.
1. Capital movements—Developing countries.
I. Title.
HG3891.D37   1986   332'.042   85–18345
ISBN 0–312–53217–2

To Vasanti
and the innumerable hours of
togetherness we had to do without

Contents

Preface

Transnational migration of financial resources, in various forms, comes only next in importance to international trade. It influences the relations between countries or country groups and, in turn, is influenced by it. For a long time transnational financial flows have been a significant factor of the multifaceted world economy. Capital has migrated from countries that have it to those who need it. It has been a carrier of industrialisation from its first home to the other areas of the world.

With the passage of time, the interest and concern in the resource flows have gone on increasing. During the last few years, hardly two days went by without the financial press carrying a news item on one kind of resource flow or the other, be they bilateral, multilateral or capital market flows. Along with this the professional interest has caught on, bringing serious scholars into this field, so much so that an institute named the Institute of International Finance was set up in Washington, in April 1983, for looking into various economic issues related to sovereign lending. The World Bank has gradually acquired a greatly enhanced, almost unprecedented, role and the International Monetary Fund has come to be the linchpin of the international financial system.

The international economy has rapidly changed, the changes occurring not only during the fast-growing decades of the 1950s and 1960s, but also during the slow-growth period of the 1970s and early 1980s. Let us, however, not confuse slow growth with a no-change scenario. The level of interdependence between countries and country-groups increased more during the second period. This interdependence extended to the realms of trade, monetary system and financial flows. The migration of financial resources is an integral part of this interdependence among the nations. In the early 1970s, the emergence of OPEC as a donor-country group added a new dimension to this scene. That apart, various shocks received by the international economy gave several twists to the situation. In the recent past, the dimension of total medium- and long-term indebtedness of developing countries from all sources grew as follows:

Year	Amount (in billions of $)
1955	8
1960	35
1970	60
1975	160
1980	401
1981	528
1982	582
1983	658
1984	717 (Preliminary)
1985	774 (Estimated)

(NB. These liability figures include neither the short-term debt nor the IMF credits used by LDCs.)

Thus, the decade of 1970s brought a substantial quantitative change in the external indebtedness of the developing countries. The average annual growth rate for the decade of 1970s was 22 per cent. This rate, however, fell to 14 per cent in 1980. The deceleration continued thereafter, and annual growth rate of liabilities further declined to 13 per cent in 1983, 9 per cent in 1984 and 8 per cent in 1985. The average for the period 1980–5 plummeted to 11 per cent, which is half of the average for the 1970s. The quantitative change happened, *pari passu*, with a qualitative transformation in the debt profile of the developing countries. In the 1960s, most of these flows came from bilateral and multilateral sources in the form of grants and concessional loans. Capital market flows consisted largely of suppliers' credit and direct foreign investment. Around 1970, this pattern gradually changed and a long-run shift towards borrowing from the capital market took place. In 1970, the official development assistance and capital market flows contributed 44 per cent each to the net flows to developing countries, in 1981 the share of official development assistance declined to 29 per cent of the total and that of capital market flows rose to 61 per cent. The multilateral resource flows soared from 2 per cent of the net resource receipts in 1970 to 8 per cent in 1981. Over the years, the volume and importance of capital market flows increased over those from bilateral sources.

The first intended objective of this book is to delve into the trends in the migration of various kinds of financial resource flows to developing countries during the post-war period. It begins with the bilateral flows and quantifies them for each creditor country-group for the period under consideration. That is not to say that it only presents a quantitative scenario and ends the story there. It relates the trends to the economic, financial and political events on the international scene and it tries to ordain their influence on the flows to developing countries. It also examines the terms and conditions of the resource flows, alterations in their geographical distribution with the passage of time and the changes in the sectoral pattern of allocation. It explains the trends in the background of the value and volume of the world trade, and the pattern of imports of the creditor countries from the debtor countries, essentially because it is this that determines the repaying capability of the latter country-group. Thus, it does not study the migration of financial resources in the manner of a chronicler. Inasmuch as it is a retrospective study, it has the advantages of hindsight.

The second focus of the book is on examining the resource flows to developing countries from the international capital markets. Initially, as indicated, these flows were only in the form of direct foreign investment and export credits. Subsequently, the developing countries started utilising other instruments to raise capital, i.e. foreign and international bonds, and Eurocredits and Eurobonds. An identical exercise has been performed with these flows as well, namely, a trend analysis, the variations in quantum of flows and reasons thereof, impact of economic, financial and political events on these flows, and their terms and conditions.

The third major source of external resources to developing countries is the multilateral financial institutions. The principal ones are the Bretton Woods institutions, the three regional development banks and the United Nations Development Programme. The capital flows from these institutions have again been given the same treatment as the other two kinds mentioned above.

Indubitably, the financial flows from these three different sources have three different characters and personalities. Therefore, in order to paint a complete canvas, all three need to be looked at. Based on these analyses, an attempt has been made to look into the immediate future. After a comprehensive qualitative and quantitative gleaning of facts and figures, and their analysis, an attempt has been made to see what the developing countries can reasonably expect in times to come, and why.

Compiling various statistical time-series from the primary sources and presenting them in a lucidly perceptible manner is a major task of this study. These time-series form the basic parametric skeleton around which the whole superstructure is constructed. A great deal of importance was given to their culling, and having done that the sources and the quality of data are talked about at length in the relevant sub-sections.

The first part of the book comprises the first three chapters and lays the background for the next three, which deal with the three substantive strands of analyses. The first chapter takes a historical overview of the migration of financial resources and culminates on the eve of the Second World War. Two of the most interesting periods in the history of capital flows are: the nineteenth century, particularly five decades prior to the First World War; and the inter-war period. There are lessons to be learned from this history. While the debate on the role of foreign capital inflows still flourishes, it is widely agreed that they have an impact on economic growth. These flows also mean an increase in financial dependence of borrowing countries and rising relative debt-servicing obligations. The second chapter looks into various macroeconomic aspects of capital inflows; it surveys and comments upon the various theoretical frameworks in this regard. Chapter 3 relates to the post-war economic scene in developing countries. How have the various sub-groups among developing countries performed? What were the economic circumstances in which developing countries came to be at the receiving end of the resource flows? How have their terms of trade have fluctuated? What is the international economic climate? How have they reacted to various exogenous shocks? These factors have a direct bearing on the financial capabilities of the developing countries. It is therefore a necessary prelude to what follows.

The thematic strands of the next three chapters have already been detailed in the preceding section. Chapter 4 divides the post-war period into smaller and functional sub-periods, and examines the bilateral flows, i.e. the transfer of official development assistance from the donor country groups, namely the OECD, OPEC and the centrally planned economies. Chapter 5 deals with the capital market flows; again these flows have been sub-divided into various sub-periods. The issues that Chapter 6 addresses relate to financial flows from the multilateral institutions.

I hope that the study will contribute to building a stronger foundation for international economic and financial policies and be of interest to academics and professionals in the field of development finance and economic growth.

Geneva   DILIP K. DAS

Glossary of Acronyms

ADB	Asian Development Bank
AfDB	African Development Bank
BOP	Balance of Payments
CPE	Centrally Planned Economy
DAC	Development Assistance Committee
FDI	Foreign Direct Investment
GATT	General Agreement on Tariffs and Trade
IBRD	International Bank of Reconstruction and Development
ICOR	Incremental Capital–Output Ratio
IDA	International Development Association
IDB	Inter-American Development Bank
IFAD	International Fund for Agricultural Development
IFC	International Finance Corporation
IMF	International Monetary Fund
LDC	Less Developed Country
LIC	Low Income Country
LLDC	Least Developed Country
MFI	Multilateral Financial Institution
MIC	Middle Income Country
NIC	Newly Industrialising Country
ODA	Official Development Assistance
OECD	Organisation for Economic Co-operation and Development
OPEC	Organisation of Petroleum Exporting Countries
UNDP	United Nations Development Programme
UNHCR	United Nations High Commission for Refugees
VIR	Variable Interest Rate
WEP	World Employment Programme

Text Tables

1 Transnational Flow of Long-term Resources – A Historical Perspective

ANTIQUITY

Transnational lending, in the sense of long-term capital movement across national boundaries, is perhaps as old as nation-states themselves. The financial market activities can be traced back to over two millennia before Christ, when Babylonian temples, under the code of Hammurabi, were the places for safe keeping funds for the wealthy people. They lent funds out to merchants who wanted to finance the transportation of merchandise from surplus markets to where there was scarcity. Babylon is considered one of the centres of ancient civilisation, its greatness began with Hammurabi[1] and declined with Alexander the Great. Several sections of the code of Hammurabi contain laws relating to personal property, real estate, trade and business relations. When Greece became the centre of civilisation, commerce and finance were also active. From 500 to 300 BC Athens' market-place or forum became the centre of life, somewhat akin to our shopping centres of today. Merchants solicited 'joint-stock' capital for financing their trips to Mediterranean ports, and shared gains on these voyages. As the political and economic power shifted to the Roman Empire, international – or more aptly interregional – trade was brisk, and the legal instruments such as bills of exchange widely used by traders.[2] The revival of European financial market activities after the Magna Carta in England (AD 1215) and the Renaissance continued through the period of mercantilism.

MEDIEVAL PERIOD AND THEREAFTER

Every country, at one time, was a developing country.[3] However formidable their resources and people, most nations depended initially

1

on foreign money and bankers to help them finance their trade and development. Opulent merchant and financial houses existed in the thirteenth century. The origin of banking in the Western world is traced to the thirteenth century, when merchant bankers began to appear in Italian cities. These banks also acted as tax collectors for the papacy, and engaged in money changing and supplying traders with foreign and domestic coins of correct weight and fineness. Wealthy families like the Fuggers, who granted huge loans to Emperors Maximilian I and Charles V, existed in the fifteenth century. The Fuggers were a German family who founded, in the imperial city of Augsburg, a textile business that grew into the biggest trading, mining and banking concern of that period.[4] Various sources of private and public finance made it feasible to colonise the Americas and establish European enclaves in Asia. French and Spanish government loans to Continental Congress helped finance the American Revolution.

It was in medieval Europe that capital and enterprise started reacting for the first time, and the profession of banker was born. These bankers, not money lenders, were international in their vision. Expansion of trade was encouraged by the Crusades against Islam. The wool workers of Florence, who imported bales of wool from Spain, England and north Africa, were financed by Florentine merchants, whose savings subsequently helped finance the Renaissance.

Italy was in the van of contemporary civilisation, while England was considered to be a developing country on the fringes of Europe. During the earlier centuries of this period Italy was wealthy, its commerce and industrial arts were well developed, its merchants were experienced and well supplied with capital. They traded with every European country west of the Rhine, where the Anglo-Saxon conquest had wiped the slate clean of all survival of Roman civilisation. In modern parlance England had a low 'creditworthiness' because of its despotic monarchs, its tribal wars and corrupt courtiers. Although its exports of wool promised lucrative profits,[5] as agricultural production increased, a natural symbiosis established between the industrial regions like Italy and the Netherlands and the primary producing countries, including England. Italian capital started going into productive investment in Europe. The most active merchant and financial houses were: the Bardi and the Peruzzi in the early fourteenth century, and the Medicis in the late fourteenth and fifteenth centuries. Thus sovereign lending was born.

The Medicis had established a fairly sophisticated international banking network, with Florence as its headquarters and branches in

Bruges, Avignon, Rome, Venice, Milan, Pisa, Bruges, Geneva and London. Each branch was run by a manager who shared in the profits. Their London branch over-lent to King Edward IV, and after several attempts at rescheduling the loans they were written off and the branch was shut down.[6] The large imports of gold from Latin America facilitated Europe to have a reliable common currency, which in turn facilitated the growth of banking. The fifteenth and sixteenth centuries saw the establishment of the first modern banks, two of which, the Banco di Santo Spirito in Rome and the Monte de Pietà in Naples, still exist. Owing to bad loans, poor management and lack of co-ordination among foreign branches the Italian banking houses went into a decline in the sixteenth century. Overseas trade and finance stimulated Holland to establish banks and securities exchange in 1611. The growth of capital market accelerated after the Industrial Revolution. The Lombard bankers of Italy, the East India Company, the Bank of England and the Royal Commission in the seventeenth century laid a foundation for the British financial supremacy that followed.

THE OLD CONCEPT OF ECONOMIC AID

Use of finance in diplomacy has a long history. The first diplomats to offer subsidies as a tool of foreign policy were the Renaissance princes of Italy. However, bilateral financial flows for ameliorating the economic lot of the recipient is a relatively new phenomenon. In the seventeenth and eighteenth centuries giving subsidies to manipulate the balance of power was considered a simple and pragmatic weapon. It could buy diplomatic or armed support, or neutrality. This depended upon the assumption that 'there is a definable unit of fighting power or defence power that can be had cheaper outside a nation's military establishment'.[7] This line of logic holds even today; the essential difference is that now the closeness between the intention of the grant and the performance of the recipient has come to be less certain.

In the nineteenth century, with the decline of autocratic government, the subsidy system was abandoned. It could no longer effectively buy support. Instead, government influence over the private financial flows came to serve the purpose of forming and strengthening alliances. It became an efficacious political weapon.[8] An outstanding example of this is the Franco-Russian Alliance in the last century. With the passage of time the loans became so large that the alliance became more important to France than to Russia. Later on France was to lose all its investment, and was partly responsible for it, because its loans had effectively propped up the Czarist regime and strengthened its resistance to demands of social reforms.[9]

AMERICA – THE DEBTOR NATION

The young American nation was a borrower of European capital in the eighteenth century. A big part of developmental funds came from England; other sources were Holland, France and Spain. A great deal of French capital went to America during the Revolution and Louis XVI repeatedly pledged the credit of his country in order to add to their creditworthiness, so that they might secure funds from other European nations. By the time the peace treaty was signed the Americans had borrowed $6.5 million.

In January 1790 foreign debts of the federal government, including the interest arrears, amounted to $12.1 million, all of which were payable in foreign currencies. In January 1803 this amount was $68.3 million. A process of paying the old loans and contracting the new ones was established and the government had excellent credit rating in the international market. These loans were raised in the London, Amsterdam and Paris markets, the interest rates on them was 6 per cent. Soon the states started borrowing for infrastructure construction. In fact they indulged in a borrowing orgy throughout the 1830s. They were almost free of debt obligation in 1820, in 1830 they owed to the international capital market $26.5 million, in 1835 this figure reached $66.5 million and in 1840 it touched $200 million. The states and the municipalities had mortgaged their credit so heavily that many of them were unable to maintain payments on their obligations during the depression that followed the panic of 1837. Some loans were rescheduled in the early 1840s, while others were repudiated, which cost the capital market around 10 per cent of the total holding. The US had been called one 'vast swindling shop from Maine to Florida'; for more than a decade thereafter the debts of the states were being scaled down. The Civil War was followed by a period of political and economic chaos. In 1883 ten of the Southern states were in default: Alabama, Arkansas, Florida, Georgia, Louisiana, North and South Carolinas, Tennessee, Virginia and West Virginia. One northern state, Minnesota, was also in default from 1858.[10]

RATIONALE UNDERLYING THE CAPITAL FLOWS IN THE NINETEENTH CENTURY

Most liberal economists hold the opinion that capital essentially followed economic opportunity. If the capital market decided to invest in railroads in the US, plantations in Malaya or tea gardens in India, it was evident that the productivity of capital in these areas was higher than that in the lending countries. Migration had a similar rationale. To be sure, investment abroad led to an initial outflow of capital at the cost of domestic investment, but it meant export of goods and services, also there would be an inflow of return on capital and cheaper imported goods. All these hypotheses did turn out to be true in some measure. In particular, return on capital did lead to considerable reverse flows. For England, at least, investments were more profitable abroad than at home.[11] No doubt the situation was more complex than these simple premises imply. For the recipient country the greatest advantage was the flow of capital into infrastructure projects which, in many cases, encouraged migration into these developing countries.

DEVELOPING COUNTRIES OF THE NINETEENTH CENTURY

Typically a developing country lacks capital relative to its endowment of labour and natural resources. The nineteenth-century developing countries, namely, the US, Canada, Australia, New Zealand, Denmark and Sweden, attracted a great deal of capital from Europe, particularly from England and put it to profitable use. The pattern of foreign investment shifted from government securities to private ventures during this period. Yet, most of the long-term foreign investment in the US was concentrated in public securities. For example, estimates for the year 1839 show that the US owed $125 million in public securities and $75 million in private securities. For 1853 the corresponding figures are $159 million and $63 million respectively.[12] During the latter half of this century foreign inflows shifted heavily in favour of investment in railroads and other non-governmental securities.

In Canada the purchase of foreign securities was dominated by government issues, followed by the railroad issues and the land mortgage companies. After 1880 the government issues fell back and the railroad issues became predominant. For example, between 1880 and 1889, of the total foreign resources inflows, government issues constituted $70 million, railroad issues $191 million and the land mortgage companies $49 million.[13]

Although there have been year-to-year fluctuations yet it is reasonably clear that the US was the largest single destination of external resources. The foreign capital never exceeded 10 per cent of the gross domestic investment. At the other end of the spectrum was Australia, where this figure was 50 per cent in the 1880s; it touched 70 per cent level for some years in the 1860s. It may well have been quite high in Canada.[14] Although the share in the gross domestic investment was relatively low, but external resources did play a significant role by being available in the right sector at the right time to break bottlenecks.

These countries used the financial inflows for the purchase of capital goods and creation of transport infrastructure; this helped growth of production and the export sector. This also applied to railroad financing in Egypt and India, but in these countries expansion of transport network, mining and plantations tended to create a dual economy.

The nineteenth century converted Japan from a small, feudal island empire to a great power. Japan needed financial resources for its transition in general, and in particular for unifying its railways, foster large-scale industrialisation, to equip its cities with public utilities and to acquire and develop Korea and Manchuria. To this end Japan borrowed abroad, primarily from England and then from France. Towards the end of the century it was found negotiating loans in all the main capital markets.

GOLDEN ERA OF RESOURCE TRANSFER

The half-century prior to the First World War was uniquely favourable to the free movement of financial resources, because of (1) the fact that the world was sharply divided into capital-exporting and capital-importing countries whose needs and opportunities complemented each other; (2) the coincidence of the demand for finance by countries trying to launch themselves into their economic take-off, and the expansion of the supply of savings from the mature economies; (3) the virtual absence of impediments to the international mobility of the factors of production; (4) the then prevailing gold standards, which meant that the currencies were anchored to gold and there were few exchange problems or transfer difficulties; (5) the institutional framework for international financial operations was better prepared than that for domestic operations; (6) the financial flows went on parallel with the migration of population and expansion of trade between the debtor and creditor nations; and, finally, (7) these were the years of political stability coupled with revolutionary developments in the ocean-going transport.[15]

This was the period when the free enterprise was in the full flush of vigour; the rules of the game and the conduct of the players were clearly defined. Since the foreign capital was the mainstay of economic development, it had to be enticed, facilitated, encouraged and guarded by the host government, so that the private enterprise gets on with its job of development. An attractive financial climate had to be maintained and obligations to be honoured. Debts had to be paid in full and on time. By and large countries made an effort to conform to the canons of orthodox finance and international good behaviour. This is not to say that there were no exceptions. The colonies followed the same set of rules, the doctrine of *laissez-faire* applied to them as well. They had to attract finance on their own and plan for their development with its help, and with whatever they could earn from their exports.[16]

The developing countries of today did not start borrowing substantially in the capital markets until after 1860.[17] Indeed, financial resources were as important for this group of countries as well, but they were not given high priority by the investing countries. Much of the resource flow was to the countries of higher per capita income. I hasten to add that the gap in per capita income was not large at this time. In 1850 countries now considered developed accounted for 26 per cent of the world population and roughly 35 per cent of world income.[18] The creditor countries had generated exportable surpluses in the process of agricultural and industrial growth, and sought most profitable avenues for investment.

London was unquestionably the leading financial centre of this period; under its shadow, in the latter half of the nineteenth century, Amsterdam, Berlin, Paris, Milan and New York also started serving the international financial community.[19] Holland's overseas investments and trade were focused largely on its Far-Eastern colonies, while France concentrated on African and Far-Eastern colonies. The geographically widening industrial revolution became the broad base of international financial activities. A large proportion of international capital flows during this period was in the form of portfolio investment, while direct investment took a back seat.

TURN OF THE CENTURY

All through the preceding century international finance was sterling-dominated and England was the dominant creditor; its exports of capital were of the order of 4 per cent of national income. This figure rose to 7 per cent during 1905–13. On the other side Canada was the biggest debtor; its foreign debts totalled 114 per cent of the GNP in 1900 and 111 per cent in 1910. These ratios are higher than that of the US, indicating higher Canadian dependence on foreign finances.[20] Comparable figures for the US are as follows: 20 per cent in 1899 and 18 per cent in 1914.[21] Australia and New Zealand followed the Canadian pattern and the ratio of external debt to GNP exceeded 100 per cent. However, unlike the developing countries of today, these countries had vast amounts of unutilised arable, unsettled land, and underutilised resources, so their development strategies had to be naturally more capital-intensive than the developing countries of today which have large supplies of labour and relatively low land-man ratio. Little wonder that, relative to output, external capital was larger for the British dominions in the early twentieth century than for the developing countries in the second half of this century.

Foreign policy motives did underlie the resource movements, and influenced their direction, but their purpose and function were strictly in keeping with the prevailing doctrine of *laissez-faire*. Types of projects to be financed were squarely based on the return from it. Only those considered commercially viable, or necessary for promoting international trade and growth of exports, were undertaken. According to an estimate, outstanding foreign-owned assets, in 1913, were £9 500 million or $44 billion. Of these more than 50 per cent were held in Europe and North America. Latin America accounted for another 19 per cent. England, the richest creditor country, contributed more than 40 per cent of the gross credits. Over a quarter of its national wealth was held in foreign assets. These were in the form of portfolio investments in railroads, harbours, bridges, power stations and the like, thereby ensuring the exports and use of British capital equipment. The pie-chart (on page 9) shows the positions of the main creditor and debtor countries in 1914.

When Arthur Lewis estimated the amounts borrowed by various countries/regions, during this period (1913) the following picture emerged:

9

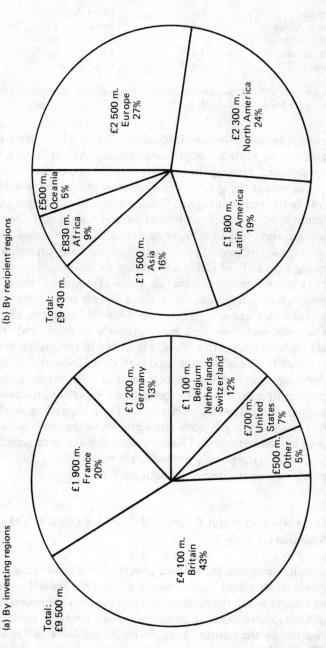

FIGURE 1.1 *Distribution of foreign capital and investments, 1914*

(a) By investing regions

Total:
£9 500 m.

£4 100 m.
Britain
43%

£1 900 m.
France
20%

£1 200 m.
Germany
13%

£1 100 m.
Belgium
Netherlands
Switzerland
12%

£700 m.
United
States
7%

£500 m.
Other
5%

(b) By recipient regions

Total:
£9 430 m.

£2 500 m.
Europe
27%

£2 300 m.
North America
24%

£1 800 m.
Latin America
19%

£1 500 m.
Asia
16%

£830 m.
Africa
9%

£500 m.
Oceania
5%

SOURCE A. G. Kenwood and A. L. Lougheed, *The Growth of the International Economy, 1820–1960* (London: Allen & Unwin, 1971) pp. 41–2.

Amount in billions of $

Canada	8.6	Other Africa	4.6
South Africa	6.3	India	2.4
Latin America	5.2	Japan	2.3
Australasia	4.8	China	2.2
Russia	4.8	Other Asia	3.3

SOURCE   W. Arthur Lewis, *Growth Fluctuations, 1870–1913* (Boston and Sydney: Allen & Unwin, 1978) p. 177.

The above figures follow the Biblical rule that to whom that hath shall be given more. More developed countries/regions were able to borrow relatively more. Turning the logic around, the figures also evidence the proposition that the greater the investment the greater would be the growth in the recipient region. This, however, is true only if the social institutions, economic structure and natural resources of the recipient region are such that investment can yield its full potential. Both the premises hold. India could productively utilise more capital, while the absorptive capacity of China was still on the lower side.

The lessons to be learnt from this period of economic history are that high foreign debt levels can be sustained and are compatible with long-term economic growth. Where the financial resources are utilised productively and their repayment properly planned, and when the world trade continues to expand, experience of the British dominions shows that it is feasible to service high debts. Nonetheless there are enough important differences between historical events and present conditions to make the past experience an imperfect forecaster of the future. These experiences portend that in an expanding world economy, foreign lending is both remunerative to the creditors and productive for the borrowers. There are, indeed, risks to be faced and, on occasions, repayment may be tardy, but over the long haul there are tremendous gains to be had by both the sides.

GOVERNMENT ROLE IN THE PRE-FIRST-WORLD-WAR FINANCIAL FLOWS

Although, there was little direct governmental involvement, yet the government-chartered monopolies, e.g. the East India Company, or companies in which the governments had substantial financial interest, played an active role. Inter-governmental financial dealings were carried out by the central banks. Although the Bank of England and the Bank of France were privately owned, they remained closely associated with their respective governments. Most central banks kept a part of their reserves in foreign bills, the purpose was to intervene in the exchange markets if necessary.[22] Co-operation between central banks was far from common, but in times of heavy gold losses they helped each other. There are numerous records of this kind documented in financial history. Experiences of borrowing from each other's treasuries, and the growth of financial relationships between the central banks as fiscal agents for their governments, prepared the way for future co-operation between central banks and, subsequently, for the creation of the Bank of International Settlements.

The governments kept away from direct financial involvements, but it did not deter them from indirectly protecting the interest of their investors and securing access to opportunities for foreign investment. They also influenced the direction of financial flows. On several occasions the US, British and other governments resorted to diplomatic, even military actions, on behalf of their nationals' financial interests.

Foreign policy objectives played a significant role in promoting and directing the private capital flows. National 'gains', not 'growth', was the prime mover of the flow of private capital; this is not to say that these resources did not benefit the recipients.[23] Former British governments did not have a formal policy or regulatory system, but they did induce the financers to purchase British colonial and dominion securities, and the capital market was responsive. French and German private capital was employed as an instrument for colonial expansion and for cementing political alliances, such as the Franco-Russian alliance. The German government exercised both positive encouragement and specific restraints on the flow of financial resources. For example, German finance served the official interests in penetrating the Ottoman Empire and parts of Africa, whereas curbs were placed on loans to Russia, Serbia and Bulgaria.[24] In the case of the US, financial flows to Latin America were not totally free from government influence.

SCENARIO ON THE EVE OF FIRST WORLD WAR

The year 1914 marks a watershed in the history of transnational financial flows. At the outbreak of the First World War long-term foreign investments of England, France and Germany represented about three-quarters of all outstanding international capital. The growth rate of their capital flows was close to the growth rate of the yield, which includes interest, dividends and profits. The average annual rate of return was measured to be in the vicinity of 5 per cent; the aggregate international investment tended to double every twelve or thirteen years, and the growth, it appears, was financed from the investment yields.[25] Taken as a group, in the three creditor countries, financial payments – that is, capital yields and capital investments – tended to by and large offset each other in the balance of payments.

The value of long-term resource flows by principal creditor and debtor countries has been given on pages 8 and 9. It should, however, be noted that short-term capital flows are excluded from the quoted figures. Short-term financial flows were confined to revolving mercantile credits, varying in accordance with the business performed, and to changes in the banking deposits held in creditor countries by debtor countries. These deposits were the proceeds of the loans raised but not utilised, or loans intended for servicing foreign debts.[26] A caveat here: the approximate balancing of financial items in the external transactions of the debtor and creditor countries during the second half of the nineteenth century, and up to 1914, does not indicate that other items in the balance of payments were not unaffected. First, the movement of capital from year to year naturally varied more than interest and dividends, which grew almost in proportion with the outstanding investments. Second, in individual debtor and creditor countries there was considerable deviation from the rule of thumb that capital movements offset interest and dividend payments, even over the long term.

Capital flows during the few decades preceding the First World War tended to work towards the integration of various national economies, into what may be referred to as an expanding international economy. The free convertibility of currencies favoured easy flow of goods and services. The movement of financial resources was influenced by periodic business depressions that occurred, but the apparent disturbances were of short duration. Several developing countries had begun to grow rapidly by contemporary standards during the three or four decades preceding the First World War. If they had maintained the growth rates achieved they would by 1950 have been unrecognisably affluent.[27] Instead, most of them were not significantly better off, in terms of real per capita output, in 1950 than they had been in 1913.

INTERNATIONAL FINANCIAL RELATIONS DURING THE FIRST WORLD WAR

All the major creditor countries and the US were involved in the First World War. Migration of financial resources was discontinued during the war. Also England and France sold about $4 000 million and $7 000 million, respectively, worth of foreign securities. Around two-thirds of the British liquidations represented US securities, largely railroad bonds. In addition, both the countries suffered losses as their investments in central and eastern Europe, and the Near East depreciated in value, or became valueless. The British losses on this account, estimated at $600 million, were small since at the outbreak of the war only a small proportion (approximately 6 per cent) of British investments were in Europe. The French losses, on the other hand, were large, and exceeded $4000 million or nearly half the French investment at the beginning of the war.[28] Germany was in the same boat, for the same reason, investing largely in Europe. Substantial losses were also suffered by other creditor countries, particularly Belgium and Switzerland. Sweden lost the bulk of investment made in Russia before the war.

On the contrary the US not only repatriated American securities held by the British and French investors, but also invested heavily in foreign securities. The turning of the tide had begun. According to an estimate the purchase of British and French securities were of the order of $1500 million, and total US investment abroad was several times this sum.[29] Accordingly, at the outbreak of war the US was a debtor nation. It emerged a creditor nation from the war. In addition, the US had granted inter-governmental loans to the tune of $10 billion during the war.

THE POST-WAR SCENE

Some of the most exciting and most depressing incidents in the financial history of the world took place during the inter-wars period. First, Europe was transformed from a substantial creditor to a substantial debtor. Second, New York became the leading financial centre instead of London. Why? Because of the weakening of the pound sterling, the strong export position of the US, the establishment of the Federal Reserve System, and the expanded capital market facility in the US. The British hegemony was substitued with American hegemony in the world economy. Also, a transition from sterling-dominated to dollar-dominated international financial world took place. The war had depleted the belligerent countries' resources and depreciated their currencies. This made the US the only major country whose currency remained convertible into gold, and where foreign bonds could be floated. Despite its prosperity the US financial market was new and inexperienced. This implies that although the US had the 'raw material', yet it was weak on the 'know-how' front. This is confirmed by the

1929 Stock Market crash, which became associated with a series of international financial crises during the 1930s.

During the early period of transition to peace economy the US exported financial resources in a big way. The general pace of movement of the financial resources quickened. While France became a big capital importer. Capital issues of Britain were relatively small. There was a considerable amount of short-term funds loaned by European countries; these funds were accumulated during the war as flight capital. The Netherlands liquidated a portion of its foreign investments, Sweden and Switzerland drew upon their funds abroad. These countries were eager to replenish their stock of goods even at the high prices that prevailed largely due to sudden release of demand.

There was a mild recession in 1920 and the prices plummeted; this hindered the transition to a peace economy. The American and British capital exports fell off, but France and Sweden entered into capital-exporting business. The period 1921–3 became the second transition phase; private long-term capital operations picked up, but they were dampened by political considerations and lack of monetary stability, particularly in Europe. As the barter terms of trade of primary exporting countries improved, capital was attracted to Latin America and Asia. Large importers of capital during these years were Argentina, Australia and India.[30]

During the 1920s a large proportion of capital went to the developed and semi-developed countries of that period; the developing countries of today had to be contented with trivial amounts. From 1924 to 1929 the largest capital importers were Germany, Australia, Japan and Italy, in that order. The list of small borrowers includes Bulgaria, China, Greece, Hungary, India, Iraq, Lithuania, Turkey and Yugoslavia. The developing countries of today received less capital, both absolutely and in relation to the size of their population. India and China, for instance, which accounted for 40 per cent of the world's population, each accounted for a capital influx of less than Argentina and Australia, with only 1 per cent of the world's population.[31]

During the 1920s a somewhat larger proportion, about a quarter, of the flows took place in the form of direct investment, i.e. investment by companies in overseas subsidiaries and branches. This portfolio investment was largely in the primary producing countries, and it was mostly devoted to income-generating activities, which in turn helped service the debts out of increased exports.[32] The transnatioanl cables and international telegraph were already introduced, therefore, the financial markets found it easy to acquire a new bank-dominated structure in most places. There was a huge surge of American international investment and credits in the 1920s, which was to abruptly recede at the end of the decade. The US also made large loans to the Latin American countries which were related to income generating activities. Until this point in time, as indicated, the US neither had the discriminating experience nor financial savvy possessed by England in this field; this resulted in a good deal of extravagant and imprudent lending. The foreign assets held by Americans rose from $3.0 billion in 1919 to $6.7 billion in 1924, and $8.1 billion in 1929.[33]

The US was followed by Britain and France in capital exports, also Germany and Holland managed to make their presence felt. Certain smaller European countries – namely, Belgium, Sweden and Switzerland – also turned into exporters. The outflow of funds from the creditor countries peaked in 1928. The slowing down of capital movements began in the middle of this year. The world-wide depression began in 1929. It had a heavy impact over the primary commodity prices. This rendered debtor nations unable to meet their international obligations; capital flows to them were curtailed or stopped. Debt-service ratio soared precipitously because of the fast plummeting commodity prices. The general price level of primary commodities fell by 60 per cent between 1929 and 1931.[34]

THE GREAT DEPRESSION: A THIN DIVIDING-LINE

The edifice of the international financial market tumbled with the economic depression. Its immediate impact was the wholesale default by debtor countries and sale of assets by creditor countries. The crisis set in motion a series of events which were cumulatively disastrous for the international saving-investment mechanism. The gold standard and free convertibility of currencies were swept aside by exchange control and regulation, and free trade gave way to import restrictions and bilateral trading. World trade declined in value from $34.3 billion in 1929 to $27.9 billion in 1930, and further to $13.5 billion in 1932. International flow of financial resources came to a near halt. When it recommenced after the Second World War its structure was radically different.

Insofar as the US was the largest creditor country it suffered most from the retrenchment which followed. Towards the end of 1930s US investments were far less than at the beginning of the decade. Almost all of this fall was due to the liquidation or depreciation of portfolio investment; direct foreign investment proved to be resilient. Britain received jolts, but to a lesser extent; it was because of the wider spread of its finances. Unquestionably all the creditor nations were adversely affected by the declining fortunes of the primary producing countries, who sought to reduce their debt burdens in various ways.

In a milieu of falling prices the burden of debt was found to be greater in terms of commodities and services than was originally visualised. The debtors, in effect, ended up paying more value than they received. Also, in the circumstances mentioned above, even if the debtors have the local currencies to repay, foreign currency may not be available. This milieu destroyed the marketability of portfolio capital; lenders became suspicious and borrowers reluctant because they thought they may not survive the debt. It can be visualised how the conditions of investment in 1939 were different from those in 1913. An estimate for 1938 reveals that aggregate world indebtedness of long-term account was $55 billion.[35] This estimate is not directly comparable to earlier ones. Among the source countries Britain maintained the dominating position; the significance of the US was growing while that of France and Germany declining. Of the debtor areas Latin America and Asia increased their independence of foreign resources. Canada remained a large recipient.[36]

The US became an absorber of long-term capital because of regular amortisation receipts, and because of the excess of foreign purchases over sales of US securities. The capital market could not be revived because of the exchange controls introduced by creditor and debtor countries. The direction of financial flows was also very limited: bonds floated in London were generally for the Commonwealth countries, Japan mainly invested in Manchuria. There were some flows based on geographical proximity or economic integration, such as those by the US in Canada, by Sweden to other Scandinavian countries and by Belgium, the Netherlands and Switzerland to France.

One of the principal effects of the break-down of the international economy was the elimination of a large portion of the triangular trade through which returns on foreign investments as well as the servicing of the foreign loans were done. The partial exclusion of the intermediary countries from the established trade circuits tended to reduce the effective demand for primary commodities in international markets. Since international trade and economic relations were out of joint, resources flows continued to be retard.[37]

Another change was in the movement of short-term finance. Until 1931 there existed in London and also – particularly since the mid-1920s – in Paris and New York, a large acceptance market financing international mercantile credits. The amount of credit outstanding, though variable, was considerable in magnitude. In London and New York alone at least £2 500 million was outstanding in the late 1920s.[38]

With the collapse of the gold standard and the introduction of exchange controls the international acceptance market declined in volume and importance. Except between countries united by monetary ties – say, those belonging to the sterling area – other methods of financing foreign trade had to be used.

IMPACT OF THE SECOND WORLD WAR

The consequences of the Second World War on financial flows were much the same as that of the first, save that the losses suffered by the leading creditors were far more devastating. Neither of the two principal creditors emerged from the war as net creditors. Although there was a slight increase in the long-term assets of the US during the war years it was more than offset by the increase in American short-term obligations, due to the expenditure of the government and armed services abroad. Britain was a net creditor of $21.6 billion. It emerged from the war owing about the same amount, but within the next two years became a net debtor to the tune of $2.6 billion. This dramatic change in her position came about through three main factors: (1) the sale of long-term investments; (2) an increase in long-term obligation to the US and Canada; and (3) an enormous increase in short-term liabilities, almost entirely in sterling balances.[39]

On the other side of the balance-sheet there was a marked fall in the obligations of the debtor nations. The Commonwealth countries reduced their debts by over $12 billion; this was largely due to an accumulation of sterling balances arising out of Britain's large war expenditure. Likewise, the Latin American countries benefited from an increased demand for strategic and essential materials by the US. Since their imports rose less quickly this group of countries was able to reduce its indebtedness from $11 billion to $5 billion.[40] As a result of the war, aggregate net international obligations – both long- and short-term – fell from $25 billion before the war to $10 billion after. The gross value declined less, from $55 billion to between $35 billion and $40 billion.

PRINCIPAL SOURCE COUNTRIES

England

During the latter half of the nineteenth century the financial centre of London was well nigh the greatest financial power in the world. Its strength came from its wealth and the sober yet daring energy running it. For many decades natural resources and industrial operations at home did not offer promising opportunities for capital as had those of foreign lands. The British saved about 18 per cent of their GNP, which was available for productive investment. The British capital during the nineteenth century remained the quickest to move and its distribution was the widest. In fact during the earlier decades it was the only source for countries which lay outside Western Europe. Around the turn of this century almost a half of the British savings were being loaned abroad. The strong financial institutions of this period played a role in fast expansion. The large commercial banks which financed commodity movements throughout the world were the biggest source of credit. They were assisted by the public and private banks of the dominions and colonies. Also, the boards of directors of giant British banks which operated abroad made their decisions in London. All this combined to form the strongest financial structure. There were few governments in the world to which the English did not loan. The financial market was capacious and supple enough to take care of large loans of governments. During this century most European governments had sought help.

The returns on English capital multiplied three to four times during the three decades preceding 1914, while the national income scarcely doubled. In the early 1880s the income from abroad was less than £50 million, but by 1914 it rose to £200 million.[41] In the closing decades of the last century France acquired financial muscle of some significance and Germany moved in the same direction. Both the countries followed England as a role model. English financing took to new opportunities in India, South America, Canada, Australia and the US. The alliance of 1902 with Japan increased sale of Japanese securities in London. In China, as well, the British investment grew. Only a quarter of the investment was in the form of loans contracted by government bodies; the rest was employed in private economic ventures. Much over half was used in infrastructure construction, that is, railroad, public utilities, roads and harbours. A major part of this investment was in securities yielding fixed return.[42]

The concept of financial aid to colonies was born in 1929. For the first time provision was made on a tiny scale, for assisting the colonial government in developing their economies by means of grants and loans for infrastructure. A subsidiary aim of the Colonial Development Act was to promote employment in England by stimulating the colonial economies and their demand for imports from England. The scope of this act was miniscule, so were the sums; less than £1 million a year. Less than £7 million was spent in seven years that the Act remained in force.[43] Throughout the 1930s, the theory that the colonies should be self-financing remained intact. In 1940, under the Colonial Development and Welfare Act, £5 million per annum was made available for development of the colonies. In 1945 a new Act made £120 million available for a ten-year period, to be spent on projects in the colonies.[44] In the 1950s the British aid to the developing countries of south and south-east Asia was co-ordinated through the Colombo Plan, formulated as a result of Commonwealth initiative.[45]

France

As mentioned, during the last part of the nineteenth century Paris came to rival London in making finances available to foreigners. It offered cheaper funds, rate of interest in Paris never rose as high as 4 per cent, during 1875–1914. French borrowers included the Czars, the Austro-Hungarian Empire, Turkish sultans and the Khedive of Egypt. Building of the Panama Canal was made possible by French credits. Besides, for the whole circle of the Mediterranean coast, Paris was the financial capital. During this period Asia did not attract much French capital; according to an estimate it was less than 1 billion francs in 1900.

These loans were arranged through a small group of sound banking houses, led by the house of the Rothschilds. In the first two decades of this century the bonds of the governments of Argentina, Brazil, Mexico, Italy, Japan and China, increased in market value, and they continued to offer higher yields than domestic securities. The flow of resources to Asia reached 2.2 billion francs in 1914. Around the close of the last century Russia was the largest borrower from the French financial market. The government and banks threw their joint efforts behind the successive flotations by Russia; the borrowers were both the governments as well as private enterprises.

French financial enterprises built and operated lighthouses and docks in the waters of the Mediterranean, the Black Sea and the Red Sea. In Latin America and Russia, French resources largely went into railroads, bridges, gas and power works, and ports. Investment in colonies was relatively small before the First World War, something over 4 billion francs, about a third of the total foreign holdings. Two-thirds of this were placed in the Maghreb countries, and the rest in Indo-China.[46] Nearly 60 per cent of French assets were in areas in which they might be expected to bring some political benefit.

Germany

Eighteenth-century Germany was a poor country. In the beginning of
the nineteenth century it was a rural land broken up into a multitude of
small states, but by the end of the century the industrial organisation of
a united Germany had become massive and strong. Its foreign trade
and financial market expanded fast. Its official discount rate was
seldom below 5 per cent, yet surprisingly German capital did move
abroad, and substantially. For much of the investment the German
banks were more than an agent; they were the controlling owner. There
were about 130 deposit banks in Germany, a dozen of them were large.
Branches of these banks operated throughout South America, with
lesser expansion in Central America, Turkey, Egypt, the Far East, the
Balkans and the German African colonies.

Until the end of the nineteenth century German capital moved
mainly towards near-by states, especially those on its eastern frontiers.
The governments of these countries felt bound to Germany either by
friendship or fear of the power demonstrated in the war with France. It
was in Turkey that the accumulation of German capital was most
notable. Securities of the American and Canadian railways were
another big investment. The government bonds of Argentina, Brazil,
Mexico, Chile, Venezuela and others were received in the German
financial market. German capital built factories in lines of industry in
which they were pre-eminent.[47] A co-ordinated system of German
banks was built south of the Panama Canal. Of the investment in Asia
only that in China was of importance, in Shantung they undertook
financing of railroad and mines. There was a good deal of investment in
Egyptian and Moroccan securities. More than half of the investment
was in the fixed-interest-bearing securities, especially the bonds of the
various governments.

United States

As noted the young American nation was essentially an importer of
capital, until the closing decades of the last century the outflow of
capital was negligible. The earliest American interest in foreign lending
began when the British began placing capital in Latin America in gold
and silver mining, some US citizens shared in the movement in a small
way. Their investments in the Caribbean railways also began during
this period, which was followed by flow of capital in foreign public
utilities. Early US investments in foreign utilities were almost all in

ocean and land telegraph cables. With the growth in foreign trade US cable companies rapidly expanded their facilities, laying their lines of communication along important trade routes, to Europe, the Far East, Mexico and later throughout the Caribbean. The last decades of the last century saw the beginning of a world-wide boom in the building of power plants, electric railways and telephone systems, in which America took an important part. They executed projects in England, Ireland, Mexico and Latin America.

Around the turn of the century Americans started investing in the foreign government securities. Bonds of a number of countries, including China, Cuba and Switzerland, were acquired. Russia made several bids for US capital. In the opening years of the new century events occurred that set the Wall Street dreaming of a time when New York would be the money centre of the world. The US portfolio at the close of 1914 included foreign securities from a large number of countries; the largest borrowers were Japan, England, Mexico, the Philippines, Argentina and Brazil. The outstanding amount was $747.7 million in December 1914.[48]

After the outbreak of the war the belligerent nations began borrowing in the US to help finance their purchases of the strategic materials. They borrowed from US bankers and the public until the US entered the war in April 1917. Thereafter they borrowed funds directly from the US government; these lendings virtually came to an end in 1920. An important episode of inter-war international finance was the huge flood of American credits and investments which invaded the world. Between 1921 and 1924 large issues of reconstruction loans were sold in the American market to repair the shattered financial systems and the damaged European economies. Almost all these loans were of short-term duration. The decade that ended in December 1924 was an extraordinary one in the financial history of the US. At the beginning of this decade the foreign securities amounted to $1 billion, at its close the amount was $4.6 billion, or $5.4 billion if short-term credits are included.[49] New York did become the money centre of the world. Apart from the involvement of the financial market the US government held foreign government securities aggregating $11.8 billion.

In the 1930s American loans were defaulted by countries like Mexico, Bolivia, Colombia, Uruguay, Hungary, Greece, Bulgaria and Austria. The immediate cause of default was the world depression, which enormously increased the burden of debts. But in retrospect it was easily seen that the defaults were the painful aftermath of the excessive and ill-advised lending of the 1920s.[50]

2 Inflow of Financial Resources and Economic Growth

INTRODUCTION

If any one scarce factor associated with underdevelopment should be singled out, it would indisputably be capital. This being said, it would be an over-simplification to regard economic growth as a matter of capital accumulation alone. Other factors are needed in addition, but economic growth is seldom possible without some increase in the stock of capital. An empirical study shows that compared to the US and north-western Europe, capital investment has been a more important source of growth for the developing countries (LDCs) of today.[1] For a great many of the LDCs, the inner mechanics of take-off involve a problem of capital formation, for which there are materially two ways: domestic savings and inflow of foreign resources.

In reality external financial resources come to an LDC in the form of a mixed bag of grants,[2] loans and direct foreign investment from bilateral, multilateral and commercial sources. They have a unique importance in the process of development. A country may have the ability to save more than it does, but more investment using only indigenous resources can be limiting and is not always worth while. Many LDCs find, for reasons beyond their control, that they neither can export more nor import less so as to leave a margin with which to buy those foreign capital goods and services which would make investment more productive, and so, in turn, make it worth while to save more. Indeed it is not plausible as a main explanation of stagnation in the developing countries today, but it can, for sure, be a contributory explanation of either stagnation or a very low growth rate. The fact that inflow of foreign resources can catalyse economic growth cannot be over-emphasised.

A large number of LDCs, for good reasons, cannot be expected to save enough to finance all the investment which is feasible and could contribute significantly to growth. In the past, countries endeavouring to achieve planned economic growth have found that foreign exchange constraint bites before the saving constraint. The structural bottleneck faced by Argentina, Brazil, Columbia and India is the case in point. A foreign exchange shortage adversely impacts upon the productivity of investment in general. There is a limit to the extent the import component of investment can be reduced.

THE SUPPLY-SIDE STORY

What factors determine whether capital exports result in a gain or loss for the donor economy? Theoretical literature on this issue is surprisingly slim. The productivity of the capital may be higher in the recipient country, but it does not mean that there is a net benefit to the social product in a capital-exporting country. For example, on what part of the production function the donor economy is operating would be of material importance. If there are no diminishing returns to capital the loss of output would be substantially greater than in the case of strong diminishing returns. Second, if there exists some unemployment in the donor economy, outflow of resources implies reduction in employment at home. On the other hand, outflow may not be at the expense of domestic economy if savings are larger than domestically available investment opportunities.

Resource outflows affect the volume and composition of trade and the terms of trade. The mechanics of factor movement work to equalise factor returns and decrease trade. Literature on this is rich but restrictive, because of assumptions it cannot hold in today's world of rapid technological and structural change. Movement of financial resources has both trade-creating and trade-diverting effects, and the static models, more often than not, miss the trade-creating tendencies. Few would dispute the change brought about in the composition of trade by financial flows between the donor and recipient economies, but the effect of this shift on welfare of the donor economy is difficult to designate precisely. The neoclassical view, that the terms of trade would have a secular movement against the donor economy, is generally considered dubious.[3] It seems possible that the literature over-emphasises the impact of normal international lending on the terms of trade. Hans Singer takes the opposite stance, that the terms of trade of the capital-importing countries, whose major exports are primary commodities, tend to deteriorate *vis-à-vis* the industrial, capital-exporting countries.[4]

Another aspect which does not readily draw attention is the loss of tax revenue to the donor government, had the capital been invested domestically, it would have yielded a constant stream of revenue. After a critical survey of the theoretical and empirical literature, Paul Simpson concluded that the following conditions are highly beneficial to the donor economy; (1) high capital returns abroad; (2) expanded output of the goods needed by the donor economy abroad as a result of the financial outflows; and (3) increased employment of labour or natural resources abroad, or exceptional external economies abroad.[5]

The principle of opportunity cost can also be used to determine the cost of transferred funds for the donor economy. This concept presumes that the range of alternative possibilities is not only open, but capable of being fulfilled, hence the financial resources which go out are essentially diverted from the productive capacity of the donor. Therefore they represent a loss of domestic productive capacity. This analysis is simplistic because one must distinguish between those donors whose factors of production are fully employed and those with spare productive capacity. This distinction is essential because in the former case outflow of financial resources would imply loss to the economic potential of the donor; the loss occurs because there is an opportunity cost of the outgoing capital. On the other hand, with no spare capacity, aggregate domestic expenditure is equal to national income generated at full-employment level. It can be explained by the following relationship:

$$E = Y$$

where E designates aggregate internal expenditure and Y national income. This can also be expressed as:

$$E = Y = C + I_d + X - M,$$

where C is consumption, I_d domestic investment, X export and M imports. Now if the donor economy diverts a part of its resources in the form of an export surplus denoted by A, then

$$Y = C + I_d + A.$$

But since, by definition, aggregate internal expenditure equals national income at full-employment level, then

$$E = C + I_d.$$

By substitution this becomes

$$Y = E + A$$
or $\quad E = Y - A.$

Therefore, aggregate internal expenditure is less than national income at full-employment level.[6] One can then identify the real cost of resource transfer as the loss of productive capacity.

Turning to the latter case of economy with extra productive capacity, here the resource outflow can serve a positive function – that is, helping the donor achieve full employment. We equate export surplus with resource outflow, which, like investment, has a multiplier effect. Therefore, the income thus generated is higher than the income which would be generated without A. One may infer that resource outflows for an economy with free productive capacities lead to its own benefit also by assisting it in obtaining a higher level of economic activity.[7]

In order to determine the factors governing resource outflows let us make a finer distinction between the flow aspect and the stock aspect of the financial resources. Saving, investment and capital flows are generally referred to as the 'flow aspect', because they have a flow dimension – that is, they change per unit of time. Whereas, the level of capital accumulation and external indebtednes are considerd the stock aspect, since they have a stock dimension. It is the flow aspect which determines the direction and magnitude of resource flows. The stock aspect does not have a direct effect, but indirectly it influences the flow aspect and so resource transfers. It influences the flow aspect through the mechanism of the international interest rate, time preference and the marginal efficiency of resources. An increase in capital stock, *ceteris paribus*, stimulates resource outflows. Second, for the donor economy an increase in the value of foreign securities or interest receipts leads to an increase in capital outflows through an increase in the aggregate domestic savings. Third, increase in international interest rate would increase the donor's resource outflows, provided the interest rate does not become so high that the recipient economies become chary. Fourth, an increase in donor's saving propensity or reduction in time preference increases the outflows. These relationships can be empirically proved.[8] As for the impact of outflows on donor's rate of growth, it is raised above its potential growth rate, if and only if the rate of return is higher than the marginal output–capital ratio at home.[9]

MACROECONOMICS OF RESOURCE INFLOWS

There are numerous growth theories; they all presume that external resources play a decisive role in the meta-process of growth, and that they take the recipient economy towards self-sustained growth. It is also assumed that the recipient economy would have a target of some minimal rate of growth and that it would, of its own accord, terminate or at least phase down the inflows at some unspecified time in future. Both the propositions may be unrealistic, and we may well get used to the idea that external resource inflows are there to stay for a while. Three related macro theories are briefly dealt with below:

The Two-gaps Theory

Inflow of financial resources assists the developmental process in two discernible ways: first, it adds to the total volume of investible resources, and, second, it increases the recipient's capacity to import goods and services of certain specific kinds which are of importance to development, but could not be produced domestically or produced at prohibitive cost. A vivid manner of showing the two gaps is as follows:

$$I + X = S + M,$$

where I is domestic capital investment, X exports, S savings and M imports. In an LDC S may be too small to permit the full amount of I for which the country otherwise has the capability. This is the saving gap. Secondly X may be too small to permit the needed M, even though some resources are idle in the economy. This is the foreign exchange gap.

Correspondingly the amount of inflows needed to achieve the target growth rate may be estimated in two ways: first, an estimate is made of the gross capital required to achieve the target, and the *ex ante* savings are juxtaposed next to it. The difference is the savings gap, to be filled by inflow of external resources. Second, import requirement is estimated, and the export earnings are juxtaposed next to it. The difference is the trade gap. In any real life situation the saving gap would necessarily equal the trade gap. What ultimately this implies is the excess of resources needed in the economy over what the economy is capable of producing. There is only one gap to be filled by the resource inflows. The necessary identity of savings and trade gap is brought about by a process of adjustment.

The Big Push

The name of P. N. Rosenstein-Roden is associated with this macro theory.[10] He asserts that in certain conditions the pace of development can be accelerated by undertaking a broad range of development projects at the same time. The main strand of the argument runs like this: if a wide range of productive activities are increased together, they create markets for each other's goods and so establish the conditions in which all of them can be successful. According to his doctrine one determines the amount of resource inflow on the basis of (1) how much an LDC has succeeded in increasing its volume of investment during the last five or so years; (2) the degree to which the LDC has widened the difference between average and marginal rates of savings over the recent past; and (3) an impressionistic judgement of its overall administrative and developmental infrastructure.

To sum up, the level of resource inflows is reflected in the target rate of growth of the recipient LDC, its average and marginal savings rates, and the initial and estimated capital–output ratios.[11]

Capital-absorptive Capacity Approach

In an attempt to be more precise some economists prefer to view the inflows in terms of specific capital projects, or measures designed to deal with specific limitations on economic growth. Resource requirement is based on the ability of the LDC to employ it productively; this, in turn, is determined by the rate of return on the resources deployed.

That there is a limit to capital absorptive capacity is seen in lack of worth-while projects ready for financing, delays in executing projects, and slow absorption of the committed funds. Opposing this view is the belief that absorptive capacity is not a rigid phenomenon and it only results from the inflexible attitude of donors. They, at times, are interested in financing only limited types of projects, or are not interested in small and scattered projects. High standards of project appraisal and reluctance to finance development programmes as a whole rather than individual projects are other factors which inhibit the inflow of resources.[12] The donors see this as an attempt to ensure a reasonable return on the resources, and to avoid undue substitution of the indigenous resources.

Absorptive capacity is not a clear line drawn between the inflows providing a positive benefit to the recipient LDC and the absence of such possibilities. It is a slow process, when increasing flows provide diminishing value, if efforts are made to increase the inflows beyond a certain point at a certain point in time. However, before saturation point is reached there are likely to be amounts of resources which have rather small developmental impact. The question is to decide what is the minimum ratio of developmental impact to the cost of resources that is sufficient to justify provision of additional resources.[13] The diminishing returns, mentioned above, occur due to a situation in which the domestic institutional resources and factors of production, e.g. skills, management, are stretched too thinly, with increased resource inflows.[14]

MICROECONOMICS OF RESOURCE INFLOWS

In the preceding section I have dealt with the issue in a macro manner. The next logical step is to see resource inflows in relation to specific objectives. These can be income, consumption, investment, imports and export earnings. Also, the short- and long-term implications of resource inflows have to be examined. Besides, since external resources make only a small part of the total investment, it is essential to consider the strategies for maximising their impact on growth.

A useful starting-point is to consider the circumstances in which resource inflows are desirable. Usually this issue is assessed in a macro framework, using the simple Harrod–Domar-like growth model. The results derived, therefore, are limited and only suggestive. A cost–benefit framework needs to be developed for making the right choice, and appraising the desirability of such inflows. This is because external resources can come as grants, or as loans at subsidised effective interest rate (say, a soft loan), or as hard term loans (say, on the Eurodollar market). In an economy with constraints on raising domestic savings fast, the acceptable rate of interest of a loan is determined by the social rate of discount. A comparison between the net present value of the marginal investment project financed from domestic resources with that financed from external resources has to be clearly made in order to assess the desirability aspect. The pattern of social rate of return, or the conditions for external resource inflows to be socially desirable, as developed by Lal,[16] is: they should be acceptable *in toto* if they come in the form of grants, irrespective of the country's other characteristics. On the other hand, assuming that there is no grant element in the capital inflows, and that the country does incur excess costs on its external-resource–inflow-financed imports through aid tying, and that the import content of the investment is unity, then a resource inflow is only desirable if the effective interest rate is less than or equal to its social discount rate. As the social discount rate is likely to be less than the social return to investment in most LDCs, where the level of saving is less than the socially optimal, this suggests that even if the social rate of return on investment is as high as 15 per cent, it would be worth while to borrow only at effective rates of interest that are lower than the social discount rate, say 6 per cent.

What is economically more efficient from the point of view of the donor, a loan or a grant? A loan is superior to a grant if the return on capital is higher in the recipient country than that in the donor country. If the annual rate of return in the donor economy is $7\frac{1}{2}$ per cent and that in the recipient 10 per cent then not only the recipient economy is benefiting from the transfer, but society as a whole is gaining by putting resources to work in a higher return endeavour. In this case, by return we exclusively mean financial return; it does not include the social benefits. On the other hand, should the opposite be true – that is, the annual rate of return be higher in the donor economy – then a grant would be preferable. This stems from the fact that every year in which capital is being used in the borrowing country, it could be used more efficiently in the lending country. Thus, the benefits to the recipient LDC can be cheaply given in grant form by the donor.

It was naïvely believed that external resources only finance that particular investment project for which they were meant and none other. It soon became clear that they were financing, not the projects for which they were meant, but marginal investment projects – that is, of all the projects in the programme, the one that ranked lowest on the list of priority, and had a meagre rate of return. This is what is meant by fungibility of foreign resources. Fungibility, however, does not stop at this point, external resources may even go into financing the marginal expenditure projects, which are as likely to be on consumption goods as on capital goods. Resource flows mean transfer of purchasing power from one country to another; to what use it would be put cannot be *a priori* determined. They may well be used to raise the consumption standards; if this is done as a short-term measure economic theory would have no qualms about it. Problems, however, would abound if it is continued for long.

The productivity of the external resources in an LDC is measured by the rate of increase in income and consumption. Its value depends upon the extent to which it makes fuller utilisation of the domestic resources possible. Failure to mobilise any one factor can frustrate attempts to raise growth, even while other factors have been successfully mobilised. If growth is stalled by the lack of capital there would be under-utilisation of other factors of production. In the short run, external resources are effective in relieving the shortages of savings and imported commodities, and promoting fuller utilisation of indigenous labour and skills. In the long run, what use was made of the initial increases of the output becomes more important. Even if the short-run productivity of the resources is high the LDC may continue to depend on external resources indefinitely, unless the additional output is so allocated as to increase savings and reduce the trade gap, and eventually reduce dependence on the external resource inflows.

RESOURCE TRANSFER AND ECONOMIC GROWTH

Few issues stir more debate than the subject of impact of external resources on growth. Because of its obvious political implications it generates impassioned arguments which lack straightforward economic analysis. The early literature was too simplistic and went along the line that each dollar of external resource inflow would result in an increase of one dollar of imports and investment. It was thought in the 1950s that, with the help of an assumed incremental capital–output ratio (ICOR), the impact of resource inflows on growth can be calculated. Or, to reverse the posture, it was possible to calculate the resource inflows required to achieve a target rate of growth. At this stage the Harrod–Domar-like models were in wide use, which were subsequently modified. The later models, including the modified versions of the one used by Chenery,[17] were more sophisticated and closer to reality.

The second stage models did not simplistically attempt to determine growth rate by investment alone; also, unlike the first-stage models, they did not believe that ICOR stays fixed; it was recognised that it changes with the rate and composition of investment. Secondly, domestic saving was considered an important endogenous variable, changing with the rate of growth and with other variables. Yet the basic premise remained the same, and the belief was continued that the external resources are additive to domestic savings and to domestically financed imports.[18] Although this line of thinking continued firmly and obstinately, it was hard to justify it by traditional economic analysis.

The 1970s saw a radical change in thinking, and the revisionistic era began. It was argued that the external resources have little impact on growth because they tend to work as a substitute for the indigenous savings, the rate of return on inflow-financed projects is low and the debt-servicing soon becomes a burden on the recipient economy. Temporarily the inflows may appear good because they may permit higher consumption levels in the recipient LDC, but they hardly have an effect on the long-term growth. Furthermore there were some who went so far as saying that these inflows have undesirable social and political influences.[19] There are articles which reached the other extreme, predicting no increases in growth and investment as a result of external resource inflows.[20] These challenges to the conventional wisdom did a good job of rocking the naïve views.

Papanek did a cross-country regression analysis of thirty-four LDCs for the 1950s and fifty-one LDCs for 1960s, making it eighty-five observations in all. It is conventional economic wisdom to regard investment as the major determinant of growth; in fact one study proved that investment is the only variable explaining growth.[21] By decomposing investment into its components – savings and various kinds of resource inflows – one can obtain some indication of their impact. This is, indeed, a very poor analysis, and a complete analysis would need more variables. Besides, cross-country analysis can only give suggestive results, not the definite ones.

The results given above are not unexpected; financial assistance has a coefficient nearly twice that of the other independent variables, which is reasonable. The results are in unison with another similar study.[22] The high coefficients for aid are due to the fact that, unlike other kinds of resource inflows, economic assistance is specifically designed for growth.

There are, however, voices of dissent. Griffin and Enos[23] do not associate capital inflows with economic growth. Data taken by them are those of fifteen African and Asian countries; which do support their hypothesis. Using 1963–4 data they show that there is no close association between the amount of financial assistance received and the rate of growth of GNP, the correlation coefficient is low and the standard error of the regression coefficient is high. The regression equation is:

$$Y = 4.8 + 0.18 \ (A/Y)$$
$$(0.26) \qquad R^2 = 0.33,$$

where Y is the average rate of growth of GNP and A/Y is the ratio of foreign aid to GNP.

TABLE 2.1 Regression equations

Equation		Savings	Aid	Foreign private investment	Other foreign inflows	corrected R^2	F-statistic
(1) Growth =	1.5 (2.5) +	0.20 (6.0) +	0.39 (5.8) +	0.17 (2.5) +	0.19 (2.1)	0.37	13.5
(2) Growth =	4.4 (8.7) +	0.07 (1.7)	:	:	:	0.02	3.9
(3) Growth =	4.9 (20.)	:	0.20 (3.1)	:	:	0·08	9.6
(4) Growth =	2.0 (3.3) +	0.18 (5.0) +	0.39 (5.5)	:	:	0.28	17.9
(5) Growth, Asia (N=31) =	1.5 (1.5) +	0.21 (4.2) +	0.46 (4.4) +	0.35 (1.7) +	0.13 (0.8)	0.46	7.7
(5.1) Growth, Asia and Mediterranean (N=38) =	1.1 (1.2) +	0.23 (4.5) +	0.47 (4.8) +	0.21 (1.3) +	0.12 (0.9)	0.44	8.8
(6) Growth, Americas (N=37) =	2.5 (2.7) +	0.11 (2.0) +	0.29 (1.7) +	0.19 (1.4) −	0.06 (−0.3)	0.11	2.4

SOURCE Papanek, op. cit. (1973).

The evidence for Latin America was found to be stronger. Taking the average growth rates of GNP over 1957–64 for twelve LDCs they found that growth is inversely related to the ratio of external financial assistance to GNP. The association is loose, but the indication is that as the external assistance amounts rise the growth rates fall.

$$Y = 42.97 - 6.78 \ (A/Y) \qquad R^2 = 0.13.$$

The above correlations make it hard to fight down a desire to think: 'One can do almost anything with statistics.' The following needs to be considered: First, the fit is not good, the R^2 value is low. Second, the period chosen is short and the sample LDCs are localised in one continent. Is an inverse relationship plausible? It has been noted that external resources are nothing but imported purchasing power and are a possible substitute for domestic savings. As far as the incremental output–capital ratio is higher than the cost of the resources, they would pay for themselves. Where does the question of their inversely affecting growth arise? Under this set of circumstances the LDC should borrow as much as possible and substitute foreign resources for domestic savings. In reality this explanation seldom works. The study done by Chenery,[24] for Latin America, revealed that external resources became a substitute for savings, not an addition to investment. In fact the saving rate fell and the growth rate of GNP stagnated.

An identical line was taken by Massell[25] when, with the help of a Harrod–Domar-like model, he concluded that external resources would contribute to growth only if the marginal output–capital ratio exceeds the interest rate.

At this stage we hardly find his conclusion a startling one. These resources would really contribute to growth of the LDC if they are absorbed in the economy, and a certain amount of complementary investment is generated and the required domestic resources are mobilised. Otherwise the side effect would be creation of a dualistic economy.[26]

In conclusion, therefore, the quantitative evidence available regarding the impact of external resources on the growth of the recipient LDC is far from conclusive. It matters little what time span or country group is taken as a sample. *External resources are neither a necessary nor a sufficient condition for growth.* This being said, there are certain sets of circumstances when the external resources can adversely affect the output–capital ratio of the recipient. These circumstances depend upon the motives of the donors and the recipients. Donors have various motives for extending financial help: economic growth is one of them, though political rationales predominate. (These issues have been dealt with in Chapter 4). They may be interested in giving large, highly visible projects, sometimes as a not-so-subtle monument to their generosity. This is not to say that the LDC governments do not favour massive projects for reasons of their own, in lieu of the ones which integrate well in their respective economies. The demand may create its own supply, but in the process economic efficiency suffers. Again there is the question of economy of scale for the donor organisation; it may prefer to finance one project of $20 million, instead of twenty projects of one million. This suits them better because it keeps the supervision and administrative costs down. One cannot assume that large projects have a higher rate of return than small ones. If anything the opposite may be true.[27] A tendency to alter the pattern of investment in favour of large schemes is likely to lower the output–capital ratio.

In the past, some donor agencies, particularly the multilaterals, had an ideological bias against the public ownership of productive activities. This bias led to an extra emphasis on financing social overhead capital and economic infrastructure. It is no doubt possible that in some LDCs infrastructure deserved priority, but this could not possibly justify the policy of discouraging the manufacturing sector.[28] A general bias against directly productive activity would go a long way to lowering the aggregate output–capital ratio.

RESOURCE INFLOWS AND DOMESTIC SAVING

The saving rate – average and marginal – is regarded as one of the key economic indicators, and foreign aid administrators admonish their clients to increase their saving ratio as a primary condition for achieving a satisfactory rate of economic growth. However, questions have been raised about the saving function being an independent determinant of economic growth. Also, policy-making about stepping up the saving propensities has suffered from some vagueness about the saving function in LDCs. The Keynesians and the neoclassicists have held differing views; while the former based on under-employment equilibrium made saving a function of investment, the latter considered saving as a determinant of investment. In this regard the wheel has come full circle and the modern capital-oriented growth models again consider it an independent variable, which may work as a constraint on investment, or as in the case of the two-gaps model, one of the two possible constraints on investment. It works as follows: investment determines the rate of growth of income out of which incremental saving takes place. But the marginal saving, which is a policy variable, not a fact of nature, is one of the determinants of the rate of increase in investment and so the rate of growth.

A priori resource inflows are expected to influence the domestic saving formation positively, apart from supplementing it. However, some studies have seriously questioned this effect of resource inflows on both level of national savings and the average saving rate. There exists a psychological theory of the relationship between resource inflows and savings,[29] according to this inflows of resources cause flagging of saving endeavour by the recipient government, and so average saving rate falls. In order to test this hypothesis the average saving propensity of 31 LDCs was regressed on the ratio of net capital import to GNP. The data for this were taken from the study of Chenery and Strout.[30]

$$S/Y = a + a_1 (F/Y).$$

The value of a_1 in this was -0.25 ($t = 2.6$). This thesis was later criticised for the selection of 31 LDCs. It was subsequently repeated with data for all the 50 LDCs considered in the Chenery and Strout article.[31] The new coefficient was positive (0.03), but its statistical significance was low because the t value was 0.4. The upshot is that external resource inflows have virtually no effect on domestic savings in LDCs. The next step was to classify the 50 LDCs into three groups, based on the level of Y per capita. The results of this exercise were as follows:

per capita income Y/Pop.	a_1	t	R^2
Up to $124	0.33	1.1	0.35
$125–$249	−0.02	−0.3	0.08
$250–$675	0.42	1.3	0.38

The above results show that no particular relationship exists between the saving rate and resource inflows. Only the middle category conforms to the pyschological theory of saving.

There are two more relevant studies, those by Landau,[32] and by Chenery and Eckstein[33] for the Latin American LDCs. Landau regressed saving on net capital inflow and GNP:

$$S = b + b_1 Y + b_2 F.$$

The partial derivative of S with respect to F was found to be significantly negative for 16 of the 18 LDCs, the derivative ranged from -0.2 to -0.9. In the two countries where it was postive, the coefficient was not found to be significantly different from zero. Chenery and Eckstein altered the approach a little by adding the ratio of exports to GNP in their equation, but again for the majority of the LDCs the regression coefficients of F were found to be negative. In order to increase the number of observations, and so the degree of freedom, Landau pooled data for the 18 LDCs. By so doing he obtained 307 observations to investigate the effect of F on the averge propensity to save. The new regression equation was:

$$S/Y = d + d_1 \log(Y/\text{Pop}) + d_2 \, (F/Y).$$

Results were not different; F was found to be negatively correlated with the rate of savings.

One of the best studies is by Weisskopf,[34] best because of the R^2 value, which is in the range of 0.9. He included exports in his saving function. The result was as follows:

$$S = a + 0.183 \, Y - 0.227 \, F + 0.176 \, E.$$
$$\quad (65.9) \qquad (-5.3) \qquad (4.6)$$

Time series data of the relevant variables for a period of seven years were obtained for a sample of 44 LDCs. According to this, the impact of F on S is highly significant; approximately 23 per cent of the net resource inflows substitute for domestic savings.

An amber signal needs to be given here; the picture that emerges from the above studies may be a trifle misleading. Although exports and resource inflows both provide the foreign exchange needed for investment, but what is often forgotten is that resource inflows also increase current account deficits.[35] Clearly, gross domestic savings, according to the national account relationship, does not rise even though gross domestic investment may have increased by the amount of capital inflows.

Papanek's reaction[36] to the critics is that when these studies point out the negative causal relationship between the external resource inflows and domestic savings they do not specify the saving function which lies behind their assumed relationship. He separates two saving functions from the above studies: (1) that of Rahman and Griffin, which implies that savings are basically a policy variable, and the policy-makers' keenness is blunted by the high level of external resource inflows, and (2) as indicated by Griffin, if the saving performance is determined by the available investment opportunities the resource inflows use up some of those investment opportunities and to that extent discourage saving.

If one were to look at it from the other end, external resource inflows can produce a rise in savings and substantial increase in investment. This is how it works: (1) if investment is a function of foreign exchange available for importing capital goods and inputs, then external resource inflows would increase both investment and savings; (2) if the rate of saving is determined by the rate of growth of income of the entrepreneurs, then resource inflows may rapidly raise savings by increasing the incomes of this group; and (3) there are certain kinds of financial inflows like export credits, foreign direct investment, capital market flows, etc., which are directly invested, this, coupled with the pressure of the bilateral donors to increase domestic investment, results in extra income and savings.

To sum up, there are plausible saving functions which could result in one dollar of external resource inflows producing from no increase in savings and investment to more than one dollar of addition; also no one needs to be surprised by a negative impact. Therefore the negative causal relationship, arrived at by all the critics, need not be meekly and passively accepted. In most instances there may be more than meets the eye; there may be exogenous factors influencing both the resource inflows and the saving rate. The relationship should not be direct, it is more likely to be a complex one. A statistical analysis which links a high level of resource inflows with more saving, should see if it would have been lower in the absence of inflows, and to what extent.

THE FOREIGN EXCHANGE CONSTRAINT

In the early stages of economic growth foreign exchange comes to acquire a vitally important part in the investment programme of the LDC. As noted earlier, there are many capital goods and services which cannot be indigenously produced, or can be produced only at a prohibitive cost, but are of great significance for the successful implementation of the development programme. Availability of foreign exchange makes it easy to acquire these goods and services. When a foreign exchange constraint is binding, and more often than not it is, external resource inflows can have a discernible impact on growth. It matters little if the transfer is of a small fraction of the domestically available resources. For example, Manne found that optimal use of a relatively small ($75 million) increase in foreign exchange availability to Mexico would step up the annual growth of the industrial sector from 5.5 to 8 per cent, if one agrees to, probably, overly optimistic interpretation of his results.[37] The ways to circumvent this bottleneck are: import-substitution, export-promotion and external resource inflows. But like the saving rate the possibilities of promoting exports depend upon the level and rate of growth of the LDC, and on the climate of the world market. The exports of the primary commodities can only go so far, and the basic industrial exports like textiles and clothing face protectionistic barriers in the world market. Some other industrial goods have managed to penetrate the market well, but the producers and exporters of these are a few small, outward-looking developing economies. However, with the help of the exports of light manufactured goods the so-called newly industrialising countries (NICs) have managed to grow out of their foreign exchange bottleneck.[38]

When the foreign exchange constraint exists, resource inflows from abroad would have a proportionately greater effect on the growth rate than when it does not. This can be intuitively rationalised, as expenditure on foreign capital goods will form only a fraction of the domestic capital investment.

REVERSE TRANSFER

Unless the resource inflows are exclusively in the form of grants, which they seldom are, the recipient LDC will have to provide for amortisation, interest and dividends. This inflicts a necessary penalty on the domestic saving and foreign exchange resources of the LDC. Thus external resource inflows entail an annual reverse transfer; it should be taken into account what impact they would have on the budget of the LDC in general and the foreign exchange reserves in particular. If for a moment we forget about the foreign exchange constraint, the essential condition for independence from external inflows is that the marginal rate of saving should exceed the *ex ante* rate of investment.

In the case of the capital market flows, payment obligations would include interest and amortisation. The time profile of repayment would depend upon the interest rate, and whether it is a long- or short-term loan. The unliquidated balance of each loan becomes smaller every year. While interest is charged on the net debt outstanding, annual amortisation may be $1/T$ of the original loan for T years. Intuitively a low rate of servicing indicates a prolonged period of amortisation and a low rate of interest. For instance, if a loan is amortised over forty years, the rate of servicing will be 4.3 per cent if the rate of interest is only 3 per cent, and 5.8 per cent if the rate of interest is 5 per cent. If the amortisation period is reduced to twenty years, then, even with 3 per cent rate of interest, the servicing rate would be 6.7 per cent.[39]

3 Developing Countries in the International Economy – Progress, Interaction and Integration

INTRODUCTION

A cursory viewer, casting a rapid glance, may find this chapter redundant. However, a reflective perusal may indicate how it fits into the rest of the jigsaw. In the context of resource transfer it is pertinent to look into the recent economic scene in the developing countries. What were the economic circumstances in which the less-developed countries (LDCs) have come to be at the receiving end of the resource flows? How have their main sectors, namely, agriculture and industry, performed in the recent past? What is the situation of their main sources of foreign exchange earnings – that is, their trade with the industrial countries and among themselves? What are the recent trends in their terms of trade? What is the international economic climate? How have they reacted to various exogenous shocks? These have a direct bearing on the financial capabilities of the LDCs, and the resource transfer to them from bilateral, multilateral and commercial sources. Thus, this is a necessary prelude to what is to follow in the next three chapters.

Throughout the 1970s, the LDCs – excluding the capital-surplus oil exporting countries[1] – grew at an average rate of more than 5 per cent annually, which is about two-thirds faster than the average for the industrial economies.

Between 1960 and 1980, the LDCs increased their share of global output by 21 per cent. The industrial countries now sell a quarter of their exports to LDCs, and the volume of these exports doubled in real terms over the 1970s. The economic growth has, indeed, been uneven. The dynamism is concentrated at certain poles of development. The OPEC countries and a group of newly industrialising countries doubled their share of the global output between 1960 and 1980.[2] But the other groups of the developing countries have made slower progress, and, in one case, even suffered retrogration. The Sahel countries, in sub-Saharan Africa, is one region of the world where most countries suffered a fall in per capita income over the last decade. Poverty is also pervasive in the populous nations of south Asia, but their economic performance has been encouraging. On the whole the economic performance of the LDCs has been varied, but, in more places than not, it has been dynamic. Their economies have come to acquire a certain degree of resilience. That apart, the perception of the LDCs regarding the pattern of growth has undergone substantial change. Now they no longer worship at the altar of the god GNP. Their aim is broader and they look for means of reducing poverty directly, e.g. improving distribution and employment, and fulfilling basic needs. Some regard this shift as just another fashion in a fad-prone discipline.

THE GROWTH SCENARIO

A large number of LDCs had not experienced any economic growth for centuries, their growth performance during the quarter-century (1950–75) was impressive and marked by three characteristics: (1) a rapid average growth; (2) a wide diversity in experiences; and (3) a widening gap between the relatively richer and the poorer LDCs. To give a quick run-down of the growth performance: income per capita increased by almost 3 per cent a year, with the annual rate accelerating from 2 per cent in the 1950s to 3.5 per cent in the 1960s; however, it fell to 2.7 per cent during the 1970s. This laid a base for further economic growth. These rates compare favourably with the growth rates achieved by the industrialised countries over the comparable period of their industrialisation. Income per capita grew at a rate which was well below 2 per cent a year, in most of these countries over the 100 years of industrialisation beginning in the mid-nineteenth century. Even in Japan, the fastest grower, the comparable growth rate was less than 2.5 per cent per annum.[3]

What has been said in the preceding paragraph is a trifle misleading because averages mask a wide variety of disparity in performance. On one hand, nine countries, with a combined population of 930 million people in 1975, grew at an average of 4.2 per cent or better during this period. A second group of nine LDCs grew at an average rate between 3 and 4 per cent. On the other hand, the large and poor countries of south Asia and many countries in Africa, with a total population of 1.1 million, grew by less than 2 per cent per annum in terms of per capita income. Thus, the growth rates have generally been lower in the low-income countries of Africa and Asia, where the majority of the world's poor live.[4] For about 33 per cent of the inhabitants of the developing world the per capita income has trebled, but for another 40 per cent the increase has been only one or two dollars a year in real terms.[5] Marked differences in the performance of the individual LDCs are spelled out below (Table 3.1):

TABLE 3.1   *Difference in growth rates of LDCs*

Average annual growth rate (per cent)		Number of countries	Percentage of population[a]
Less than 0		3	1
	0–2	25	48
Above	2–4	33	35
	4	11	15

[a]Share of the total population in the 72 developing countries covered. These 72 countries accounted for 88 per cent of the total population of developing countries in 1976.

SOURCE   *World Development Report, 1978.*

The disparity between the rich and the poor LDCs has increased significantly. At one end of the spectrum several LDCs concentrating on exports of manufactures achieved an impressive growth rate of 6.4 per cent a year in the 1960s, and attained a record level of 7.1 per cent in the 1970s. These LDCs, geographically concentrated in South-East Asia and Latin America, are few in number and represent only 13 per cent of the total population of the developing world, but they account for over a third of the GDP of the developing world. Their economies differ in scale and endowments, but there are certain common features: they all followed outward-looking polices favouring export promotion, they all have a high-quality labour force, entrepreneurship and an ability to respond quickly and flexibly to an adverse economic climate. At the other end the least-developed countries (LLDCs) were unable to expand production at a satisfactory rate. They also did not make a good job of absorbing the exogenous shocks, because of structural rigidities in their economies. As seen in Table 3.2, their real income did not increase in the 1960s and declined in the 1970s.

TABLE 3.2   *Growth rates of total and per capita GDP and real income in LDCs*
(per cent per annum)

	1960–1970	1970–1980
GDP		
Total developing countries	5.7	5.6
* Fast-growing exporters of manufactures	6.4	7.1
Least-developed countries	2.6	3.2
PER CAPITA GDP		
Total developing countries	3.1	3.0
* Fast-growing exporters of manufactures	3.6	4.5
Least-developed countries	0.0	0.6
REAL INCOME		
Total developing countries	5.0	7.1
Major oil-exporting countries	3.6	14.0
* Fast-growing exporters of manufactures	6.3	6.6
Least-developed countries	2.6	2.3
PER CAPITA REAL INCOME		
Total developing countries	2.4	4.5
Major oil-exporting countries	0.9	11.1
* Fast-growing exporters of manufactures	3.5	4.0
Least-developed countries	0.0	− 0.3

SOURCE   UNCTAD Secretariat estimates, based on international sources.
NOTE   The GDP series is based on annual chain-weighting of production by sector. Real income is gross domestic product adjusted for the terms of trade effect. In this table and in subsequent tables in this section (A), unless otherwise specified, the country classification used is that of the UNCTAD *Handbook of International Trade and Development Statistics: Supplement, 1980.*
* According to UNCTAD classification the following are the fast-growing exporters of manufactures: Argentina, Brazil, Korea, Singapore, Uruguay, Yugoslavia and Hong Kong.

In the 1970s about one-half of the countries recorded per capita growth less than 2 per cent per annum, the corresponding proportion in 1960 was one-third. It should also be noted that only twelve countries registered a decline in GDP per capita in the 1960s, and that about 60 per cent of the LDCs surpassed the per capita growth target set for the First United Nations Development Decade.[6]

If LDCs are divided into income groups on the basis of 1975 per capita income the relation between income and growth rate appears to be uniform. On average today's highest income LDCs grew fastest, whereas the low-income LDCs grew slowly. It is not surprising that there should be a positive correlation between income and the growth rate. The ranking of 80 LDCs by GNP per capita done by Morawetz,[7] remained remarkably stable between 1950 and 1975, while at the same time the absolute disparity between the richest and the poorest LDCs increased by a factor of three.

With the growth in output and income, substantial structural changes took place in the economies of the LDCs. The industrial sector increased its share in the total at the expense of the agricultural sector. Industry has been the fastest-growing sector in virtually all LDCs during the post-war period. Table 3.3 is a revealing one:

TABLE 3.3   *Distribution of GDP* (median values, at current prices)

	Distribution of Gross Domestic Product *(per cent)*					
	Agriculture		*Industry*		*Services*	
	1960	*1975*	*1960*	*1975*	*1960*	*1975*
Low-income countries	52	43	12	23	35	45
Middle-income countries	26	15	23	38	46	47

NOTE   Sectoral shares do not add up to 100 per cent because median values have been derived separately for each sector.
SOURCE   *World Development Report, 1978* (1979).

It would have been more revealing had it been updated to the 1980s. For the period covered it shows that for the low-income LDCs, which are also the slow-growing LDCs, the agricultural sector is still large, though its proportion has declined. Agriculture continues to be the principal economic activity in LDCs, accounting for 60 per cent of the labour force in 1978. However, as a source of income the importance of this sector had declined. In 1960 it contributed 31 per cent to GNP; this dropped to 19 per cent in 1978. The disproportionately large share of agriculture in total employment in relation to the sector's share in total value-added reflects the low productivity in this sector. One of the major structural transformations in LDCs that occurred in the 1960s was the reversal in the relative contributions of agriculture and industry to GDP.[8]

The scope of economic changes in these economies over the last thirty years or so can be visualised from the fact that many of them have modernised their agriculture and sustained high growth rates in it. Also, many of them now manufacture technologically sophisticated equipment; some are even able to compete successfully in the international market for turnkey projects. Their growing sophistication is marked by large and modern institutions of increasing complexity, ranging from industrial corporations to first-rate universities. A whole range of development-related institutions have proliferated, for example, development banks, farm credit institutions, extension institutions, training institutions, macro- and micro-planning agencies. This is not to say that all these function at peak efficiency, or all the LDCs have the needed institutions. For sure, there are gaps to be filled.

Several LDCs demonstrated their proficiency in economic management through their adjustment to a series of exogenous shocks in recent years, including: (1) wide fluctuations in international commodity prices; (2) sudden increases in oil prices; (3) the prolonged recession in the industrial market economies; and (4) the unpredictable gyrations of international exchange rates. Through measures affecting the structure of domestic production and prices, as well as external trade and borrowing, they have been able to withstand these exogenous shocks, maintain their growth and control inflation. Those following export-oriented policies have generally fared better than others.

As regards the management of their economies, a major econometric exercise was conducted by Euromoney[9] to rank each country according to the performance of its economy since the first oil price hike. The indicators chosen were: (1) real GDP growth; (2) consumer price inflation rate; (3) currency strength in terms of SDR; (4) current account balance relative to GDP; and (5) strength of exports. These were considered the most important indicators of economic health. Using a computerised technique, a country's scores for each of the five indicators were combined into a single index which measured economic achievements over 1973–83. According to the index the five best performers were developing countries, namely, Singapore, Taiwan, Hong Kong, Malaysia and Thailand, in that order. Again, nine of the first ten performers were developing countries, of which seven were non-oil and two OPEC members.

AGRICULTURAL SECTOR

That it is a crucial sector is revealed by the following facts: first, at present this sector employs 65 to 70 per cent of the active population in the LDCs, provides 35 per cent of the GDP and accounts for over 40 per cent of the foreign trade, excluding oil. A sector as significant as this must play a crucial part in the process of take-off. It would be inconceivable to think of it without the participation of such a large part of the population who are also consumers. The level of food and agricultural production of the LDCs as calculated by the Food and Agriculture Organisation of the UN is shown in Table 3.4:

TABLE 3.4   *Agricultural production indices in LDC's (1961–5 = 100)*

| | Food products only | | All agricultural products | |
	Total	Per capita	Total	Per capita
1948–52	66	90	66	89
1953–7	79	96	78	96
1958–62	92	99	92	100
1963–7	105	100	105	99
1968–72	121	101	121	101

[1] Excluding Communist countries.

Author's estimates based on *Production Yearbook 1972* (Rome: FAO, 1973); *The State of Food and Agriculture 1970* (Rome: FAO, 1970); and *Monthly Bulletin of Agricultural Economics and Statistics* (Rome: FAO, various issues).

Considering the entire period the growth rate of agricultural production was in the vicinity of 2 per cent. As may be visualised, it was far from uniform; it was moderate up to 1952 and rapid during the following decade. A slackening was visible during the 1960s. High rates of population growth were responsible for absorbing nearly all increments of production, at times even lowering the per capita food production.[10]

During 1950s and 1960s total agricultural production in the LDCs expanded at an annual rate of 2.9 per cent, which is a meritorious performance both historically (no other period is known when such a rapid growth of agricultural production was shown by so many countries) and in comparison with the industrial market economies, whose production rose no faster. Yet, the overall picture of this period is a bleak one, the reasons for which are: first, an uneven performance among the LDCs; second, uneven performance over time. For example, there was a quick rise in production after the widespread bad harvests of 1965 and 1966, but there was a long period before that when progress was extremely low. The most important snag is that the rapid and in many cases accelerating population growth in per capita terms often wipes off production gains. Food crops sector production has not kept pace with population growth during this period. It failed to keep up with population growth in 30 LDCs in the 1950s and 27 during the 1960s.[11] In LDCs, which recorded improved performance, different studies point to different reasons: it has been attributed to area under crops, fixed and working capital per hectare, level of farm technology and the size of the agricultural labour force. In fact a prudent analysis would indicate that far more than any one of these factors it is the response and adaptations by the cultivators that determine an LDC's success in increasing agricultural output and productivity.

A new variable has entered the food–population equation; it is generally referred to as the Green Revolution, and has been brought about in the rice and wheat crops with the help of chemical–biological agents. It is estimated that by 1971 about 13 per cent of rice cultivated in south and east Asia was sown with the new varieties of seeds. As mentioned in the preceding paragraph, farm production suffered in 1965–6 because of poor harvests, the very next year it leapt ahead by nearly 5 per cent, much of this increase being attributable to the use of new seeds. It is possible that the new seeds did play a role, but the real impact is difficult to measure, since there is usually a rapid growth in production after a bad harvest when the land has the time to recoup its fertility. Despite the new seeds and its expanding use, food production in LDCs increased by only 2.5 per cent between 1967 and 1972, a growth rate below that of population.[12]

The index numbers of food and agriculture production after 1972 are as shown in Table 3.5 overleaf.

Between the years 1972 and 1981 the food production in LDCs soared by 38 per cent while agricultural production increased by 36 per cent. However, this growth performance does not appear to be so spectacular in per capita terms, where it is 10 per cent for both the indicators. The reason, obviously, is population growth. The inference is that the 1970s have been better for the LDCs compared with preceding decades. Agricultural production soared with an annual rate of 4 per cent, while food production rose at an even higher rate. Also during this period, food production outpaced the population growth, leading to a hike, though a small one, in the per capita food as well as agricultural production. How much contribution was made by the Green Revolution in brightening up the agricultural picture is a moot question; yet, to be sure, it is deepening as well as spreading to larger areas in the developing world and gradually working a structural change into the farm sector.

TABLE 3.5   *Food and agricultural production in LDCs*
(1969–71 = 100)

| Year | Production | | Per capita production | |
	Food	Agriculture	Food	Agriculture
1972	102	102	98	98
1973	106	106	100	100
1974	109	109	101	101
1975	116	115	104	103
1976	119	117	105	104
1977	123	122	105	104
1978	128	127	107	106
1979	128	127	107	106
1980	133	131	108	107
1981	140	139	n.a.	n.a.

SOURCE   FAO, *Production Year Book*, vol. 34 (Rome: FAO).

MANUFACTURING SECTOR

Industrialisation has been one of the cardinal objectives of the development policies in LDCs in the post-war period. The degree of industrialisation is frequently used as an indicator of the stage of development an LDC has acquired. According to the UN Statistical Office, which compiles the index number of industrial production for all LDCs, the picture emerges as follows: between 1948 and 1953 the pace of growth accelerated at an annual average rate of 4.4 per cent, or about 2.2 per cent per capita. Between 1953 and 1956 the rate of growth was rather high, reaching 9.5 per cent, or 7.3 per cent per capita. Between 1956 and 1970 growth rate was high though it was below that of the last period, 6.5 per cent or about 4 per cent per capita for the whole period. It should be noted that per capita growth rate of 4 per cent in manufacturing is fairly close to that attained by the industrialised countries since the end of the last war. Besides, during the eighteenth and nineteenth centuries, when these countries were on their way to industrialisation, their growth rates were lower at about 2 per cent.[13]

Table 3.6 below set out changes in the index numbers of industrial output of the LDCs since 1953 in some of the main sectors of industrial activity. In the initial periods, heavy industries, e.g. steel-making,

TABLE 3.6 *Index of production in manufacturing industries in LDCs*
(1963 = 100)

	1953	1958	1970
1. Light industry	60	82	144
2. Heavy industry	39	67	179
3. Total manufacturing industry	50	73	158

SOURCE *The Growth of World Industry 1938–1961* (New York: United Nations, 1965).

played a large role in the immense growth of manufacturing. The rate of growth in heavy industry was far higher than that in light industry, they were 7.4 per cent and 4.4 per cent, respectively.

Prior to the Second World War heavy industries were almost completely absent in the LDCs. After their independence priority was accorded to these sectors, with more or less justification. Besides, the myth of steel works and catalytic-cracking towers looming over the horizon, as a symbol of economic progress and independence was widespread among the policy-makers of LDCs; these large mills having a halo around them in the 1950s, and succeeding in creating an illusion of progress. The conversion of other metals, although rapid, was relatively slow in growth. Another fast grower was paper-making industry–although admittedly, the original level was extremely low. The creation and expansion of oil-refineries was responsible for the relatively high rate of growth in the chemical sector. In contrast, in the initial stages the slow expansion of light consumer industries, e.g. food and textiles, in most LDCs must be emphasised. This is especially true of Latin America, where these sectors hardly kept pace with the growth of population.

Paul Bairoch[14] compared the LDCs with the developed countries at their corresponding stage of industrialisation, and concluded that African countries are at a lower level of industrialisation than the western countries were when they were still in their 'traditional' stage. The present level of Asian LDCs (excluding China) corresponds to those in the developed nations in the first few decades of their industrialisation.

The growth in manufacturing industries in the LDCs started picking up in 1969. In fact this period can be clearly divided into two: pre- and post-1969. The first was one of rapid industrialisation throughout the world and the LDCs roughly matched the pace of the industrial market economies. As a result their share in the manufacturing value added (MVA) remained unchanged despite their larger proportion of the world's population and lower level of per capita income. During the second phase LDCs recorded minor but steady gains. The general economic climate during this phase was first characterised by continued growth, followed by recession. Despite the vicissitudes the share of LDCs showed annual gains in each year during this period.

TABLE 3.7   *Share in manufacturing value-added (MVA) (1960–80) (in per cent)*

Year	LDCs	Industrial market economies
1960	8.2	77.8
1965	8.2	76.2
1970	8.8	72.6
1975	10.3	66.7
1980	10.9	65.3

SOURCE *World Industry in 1980* (Vienna: UNIDO, 1981).

The insensitivity of the LDCs' industrial sector to the cyclical fluctuations could be due to several factors: First, LDCs are less subject to a deceleration in the demand for capital goods because the capital goods sector plays a very small role in most LDCs. Second, the export growth of LDCs was aided by the rapid inflation in the industrial market economies in the recent past.[15] Industrial progress, however, has not been uniform among the LDCs, the share of Africa has remained unchanged over the twenty-year period under review. Manufacturing in South and South-East Asia enjoyed a period of rapid growth before 1978, but recession in the West broke down the growth momentum in many of them. Since the successful economies of this region are export-oriented, new protectionism slowed them down.

A study of all the LDCs with population more than 10 million (in 1980).[16] was undertaken, it concluded that the manufacturing output did grow fast in all the 41 LDCs, which qualified for the study. The manufacturing share of their GNP grew substantially, in 1950 the median manufacturing share was 10 per cent, in 1980 the median had risen to 16 per cent; 12 out of 41 countries were in the 20 to 30 per cent range, which implies that they were approaching the structural characteristics of the developed countries. In most of the LDCs falling in Asia and Latin America, but not in Africa, import-substitution in consumer goods is now substantially complete. Over half a dozen have substantial exports of consumer goods. Except in China, Brazil and India, import-substitution in intermediates is less far along the way, many of the LDCs in this study were found to import one-third to two-thirds of their requirements of the intermediate goods.

The diversity in performance is not only among the LDCs, but also among industrial sub-sectors. Growth in eleven industrial sub-sectors (out of twenty-seven) accelerated after 1976. Most of the expanding activities were closely related to the processing of raw materials or natural resources, e.g. food, beverages, tobacco, wool products, paper, petroleum-refining, iron and steel and non-ferrous metals. However, two disturbing trends emerged after 1976: First, several sub-sectors that were important sources of export and employment recorded lower rates of growth, e.g. textiles, clothing and footwear. Second, the rate of growth in the capital goods industries also declined relative to the pre-1976 years.[17] Admittedly, these branches had only a small share in the manufacturing sector's total output, but a slow-down in their growth would have serious implications for national development objectives of several LDCs.

TRADE

Around the 1950s some LDCs and the African colonies depended heavily on a handful of commodities for exports. Presently most of them have diversified their agricultural exports and some of them have taken to export of manufactures in a substantial manner. The commodity concentration of their foreign exchange earnings has declined. The creation of trading blocs like the EEC, the US, Japan, and CMEA played a decisive role in it. So has the trade among the LDCs themselves, which has grown although inadequately. Various attempts at formal integration schemes in this regard had mixed success because of politico-economic disruptions. South and South-East Asia have done better in this regard; trade among these countries has been growing, albeit slowly.

Because of the Great Depression psychosis it was generally believed in the 1950s that the net effect of industrialisation of LDCs would be negative on their manufactured imports.[18] An empirical study analysing this issue showed that industrialisation had a stimulating effect on the manufactured imports, the opposite of that expected.[19] By early 1960s LDCs were paying increasing attention to the export potential created by their continued industrialisation. They aimed at increasing efficiency of their manufacturing sector by participating in international specialisation made possible by the gradual liberalisation of the world trade.

An interesting shift in the pattern of world trade between the 1950s and the 1970s took place, the share of manufactures and fuels rose steadily and that of primary products steadily declined. The reasons were: (1) the lower income elasticity of demand for foodstuff than for manufactures; (2) the effect of protectionist agricultural policies; (3) supply problems in the exporting countries; (4) the declining input of raw materials per unit of manufactured output; and (5) the growing substitution of synthetics for natural raw materials.[20] These changes in demand and supply affected the exports of the LDCs; in the early 1950s the non-oil LDCs predominantly exported primary products, which fell to 47 per cent of the total by 1976. Likewise the share of manufactures in the total exports more than trebled; in 1976 it stood at 35 per cent. On the import side manufactures remained the most important product group, accounting for over a half of the total imports in 1976 for non-oil LDCs, and more than 80 per cent for the oil-exporters.[21]

After the first oil-price hike (the period 1973–80) the annual increase in the volume of imports of LDCs was $6\frac{1}{2}$ per cent, the fastest growth being recorded by the imports of manufactures. The industrial market economies continued to be the main suppliers during this period, though their share of the total declined. The share of oil-exporting LDCs in the total imports of the non-oil LDCs reached 20 per cent in 1980, whereas exchange among the non-oil LDCs stabilised at around 16 per cent. Exports by the non-oil LDCs increased by an average of 6 per cent per year during the same period. Industrial countries remained the main market for them, though their share declined from 70 per cent in 1973 to 62 per cent in 1980.[22] The share of non-oil LDCs in world exports of manufactures rose to 9 per cent in 1980, most of the rapid increases were recorded by exports of engineering products, steel and chemicals. Exports of miscellaneous finished consumer goods (footwear, travel and sporting goods, furniture, etc.) also grew rapidly, while exports of clothing rose with a less than the average rate. Two important categories, namely, textiles and miscellaneous semi-manufactures (plywood, leather, paper, etc.) recorded the lowest rates of growth over this period.[23] The share of the non-oil LDCs in world exports of non-fuel primary products remained unchanged at around one-quarter, with an increase in the share of agricultural raw materials being offset by a decline in the shares of ores, minerals and non-ferrous metals.

An explanation is in order for the fact that the rate of growth of exports by the non-oil LDCs did not decline despite the recent slow-down in the industrial market economies. There are three main points to be made: (1) the mutual trade among the LDCs expanded more rapidly than their exports to industrial market economies; (2) in the industrial world imports slowed down much less than domestic de-mand (or production), particularly in the case of manufactures; and (3) the growing importance of subcontracting abroad.

To sum up, since 1965 exports as well as the production of manufac-tures grew faster in the LDCs than in the industrialised market economies. With growth the manufacturing sector underwent a struc-tural change and diversification, which led to a change in the product composition of exports from LDCs. The basic impetus for this comes from the development process itself, but, to be sure, the appropriate policy-mix accelerates it, and more and more LDCs are beginning to compete in the international market in an ever-lengthening list of products, processes and activities. Some of the Far-Eastern economies pioneered in adopting the right policy-mix in the 1960s; there are other LDCs which are following suit. The latest converts are Sri Lanka and Thailand. The effect of this policy was not limited to the manufacturing sector alone; it was pervasive and has influenced numerous primary products and processing industries and services. The share of manufac-tures in LDC exports soared from 13 per cent in 1960 to 38 per cent in 1981.[23] Within the manufacturing sector some exports expanded much faster than others. Technically sophisticated products and finished goods were among the fast-growers, while products which suffered a decline have already been noted earlier.[24] Exports of sophisticated products come from the relatively advanced, 'top-tier' LDCs. This observation also applies to finished manufactured goods where product design and delivery must be closely tailored to customer demand. On the other hand, the less-developed and smaller exports do better in standardised semi-finished products and a wide range of other pro-cessed natural-resource products.

COMMODITY TRADE TRENDS

Although the share of primary commodities in the total exports of LDCs has fast declined over the last few decades, they still are a source of about half of their foreign exchange earnings. In value terms, in 1960 the non-oil LDCs earned 84 per cent of their foreign exchange by exporting primary commodities; for 1979 the corresponding figure is 47 per cent.[25] If we consider commodities in one group, the enormous increases in the price of oil over the past decade has tended to eclipse the large increases in the prices of other primary products which took place over the same period. Many of these prices, particularly those of minerals, began to rise sharply before the quadrupling of oil prices in 1973–4, and, having risen to very high levels in the early 1970s, most of them have tended to remain there. Commodity prices have been much more sensitive to changes in the world economic activity and demand in the post-1973 period than they were during the 1950s and 1960s – that is, following the Korean War boom.

Two of the most widely employed composite indices of commodity prices are those compiled by the UN and *The Economist*. The two sets of indices show a broadly similar pattern of changes in commodity prices. Figures 3.1 and 3.2 show a slight but steady decline in commodity prices, measured in dollars, between the Korean War boom and the early 1960s. This was followed by a modest recovery in nominal prices until the beginning of 1970s, but real prices (that is, commodity prices relative to those of the manufactured goods) continued to decline, though less sharply than during the 1950s. In fact, given the acceleration in the growth of world industrial production (from an annual average of 4.5 per cent in 1952–61 to 6.75 per cent in 1961–71) the annual increases in nominal terms during the 1960s were extremely modest – about 0.7 per cent according to *The Economist* all-item index and 1.8 per cent according to the overall UN index.

However, the scene changed suddenly and the prices for most primary commodities began to rise rapidly in 1972, a few taking off in 1971. They hit their peaks in the summer of 1973, or, in the case of metals, in the spring of 1974, with some of the agricultural products having a second peak, typically lower than the first, in early 1974. This surge in prices was one of the biggest increases in commodity prices on record. *The Economist* index hit its high in May 1974, 115 per cent above the level of two years earlier, and then declined irregularly by 21 per cent by June 1975. These are changes of extraordinary magnitude. During the 115 years that *The Economist* index for all commodites has been compiled, in no year have the prices risen as rapidly (63 per cent) as they did from 1972 to 1973. Thus, this commodity boom and bust is striking against the relatively stable background of the preceding twenty years.[26]

At the end of the 1970s commodity prices were higher in nominal

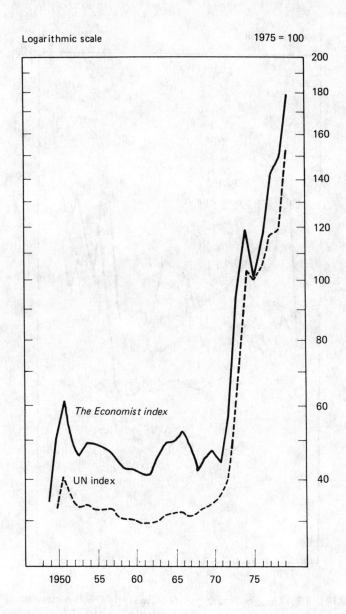

FIGURE 3.1 The Economist *and UN indices of 'nominal' commodity prices, 1949–79*[a]

(a) All price indices are defined in dollars.

56

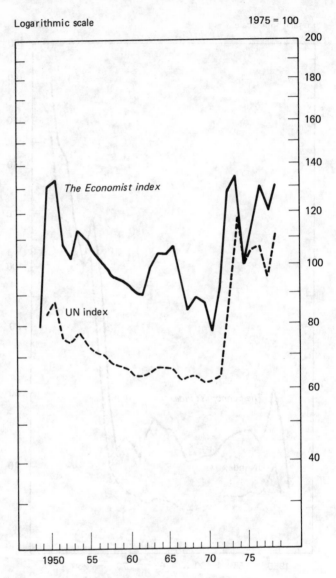

Logarithmic scale   1975 = 100

The Economist index

UN index

FIGURE 3.2 The Economist *and UN indices of 'real' commodity prices,* *1949–79*

SOURCE *Bank of England Quarterly Bulletin* (Mar. 1981).

terms than in 1974, and in real terms they almost recovered to 1974 levels, despite a substantial reduction – from 6.75 per cent to 3.4 per cent in 1979 – in the annual rate of growth of world industrial production. The increases in the 1970s were not confined to any single group of primary commodities. Prices of foodstuffs, agricultural raw materials and metals all increased sharply in 1972–4, fell in 1975 and went up again strongly in 1976–7 and 1978–9.[27] The frequency and the scale of changes in the commodity prices appear to be rather different from their behaviour during the previous two decades, when there were only two increases of any note in food prices between the Korean War and the early 1970s – in 1954 and 1963.

In the 1980s the tempo changed and since the closing months of 1980, prices fell sharply. This fall drove many prices to their lowest levels in real terms for half a century. They registered a fall of 16 per cent between 1980 and 1981, and again of 17 per cent the very next year. A substantial part of this decline was accounted for by the appreciation of the US dollar, but even in terms of SDR the fall was 10 per cent and $7\frac{1}{2}$ per cent, respectively.

Until now we have talked about the commodity group as a whole, which includes food, raw materials, minerals and non-ferrous metals. It is worth remembering that the industrialised market economies export more primary commodities than LDCs.[28] The LDCs depend heavily upon the export of primary agricultural commodities. If we select fifteen major agricultural commodities, representing exports of over $80 billion in 1981, of which about half is accounted for by the LDCs, principally due to their predominant share of exports of sugar, coffee, cocoa, tea, bananas, rice, palm-oil, rubber, jute and sisal. The other selected commodities, namely, wheat, maize, soyabeans, beef, and cotton, are principally exported by developed countries. An analysis of price trends in these commodities since 1960 lends support to the proposition that the terms of trade on which producers of these commodites exchange their exports for imports, notably of manufactures, have a long-term tendency to decline. However, the adverse impact on the purchasing power of export earnings at global level was, in many cases, mitigated by increases in the volume of trade. The LDCs which relied heavily upon one of the primary agricultural commodities for their foreign exchange earnings, had to scurry to the IMF's Compensatory Financing Facility, as a result of shortfalls in their commodity export earnings.[29]

Numerous short-term factors which contributed to the collapse of commodity prices in the 1980s are: First, real output in the OECD countries (which are 65 to 70 per cent of the market for the LDCs' commodity exports) grew hardly at all during 1980–2. Industrial production remained stagnant or declined in such key sectors as steel, automobiles and construction, thus significantly depressing demand for raw materials. Second, extraordinarily high interest rates greatly increased the cost of holding stocks of raw materials; it further reduced the demand for these primary commodities. Third, the squeeze on international liquidity in 1981–2 affected demand for a number of commodities as 'stores of value', and caused portfolio redistribution towards more liquid assets. Fourth, large increases were recorded in the supply of a number of food and beverage crops. Lastly, stocks of substantial amounts were accumulated in the producing countries, therefore the burden of global adjustment fell entirely on them.

TERMS OF TRADE

That there is a secular long-run tendency of the terms of trade to turn against the primary product exports of LDCs is widely supported in the United Nations. It remains to be seen whether it is buttressed by the facts and figures. There are several parallel terms of trade calculations put out by the UN, the World Bank and the IMF. For this study we choose the UN series because it covers the whole period under study. This controversy first attracted attention in the 1950s, through the writings of Raul Prebisch,[30] and revived dramatically in the 1970s. Heightened world inflation brought a series of windfall gains and losses to LCDs. Higher world grain prices in 1973–5 inflicted some $12 billion in additional cost on those LDCs that imported food. Besides, the oil prices quadrupling in 1973 raised the import bill of LDCs that must buy oil, by $12.5 billion annually for the years 1974 and 1975.[31]

According to the UN series the aggregate terms of trade for non-oil LDCs fell between 1954 and 1960, reached a relatively high level in 1968–70, although not as high as they were in 1954–5. Table 3.8 shows that they stayed at a relatively lower level in 1961–7, and in 1971–2 they declined again. The years 1971 and 1972 are a good base for examining the experience of the inflationary years 1973 and 1974, and the recessionary year 1975, since they are relatively representative of the whole period 1960–70. The aggregate terms of trade of non-oil LDCs showed (1980 = 100) a small improvement in 1973 and 1974, and a substantial drop by 1976. The index of aggregate terms of trade registered a spurt in 1977, followed by a monotonic decline till they sank to 91 in 1983, the lowest in the last twenty years.

TABLE 3.8   *Index numbers of terms of trade of non-all LDCs*
(1980 = 100)

1960	1961	1962	1963	1964	1965	1966	1967	1968	1969	1970	1971
120	114	111	114	116	115	120	112	117	122	125	119

1972	1973	1974	1975	1976	1977	1978	1979	1981	1982	1983
119	120	131	129	117	124	116	109	92	98	91

SOURCE   *Handbook of International Trade and Development* (UNCTAD, 1984).

Towards the end of the period (1980) a large number of non-oil LDCs suffered a decline in their terms of trade. Those with substantial decline included several populous LDCs:

	(1975 = 100)
Bangladesh	83
Brazil	72
Egypt	80
Ethiopia	71
India	70
Korea	75
Pakistan	71
The Philippines	78

Higher oil prices and declining commodity prices relative to industrial prices, joined hands to erode the terms of trade of the non-oil LDCs.

The terms of trade of the other group of LDCs, namely, the petroleum exporting countries, present a radically different picture. On the same scale of index numbers, they were 38 in 1960, fell to 33 for the years between 1967 and 1970, and shot up to 101 in 1974, on the heels of the first wave of the oil price rise. Thereafter, they, almost consistently rose till they touched 170 in 1980. Between 1970 and 1980 the terms of trade for this group of countries soared by 446 per cent, on the contrary they fell by 28 per cent for the non-oil LDCs during the same period.

RE-EMERGENCE OF PROTECTIONISM

The LDCs have gradually been making inroads into international markets in product lines in which they possess comparative advantage.

These products are primarily labour-intensive, low-technology manufactures and semi-manufactures. A small number of LDCs have started competing successfully in high-technology items as well. Textiles and clothing is one low technology sector where LDCs have a strong comparative advantage. Besides, several LDCs produce wheat, beef, rice and sugar for export and have a cost advantage in the international market. These exports from LDCs created pressure for structural change in the import-competing sectors of the industrial market economies, which resulted in application of protectionistic measures in several sectors.

The rapid industrial growth of the two post-war decades was exceeded by the more rapid expansion of world trade, particularly in manufactures. Initially this was aided by the general dismantling of tariff barriers that took place under the auspices of the General Agreement on Tariffs and Trade (GATT). From 1950 to the 1975 recession there has been a trend towards reduced protection. Tariff cuts in various GATT rounds, particularly the Kennedy Round, bit deep and brought weighted average nominal tariffs on finished and semi-finished industrial products down to 8 or 9 per cent.[32] In 1975 both tariff and non-tariff barriers were weak. Leaving aside the textile products, only about $1\frac{1}{2}$ per cent of the manufactured exports of LDCs were subjected to quantitative import restrictions in the industrial market economies.[33] This does not include exports from the 'transitional' countries like Greece and Spain. The game started changing its complexion in 1976, when protectionism increased and the pressures for further measures gained momentum. To begin with, except in a few industries (e.g. textiles, footwear and clothing) these new barriers were aimed at Japan. However, soon these measures started operating against successful export performers among LDCs, like Brazil, Hong Kong, Korea and Taiwan. The most disturbing restrictions from the point of view of LDCs are those on textiles and clothing. The maximum damaging is the device of 'voluntary export restrictions'. Here, one can see a clear return to the bilateral exercise of commercial, political and financial power, it manifests itself in the imposition of protective policies of the strong over the weak. This is the most obvious departure from the principles on which the GATT was founded.[34] The Multilateral Trade Negotiations (MTNs), which ended in November 1979, proved to be a complete disappointment to the LDCs, because they failed to achieve results in substance or scope for the trade of LDCs, given the objectives of the Tokyo Round Declaration. The LDCs were particularly concerned with the quantitative restrictions where the industrial economies, by procedural manoeuvring, avoided any solution, and where so many illegalities existed *vis-à-vis* the General Agreement.[35]

The outstanding feature of the new protectionism is its rapid growth. By 1977 import restrictions introduced by the developed market economies seriously threatened or affected 3 to 5 per cent, or roughly $30 billion to $40 billion, of international trade.[36] The quantitative estimate for 1981 is: nearly 40 per cent of world trade between private traders and manufacturers in various countries is under quantitative restrictions, and they are growing.[37] It can be plausibly argued, however, that the present extent of protection is already a major cause of the poor performance of the industrial economies, inhibiting the expansion of their potentially dynamic industries both by reducing the foreign demand for their products and by locking up resources in the protected activities, where their economic efficiency is low.[38]

(A) Protectionism in the Manufacturing Sector

The Multi-Fibre Arrangement (MFA) is one of the best-known protection measure. It was renewed in 1981, which means tightening the restrictive measures further on the imports of textiles and clothing from LDCs. The MFA provides for a 6 per cent annual increase in the textiles exports of individual countries, but the industrialised countries always find ways to circumvent the target. New protectionist measures have been introduced for steel. Marketing agreements have been established for other products such as TV sets and footwear. There is strong pressure for protectionist control on electronics, railroad equipment, bicycle tyres and tubes, copper and zinc.[39] At the end of 1982 the US had bilateral agreements with 22 LDCs for voluntary export restrictions and the EEC with 29.[40]

Non-tariff barriers are rampant; the following example gives an idea: for 1 051 export items from Latin America with total value exceeding $8 billion annually, the US applied over 400 retrospective measures. One hundred non-tariff measures were applied to 479 items imported by the EEC, with an annual export value of $8 billion.[41] In the industrial world, government aid to industry, often granted as a means of rationalising the industrial structure, have become endemic since the 1975 recession. It takes the forms of direct subsidies, of preferential tax and credit treatment, amounting to indirect protection of domestic industry by reducing production or sales cost. Many of these subsidies go to labour-intensive industries, for preserving employment. These are precisely the industries in which LDCs are thought to have high comparative advantage, and so the best opportunities for export. Also, these are the industries where LDCs have had export successes.

It is easy to overstate the case. The manufactured goods imported from LDCs have increased from 1.7 per cent of the total consumption of industrialised countries in 1970 to 3.4 per cent in 1980. Only in the US this proportion rose from 1.3 per cent to 2.9 per cent over the period mentioned above. Exports of textiles and clothing have increased. It would be more correct to say that the whole gamut of restrictive measures have slowed down the exports of LDCs, but far from stopped them.

(B) Protectionism in the Agricultural Commodities

Agriculture has been a protected sector in the industrial countries for a long time. Due to producer subsidies provided under the Common Agricultural Policy, the farm prices in these countries have become increasingly divorced from the world market. The Common Agricultural Policy adversely affects many LDCs which export agricultural commodities. An FAO study unearthed some interesting facts: the value of subsidies on sugar to producers in the US and the EEC combined in 1978 was $5.1 billion, which exceeds the total value of sugar exports from the LDCs. A 50 per cent reduction in protection to agriculture in OECD countries, would lead to a $3 billion increase in the annual exports of 57 populous LDCs. Free trade in agriculture would double the benefits.[42] It should, however, be clarified that the Common Agricultural Policy not only discriminates against the LDCs, but also against the other temperate zone exporters like Australia, Canada and New Zealand.

EMERGENCE OF THE NICs

In the recent past much attention had been given to the emergence of newly-industrialising countries (NICs) on the world scene. The World Bank defines NICs as the developing countries that had per capita income in excess of $1 100 in 1978 and where the share of manufacturing sector in the GDP was 20 per cent or higher. The countries that qualified were Argentina, Brazil, Chile, Mexico and Uruguay in Latin America; Israel and Yugoslavia in the Europe–Middle East area; and Hong Kong, Korea, Singapore and Taiwan in the Far East. Sometimes

Colombia and India are also retained in this group.[43] The dynamism of this group of LDCs is attributed to the 'cumulative virtuous circle' of growth, technical progress and international trade – and slowly and stealthily growth began to gain momentum with the assistance of the capital goods sector as an embodiment of productivity.[44] The shift to outward-looking growth policies and to the fuller exploitation of comparative advantage by the NICs had started in the early 1960s. By the time the world economy reached the 1975 recession the NICs became a source of concern to the industrial market economies. The NICs are a highly heterogenous group, yet they are all characterised by a fast growth-rate in industrial production and employment, and an enlargement of export market share in manufactures. This resulted in reduction of the real per capita income gap separating them from the industrial market economies.[45] A few other LDCs are in fast pursuit of outward-looking growth policies and so may soon become serious candidates for joining the ranks of NICs.

The four Far-Eastern NICs adopted outward-oriented strategies on the heels of completion of their first stage of import-substitution, which entailed replacing the imports of non-durable consumer goods and their inputs with domestic production. The growth rate of gross capital stock (at constant prices) grew at the rate of more than 6 per cent in all these NICs, between 1955 and 1975. The growth rate of capital stock is directly related to the rate of increase in investment. Korea and Singapore started with relatively low investment rates, were able to step it up briskly, and the investment rate hovered around 20 per cent or more for all the four of them.[46] The Latin American NICs moved on to the second stage of import-substitution, which entails domestic production of the previously imported intermediate goods and producer and consumer durables. Having reached this stage they reduced their export bias. The NICs of Europe and the Middle East went into export promotion at an early stage, but subsequently they slackened. The last group – that is, Chile, Colombia, India and Uruguay – continued to pursue inward-oriented strategies until quite late.

Between 1963 and 1973 the volume of exports of manufactures for these countries increased at the rate of 12 per cent per annum, and between 1974 and 1977 this average fell to $9\frac{1}{2}$ per cent. What is important is that, in both the periods, exports increased much faster than production. Another noteworthy fact is that for the whole period, the bulk of increase in the manufacturing output was destined for their domestic markets; the export-production ratio rose only modestly. Thus it is true that, in some branches, in clothing and electrical machinery, a significant proportion of production was exported; these branches, however, accounted for only a part of the total manufacturing production. It is worth noting that the ratio of exports to production in NICs has stayed much lower than that in the industrial countries. This means that if in a few sectors some NICs were able to reap the benefits of international specialisation, in most manufacturing branches the foreign-trade-induced economies of scale appear to be still at an early stage.[47]

EXTERNAL SHOCKS AND THE LDCs

The exogenous shocks that the LDCs received during the 1970s were: the quadrupling of oil-prices, which took full effect in 1974, the world recession of 1974–5, the second oil-price hike in 1979, the recession after 1979 and the pressure for raising of tariff walls. These shocks adversely affected the balance of payments of most non-oil LDCs, particularly the large ones. These effects were aggravated by deterioration of the non-oil terms of trade in case of some LDCs, whereas for some other non-oil LDCs improvements in terms of trade took place, alleviating their situation. For several non-oil LDCs, in particular those exporting cocoa and coffee, a net improvement in the terms of trade ensued, representing a favourable external shock. This improvement in their terms of trade more than offset the negative export-volume effect.

The LDCs, which were at the receiving end of the unfavourable external shocks, had several policy measures available to them to adjust from these shocks. The oft-utilised ones are: reliance on the inflow of external financial resources, export promotion, and temporary lowering of economic growth through restrictive macroeconomic policies. The World Bank commissioned a study to delve into the effects of exogenous shocks, 28 representative LDCs were chosen for this purpose.[48] All the NICs experienced adverse exogenous shocks but they differed in terms of the policies applied to handle them. Korea, Singapore and Taiwan continued to adopt outward-oriented strategy, providing identical incentives to sales in domestic and foreign markets. They were joined by Chile and Uruguay, which had earlier applied an inward-oriented strategy but reversed their policy structure after the shocks of 1974–5. After earlier efforts to reduce the bias in the incentive system against exports, Brazil, Israel, Portugal and Yugoslavia again increased the degree of inward-orientation, whereas Argentina, Mexico and Turkey maintained their relatively inward-orientated stance. This study also analysed the experiences of twelve LDCs, which cover the spectrum between the NICs and the least developed countries (LLDCs). Four of them – Kenya, Mauritius, Thailand and Tunisia – may be categorised as having applied outward-oriented policies, while the remaining eight followed an inward-oriented policy. Within the latter group Jamaica, Peru and Tanzania experienced internal shocks in the form of economic disruptions resulting from government policies; however, this was not the case for the remaining five LDCs, namely, Egypt, India, Morocco, the Philippines and Zambia. The investigation also included four LDCs that experienced favourable external shocks. These LDCs are: Indonesia and Nigeria, which benefited from the rise of oil prices; Ivory Coast, where increases in the price of cocoa and coffee more than offset the adverse effects of higher prices; and Colombia, which enjoyed the rise in coffee prices without being burdened by the higher prices of oil.

The study unambiguously concludes that the outward-oriented policies are superior for coping with exogenous shocks. Of the economies chosen in this work the outward-oriented ones suffered greater external shocks than did the internal-oriented ones, yet the first group was more successful in overcoming the effects of shocks. Apart from the export expansion, economies pursuing an outward-oriented development strategy experienced more import-substitution than did the other group. Furthermore, after a temporary decline, their economic growth accelerated, whereas growth rates fell in economies following an inward-oriented strategy. The differences in growth rates also reflect differences in incremental capital–output ratios, and in domestic saving ratio. Higher efficiency in allocation of existing resources and of increments in resources, together with the exploitation of economies of scale, permitted the maintenance of incremental capital-output ratios at low levels in outward-oriented economies.

THE THEME OF INTERDEPENDENCE

A salient feature of the post-war economic scene is the heightened interdependence among country groups. It has two logical aspects: what happens in other countries will affect the economic performance of an individual country, and, conversely, what an individual country can or wishes to do would, to some degree, depend upon the actions and policies of other countries. Interdependence, *prima facie*, is a simple concept, but it hides many complexities. First, interdependence is a matter of degree, no country is totally dependent upon others and none is completely isolated. The extent of interdependence varies from country to country, depending upon how well integrated it is in the international economy. Second, a country may be dependent on another country, country-group or the international economy at large. Third, interdependence is a dynamic concept, it changes with time. If anything, the awareness of financial and economic interdependence has sharpened during the last decade. Its credit can be partly attributed to institutions like the Brandt Commission. The world economy is far more internationalised today than it was during the 1950s. Take any indicator, trade/GNP ratios, financial resource flows, or the current account balances; they all indicate in the same direction. This inter-relationship has been enhanced by the emergence of three sub-groups among the developing countries, namely, the newly industrialising countries (NICs), the middle income countries (MICs) and OPEC. These sub-groups have their own economic dynamics which have had a decisive impact on the international economy. The NICs and the MICs have a fast evolving institutional infrastructure, and they are progressively more integrated in the international economy than the other developing countries, by the same token they play a more active role in the international capital markets.

One important macroeconomic link is trade. Expansion of real income in one country or country group is transmitted to other countries via increased import demand. The developing countries comprise a buoyant market for the developed ones. The US trade across the Pacific was larger than that across the Atlantic in 1984. Shrinking developing country imports can adversely affect the industrialised economies. For example, between 1981 and 1983 the major Latin American countries cut down their imports dramatically. These cuts were due to the austerity measures that these countries took to make their financial position viable. The import compression reduced the exports of the industrial economies, which hurt them. The US alone lost $21 billion in net exports to Latin America between 1981 and 1983. According to a rule of thumb, that the US government uses, that translates into some 500000 Americans unemployed and at least $2.2 billion lost in profits. These are only the direct costs.[49]

A good indicator of heightened interdependence is the growth of international trade relative to the growth of GDP. Trade has grown more rapidly than income. The nominal value of world trade in goods and non-factor services rose from $605 billion in 1960 to $2170.5 billion in 1980. In real terms this translates into 6.7% annual growth rate. Over the same period, world GDP grew at an annual average rate of 4.4% in real terms. The ratio of world exports to GDP rose from 12.2% in 1960 to 21.8% in 1980.

The degree of interdependence has been particularly conspicuous in the international financial markets and monetary system. Financial liberalisation has led to the creation of offshore markets, which have expanded with a phenomenal rate. The size of the Eurodollar market in the 1960s cannot be compared with that in the 1980s. After the advent of flexible exchange rates in 1973, the Euromarkets mushroomed into a gigantic financial system and have successfully bound the world's finances together. The nature of these markets, and the economic and regulatory factors, have made these markets highly internationalised. The financial resources mobilised by these markets for the developing countries during the 1970s were of unprecedented proportion. The developing countries value the efficient operation of these markets highly and have participated in their development. A small number of developing countries have become financial centres of international significance. This has led to ballooning of financial flows to developing countries from the financial markets, and they have far outpaced the bilateral flows.

The large-scale international movements of unskilled, semi-skilled and skilled labour also manifest an increase in interdependence. These migrations not only took place between developing and developed countries, but also between two groups of developing countries. A World Bank estimate of migrant workers put their number at 20 million in the late 1970s, of whom 12 million were from LDCs. Movement of labour means movement of funds in reverse order. The remittances made to LDCs yielded about $24 billion in 1980, up from an estimated $3 billion in 1970. The middle-income oil importing LDCs were the main beneficiaries of these transmissions.

The other overlapping spheres are commodity trade, transfer of technology, transnational corporations, energy and environment. Metaphorically, the world is increasingly becoming a rollercoaster, where we all go up and down almost together. Therefore the conventional wisdom of thinking about countries in terms of rich and poor, or developed and underdeveloped has to change because both the country groups export primary products, both are borrowers and lenders in the capital market, both of them have had problems regarding structural rigidities. Little wonder, both of them are interested in the efficient functioning of the international economy.

The upshot is that in today's multifaceted world, it is well-nigh impossible for a country or country group to stay marooned, without interaction with other identical units. International interdependence is inevitable. To be sure, these would be LDCs which are more or les integrated in the international economy. The extent of integration would have a direct positive correlation with the stage of economic development of the LDC in question as well as the degree of openness of its economy. No country — industrialised or developing — can afford to overlook the importance of global interdependence because of its direct and indirect consequences on that country's economic welfare.

4 The Structure and Volume of Bilateral Resource Flows

INTRODUCTION

The concept of transnational resource flows and/or international lending is now a clearcut one, though for a couple of decades it was nebulous and discipline lacked precision. The haze has now been dispelled, for all practical purposes it implies extension of grants and/or loans to non-residents by governments and government agencies, and the multilateral organisations. A great deal of ambiguity is caused by the expression 'aid'. Strictly defined, it should refer only to the value of the subsidy implicit in the total flow of resources. Accordingly, grants in convertible currency can be called 'aid' to the full extent of their value, while loans cannot, because they will only have an element of aid, at times an insignificant element. One must not lump these and other kinds of 'aid', while trying to reckon cost to donors or benefit to recipients. Indubitably the donor assists the recipient by providing financial resources at the right time and in the right sector, but can one always refer to it as 'aid'? Moneylenders generally benefit the clients, but we do not think of them as 'aid' givers.[1]

In connection with its task of co-ordination of economic assistance to the LDCs the Development Assistance Committee (DAC) had to grapple with the slippery concept of 'aid'. For them the term 'aid' has come to mean flow of government grants and official lendings, with a maturity exceeding five years, as well as the contributions to multilateral agencies. These resources are made available to LDCs as grants, or as loans at concessional terms, primarily for development purposes. These resource flows are the only ones which deserve to be called 'aid' or 'assistance'. The DAC Reports clarify that all the kinds of resource flows cannot be called 'aid', because many governments and government agencies provide credit for more than five years for commercial motives. Private capital exports are made in the expectation of higher returns. They may, indeed, have an element of aid because they are officially guaranteed against some element of risk, or are the result of a policy of special incentives. A policy of encouraging official or commercial outflows, or merely permitting the free flow of financial resources, can, in addition to any budgetary incidence, involve certain costs to the donor[2] country in terms of forgone investment. Besides, the strain on the balance of payments is not inconsequential.

In theory, there is a continuum between a strictly commercial transaction, with no grant element, and a pure gift, with no element of *quid pro quo*. Every financial transaction between the LDCs and the donor economies could find a place on this continuum. The proportion of grant element can be calculated and can vary between 0 per cent and 100 per cent.[3]

A word about the DAC would be in order: it is a forum in which representatives of the OECD's major donor members meet on a regular basis to discuss ways in which the quantity and quality of their economic assistance to LDCs can be improved. It came into being in January 1960, its original membership was thirteen. Since then, despite the later departure of Portugal, membership has grown steadily with the addition of Australia, Finland, New Zealand, Sweden and Switzerland; its present membership is seventeen. Representatives of the IMF and the World Bank attend committee meetings as observers. The participants in the meetings are usually members of permanent national delegations to the OECD, but they are often joined by officials from the ministries that deal with the decisions in the national capitals. The top-level meetings are attended by ministers.[4]

A QUESTION OF MOTIVATION

The question of what triggers the flow of capital from the donors to recipients can be answered thus: As for the commercial flows, the profit motive is preponderant; they flow in response to the market mechanism seeking higher returns. Looking for more profitable avenues, capital roams the world over; this is a time-tested story.

To put it plainly, countries give bilateral aid[5] because they expect something in return. It would be a trifle naïve to assume that the major objective of external resource inflows, in any form, is the economic rejuvenation of the recipient LDC. Many motives can inspire bilateral assistance, philanthropy is one of them. In reality, few transfers are completely unilateral. If the humanitarian motives were the only motives, much less than the present level of flows would result. Undoubtedly the Cold War gave a boost to resource flows,[6] but ideology is not the basic determinant. One does see capitalistic lenders financing programmes in socialist countries (e.g. French aid to Algeria) and the other way round, that is, authoritarian countries sponsoring decentralised projects in democratic nations (e.g. Russian aid to India).

Although for a candid eye it is easy to see the overriding importance of self-interest, but it is difficult to pin down precisely what the donors' interests are. One observes that bilateral flows are an instrument of power politics; they have flowed from weak to powerful countries, and from metropole to former colonies. How much a donor gives to a recipient cannot be decided by a simple formula like the need of the recipient or the capacity of the donor, or the potential or past performance. Political variables are more relevant here. Economic efficiency or social justice is subordinate to national interest. It is no exaggeration to say that economic assistance is just another instrument, like diplomacy, cultural exchange, military intervention and war.[7] It may serve the donor politically, commercially or from a strategic point of view.[8] As to what donors expect, various scholars have suggested differing considerations:

1. The elected officials in the donor country may feel that the LDC would behave more favourably towards them in the international fora, lending its support to their national and political interests.
2. They may expect (at times demand) a *quid pro quo*, for example, that the LDC import more from them.
3. They may expect some indication that they have had a favourable impact on the recipient.

The value of the above-mentioned gains, tangible or intangible, would depend upon the volume of resource inflows. An empirical study indicates that the elasticity of aid impact, calculated with respect to aid as a proportion of the recipient GNP, has a decreasing return of scale in the matter of the creation of impact.[8] Also, there is no uniform evidence of distortion in the direction of small LDCs. It is sometimes suggested that external resources have a bias toward small LDCs. The study also found that the economic links represented by the lagged exports from donor to recipient (as per capita of the latter) is significant.

INTERNALISING THE EXTERNAL RESOURCES

The monetary mechanism regarding how the external financial resources are used by the recipient economy is puzzling and generally dimly perceived. The external financial resources usually come to a developing country in a currency other than domestic, called foreign exchange. The recipient government can sell it to the central bank or the commercial banks. The central bank can add it to its international reserves, which are a part of its assets. The local currency proceeds can then be used by the recipient government as its budgetary resources. The central bank can finance its purchase either by printing currency or by floating bonds and securities in the financial market. The first operation would be inflationary while the second one would reduce the money stock in the economy. This mechanism applies to resource inflows from all the three sources, namely, bilateral, multilateral and capital market.

The resources coming in as project assistance do not generate any revenues for the recipient government, this is not to say that they do not have a favourable impact over its budgetary resources. The aid-financed capital goods imports for the project render it unnecessary for the government to raise the equivalent wherewithall in the local currency to purchase enough foreign exchange for the project-related imports. Initially the World Bank project loans financed only the foreign exchange part of the investment and the recipient country was expected to meet the local currency expenditure. This strategy, however, has undergone substantial changes, yet in most cases the recipient LDC still has to supply the counterpart funds. Drawings on the International Monetary Fund by the central bank of the recipient country have to be kept effectively out of the domestic circulation or, in principle, sterilised.

THE FIRST POST-WAR DECADE: 1946–55

First, a caveat regarding the quality of data: the first post-war decade is the scratchiest in terms of the quality of data. This discrepancy, though substantial on an individual yearly basis and from country to country, does not, however, disturb the overall pattern of financial flows from the industrial market economies to LDCs. The first post-war decade was one of the most prosperous in recent economic history, the statistical indicators confirm the extraordinary cadence of economic activity. This rhythm was achieved in the upswing state of the world business cycle, which naturally influenced the rate of growth in world trade, which in turn substantially facilitated the resource transfer. Therefore, international resource flows of substantial magnitude could take place without any major interruption. During the first quinquennium after the war, large-scale US aid to Western Europe occupied a central place in the aggregate resource flows. Assistance was given to Europe in the form of grants and loan for reconstruction and to meet temporary deficits in current supplies and inventories. A large part of these flows took place under the Marshall Plan. Once the reconstruction was accomplished, public funds to Europe tapered off. The LDCs also received long-term financial resources during the first half of this decade, but only in a small way. The flows accelerated in the second half of the decade, as shown in Table 4.1. Towards the end the non-European countries became the major recipient.

From year to year the rate of growth has been erratic; also the grant element lacks trend. It is, however, clear that it was higher during the pre-1950 years than for the post-1950.

Taking an over-view, the gross amount of public long-term capital that was transferred internationally from 1946 through 1950 amounted to more than $61 billion. That the amount is large is indicated by the fact that it was equal to one-fourth of the value of world exports during this period. The utility of these resources was high for rehabilitation of the war-torn economies, for the settlement of the war accounts and also for the efforts made after the war for the development of the underdeveloped countries.

The US and Canada were the two countries not ravaged by the war, and therefore were also the largest exporters of financial resources during the first quinquennium. They contributed almost 60 per cent ($35 billion), more than two-thirds of it went to Western Europe, which accounted for $15 billion, or one-fourth of the total. Regarding the net transfer, the following pattern emerged:

1. The US and Canada were the only net exporters of public resources to other areas; between 1946 and 1950 they exported $29 billion net.
2. The lion's share of the resource movement was between developed countries. The developing countries received only $3 billion net from the rest of the world.

The relatively small net amount of inflows to LDCs was due to the fact that the $8 billion which they received from Western Europe and

TABLE 4.1   *Gross long-term capital inflows, 1946–1955 (in billions of $)*

Year	Grants	Loans	Total	Percentage increase over last year
1946	1.3 (77)	0.4 (23)	1.7	—
1947	1.0 (59)	0.7 (41)	1.7	0
1948	1.1 (73)	0.4 (27)	1.5	−22
1949	1.3 (65)	0.7 (35)	2.0	+33
1950	0.8 (50)	0.8 (50)	1.6	−20
1951	1.1 (61)	0.8 (39)	1.8	+13
1952	1.2 (55)	1.0 (45)	2.2	+22
1953	1.3 (50)	1.3 (50)	2.6	+18
1954	1.1 (42)	1.4 (58)	2.6	0
1955	1.5 (52)	1.4 (48)	2.9	+12
	11.7 (57)	8.9 (43)	20.6	

SOURCE   The statistics relating to grants and loans were prepared by IBRD staff, with the help of the following two articles: (1) M. L. Weiner and R. Della-Chiesa, 'International Movements of Public Long-term Capital and Grants 1946–1950', *IMF Staff Papers* (Sept. 1954), and (2) J. Barnéris, 'International Movement of Public Long-term Capital and Grants, 1951–1952', *IMF Staff Papers* (Feb. 1965), pp. 108–27. They were first published in D. Avramovic and R. Gulhait, *Debt Servicing Capacity and Postwar Growth in International Indebtedness* (Johns Hokins University Press, 1958), p. 6. Other calculations were made by the author.

The figures in parentheses = the percentage of total.

the US, was offset in large part by debt-servicing.[9] Some of these reverse transfers were made to the US, but for the most part, they were made to Western Europe. The gross outflow of public capital from Western Europe to the LDCs was greater than the gross outflow from the US. Western Europe's net export of resources to LDCs amounted to only $0.6 billion, compared with $1.9 billion from the US.[10] During the second quinquennium of this decade the movement of funds to LDCs increased because the reconstruction in Europe was well on its way and in some cases it was complete. In 1953 LDCs equalled Western Europe in terms of gross inflows. During the remaining two years of the decade this trend continued.[11]

The large resource transfer from the US to Western Europe, and then its brisk recovery, enabled several countries to start resource

ransfers of their own. Before the end of the decade under review
Western European countries extended considerable amounts of grants
and loans to LDCs, particularly to their colonies.

Geographical Distribution

The distribution was on the following lines:

TABLE 4.2   *Geographical distribution (in billions of $)*

Area	Grants	Loans	Total
1. Latin America	0.3	2.9	3.2
2. Independent countries in the Sterling Area[a]	0.8	1.9	2.7
3. European dependent territories	3.4	2.1	5.5
4. China–Taiwan, Korea, Indochina and the Philippines	3.4	0.4	3.8
5. Others[b]	3.7	1.6	5.3
	11.7	8.9	20.6

SOURCE   Same as Table 4.1.
Australia, Burma, India, Iraq, Jordan, New Zealand, Pakistan, Rhodesia, Sri Lanka, Republic of South Africa.
Japan, Israel and Iran.

The amounts indicated in Table 4.2 include grants to several Asian
countries, namely, China–Taiwan, Indochina, Korea and the Philippines. This was meant for post-war rehabilitation. If these amounts are
excluded, the gross inflow on public account over the decade might be
estimated at $17 billion, distributed almost equally between grants and
loans. Grants to European dependencies were used in part for the
construction of social overheads and for services in the field of
education and health. The resources going to Latin America went in
the form of loans to develop utilities and to finance industrialisation.
The inflow into South and South-East Asia was relatively small during
this period; it was accelerated towards the end of the decade. There
were reverse transfers from Latin America and the independent sterling
area countries (e.g. Australia and South Africa) largely because of
debt-servicing and foreign-owned railways and other utilities.

Financial Terms

During the first quinquennium the interest rates were low, in fact the reconstruction loans were made by the donor governments on exceptionally low-interest rates. Refer to Table 4.3, which shows extraordinarily low interest rates for Europe. As the decade advanced, interest rates in the donor economies started rising; this was mirrored in the interest rates of foreign lending. Since the exact rates for this period are not available they were calculated by expressing the actual interest payments made during the given year as a percentage of the average debt outstanding at the beginning and at the end of the year.[12] These 'effective' rates are understatements, because interest payments are related to debt outstanding, which includes both disbursed and undisbursed amounts of the loan. Yet these estimates are a good indicator of change over time. This reservation being expressed, the effective rates for the first decade were as follows:

TABLE 4.3   *Effective interest rates*

| Region | (in per cent) | |
	1946–8	1953–5
1. Europe	0.8	2.3
2. Africa	3.3	3.3
3. Australia	3.8	3.7
4. Asia	0.8	3.1*
5. Western hemisphere	1.9	2.7
6. Non-European countries	2.7	3.4
Weighted average	1.5	2.6

*Only for 1955.
SOURCE IBRD, quoted in Avramovic and Gulhati, *Debt Servicing Capacity and Postwar Growth in International Indebtedness*, op. cit. p. 35.

The above data testify that, starting from a low level after the war, the 'effective' interest rates increased to 2.6 per cent; it was 3.4 per cent for the non-European countries at the end of the decade.

ECONOMIC SETTING DURING THE FIRST POST-WAR DECADE

This period, as noted, was characterised by a rapid growth in the world income, increased investment and a substantial expansion in international trade. It is apparent that in this decade the growth of the

European economies, which were being reconstructed, and the developing countries, was greatly influenced by the resource flows. Both the activities – that is, the flow of resources anbd the growthg of income, investment and trade – were favourably influenced by the upswing in world economic activity which took place after the war. The post-reconstruction rate of growth of the world economy was higher than the pre-war rate of growth. This is confirmed by the growth in principal industries, e.g. steel and energy. It is also confirmed by the developments in the two largest centres of growth in that period, namely, the US and Western Europe. Although no comparable series are available for the LDCs, the rate of growth in a large number of them during this period, compares favourably with the experience of the developed countries.

The rate of investment in this period was discernibly higher in most of the countries for which evidence is available. It was substantially higher in the European economies, than their pre-war average, according to one estimate the median value increased from 14 per cent in the 1920s to 18 per cent after the war. In Australia and Japan it was 27 per cent, which is higher than the long-term rates in North America and Western Europe. The gross rate of investment in Latin America has been estimated to have increased from less than 13 per cent in the 1920s to about 16 per cent in 1951–4.[13] An acceleration of development spending occurred in most of the LDCs as well, which was financed by indigenous funds as well as external resource inflows.

These increases in income and investment led to a rapid increase in the world trade. Since the increases in output were faster than the long-run trend the post-war rate of growth in trade followed the same trend. In the four decades preceding the First World War industrial production increased at an annual average rate of 3.9 per cent and the growth rate in world trade was 3.3 per cent. As opposed to this, in the seven years preceding 1955, industrial production advanced at a rate of 6.3 per cent and the world trade at the rate of 7 per cent. A comparison between long-term averages and the rates recorded over the short-term is apt to be a trifle misleading. All comparisons which extend over long periods in the past are statistically suspect because of the quality of data and differences in definitions.

The above data show that the volume of world trade increased by 60 per cent in this decade. One characteristic stands out for this period: the volume expansion was higher in the field of manufactured exports, and the price increases were higher in the case of primary commodities. According to the GATT estimates the volume of manufactured exports approximately doubled;[15] this was largely due to the stepped-up exports

TABLE 4.4 *Value and volume of world trade*
1946–55*

Year	Value *(in billions of $)*	Volume *(1937 = 100)*
1946	33.4	n.a.
1947	48.3	93
1948	53.8	97
1949	53.5	104
1950	56.5	118
1951	76.5	132
1952	73.8	131
1953	77.5	139
1954	77.5	146
1955	84.1	157

*Excluding the USSR, Eastern Europe and China.

SOURCE UN, *Monthly Bulletin of Statistics*, various issues.

of capital goods. Their share in the total exports of industrialised countries, in the mid-1950s, was much higher than before the war. This reflects the aforementioned upswing in savings, investment and productive resources in general.

The volume of trade in primary commodities increased considerably less than that in manufactures. The rate of growth varied from commodity to commodity. The slow expansion of trade in food products was partly due to low-income elasticity of demand, and partly due to the development of home output of competing products in the importing countries. The synthetic substitutes created a dent in the textile fibre exports. The demand for fresh food rose, reflecting the changing composition of the consumer basket.

The different rates of growth in the volume of manufactures and primary commodities were accompanied by a diverse trend in prices. The higher post-war prices of primary commodities were due to better demand conditions arising from acceleration of income growth. In contrast to the trebling of primary goods prices, the prices of manufactured exports had approximately doubled since the pre-war period. Therefore the terms of trade of the LDCs improved by about 40 per cent to 50 per cent during this period.

Patterns of Imports of the Creditor Countries

The reason why special attention needs to be focused on the behaviour of imports of the creditor countries is the fact that they are a major determinant of the foreign exchange resources of the debtor countries. The expansion of world trade and higher price levels of primary products managed to sustain an increased rate of economic activity in LDCs. On the whole the import demand of the creditor countries rose in response to growth in income. This favourably influenced the flow of financial resources available to LDCs for smooth debt-service payments. The US was the creditor *par excellence* in the post-war period; because of its increased imports the dollar stock of the LDCs was full. The US imports increased faster than the GNP since the war. Similarly a higher increase in imports than the increase in income was recorded for other donor countries. For this period the ratio of commodity imports to GNP rose for Canada and thirteen other European countries.[16] This proved to be a big help to the LDCs; their external resource position was sound in general.

THE SECOND POST-WAR DECADE: 1956–65

Table 4.5 documents the annual quantum of the net disbursement of bilateral resource flows to the LDCs and multilateral institutions from

TABLE 4.5 *Bilateral flows (net disturbance) (in millions of US$)*

Year	Grant and grant-like flows	Long-term development lending	Total	Percentage change over last year
1956	1 843.0 (60.5)	1 203.0 (39.5)	3 046.0	5.0
1957	2 071.0 (60.1)	1 373.0 (39.9)	3 444.0	13.0
1958	2 415.0 (60.1)	1 601.0 (39.9)	4 016.0	16.6
1959	2 265.0 (56.6)	1 736.0 (43.4)	4 001.0	− 1.0
1960	2 511.0 (58.7)	1 766.0 (41.3)	4 277.0	6.9
1961	3 644.5 (69.9)	1 269.0 (30.1)	5 213.7	21.9
1962	4 024.2 (74.7)	1 364.1 (25.3)	5 388.3	3.3
1963	4 047.1 (70.8)	1 671.8 (29.2)	5 718.9	6.1
1964	3 881.5 (70.8)	1 604.3 (29.2)	5 485.8	− 4.1
1965	3 780.4 (65.6)	1 980.7 (34.4)	5 761.1	5.0

SOURCES Up to 1960 from *The Flow of Financial Resources to Less-developed Countries, 1956–1963* (Paris: OECD, 1964); and thereafter from various issues of the *Development Co-operation Review* (OECD, published annually by the DAC).

The figures in parentheses = percentages of total.

the OECD countries – that is, those who were members of the DAC. The annual totals represent the summation of different types of financial flows, provided under different sets of terms and condition. All figures are in terms of current dollars; it is important to clarify that the figures for lending are net of amortisation and interest payments. This concept corresponds closely to the actual increases in goods and services made available to LDCs, which might be associated with an on-going assistance programme. It should also be clarified that grants and grant-like contributions are those for which no repayments in convertible currency is required. These data are prepared and published annually by the DAC, and are as consistent over time as it has been possible to make them.

A second caveat regarding the above data – statistics nearly always make dull reading, and sometimes they are confusing as well. The change from one year to the next in the value of net disbursements measured in the local currencies of the donor countries becomes somewhat detached from the real value of the goods and services transferred when inflation is high and widespread, as was particularly the case after 1969 in several OECD countries. Besides, in order to make inter-country comparisons, the figures must be converted into dollars. With frequent changes in exchange rates and with some of the important currencies floating, it is not always easy to know what rate best represents the average value prevailing during the year.

As seen in Table 4.5, between 1956 and 1960 the bilateral flows went up by 44 per cent. The grant element in the resources hovered around 60 per cent. Only 1959 can be termed a lean year, because the aid amount as well as grant element fell. On the whole this was a decade of fast growth in bilateral resource transfers, the average annual rate of growth was 13.5 per cent, as against 6.2 per cent for the preceding decade. Almost all the donors contributed to the increase which took place during this period. By far the largest absolute increase was recorded by the US, and there were substantial increases in the amounts provided by France, the UK and Belgium. These were the donors which had special long-established relationships with various LDCs. Japan and Germany did not have particular links with any large groups of the LDCs, but they also recorded impressive rises.

The 1960s marked a transition period in the policies of donors. There were two reasons for this: first, the early 1960s marked the end of colonialism, and, second, a new focus was sought in the context of the First UN Development Decade, and the commitment to a 1 per cent of GNP target for each donor. This target was to remain a theoretical one.

The year 1961 remains an impressive one from the point of view of total flow and its grant element. After 1962, there were changes in the performance of individual donors. Eleven of the 13 erstwhile donors recorded increased bilateral disbursement, Italy showed a slight fall, but there was a reduction on the part of the largest donor, the US. The slackening in aid efforts after 1962 will be dealt with at length.

Part of the reason for flagging lies with the bewildering complexity of factors which motivated these programmes in their earlier years. The complexity of objectives and, in many cases, lack of a clear definition of the nature of these programmes made them vulnerable to economic and political changes. To a great extent the economic milieu of the period was responsible for determining the level of budgetary appropriations for development assistance. It has been claimed that (1) domestic inflation; (2) balance of payments; and (3) budgetary difficulties, all imposed constraints on the amount available for development assistance. A simple statistical test was conducted of the relationship, for each of the six major DAC countries (the US, France, the UK, Germany, Japan and Canada) of the above three variables and the relevant budgetary appropriations for development assistance.[17] It was found that these three variables, in combination, explain budgetary appropriations to differing extents – 92 per cent in the case of Canada, and 22 per cent for Germany, while the other donors lie in between these two extremes.

The years 1963 and 1964 are notable for the emergence of a vigorous effort on the part of the donors to appraise the qualitative performance of the assistance and improve the policies and operations of their assistance programmes. The following are the noteworthy results of the appraisal:

1. A wider interest and participation was shown by more donor countries, both geographically and functionally.
2. For the first time there was increased awareness of long-run problems, notably the rising debt burden resulting from present terms and conditions of economic assistance was shown.
3. Economic assistance policies had to be developed on a trial and error basis, and the donor countries for the first time endeavoured to harmonise these policies. For example, the effort of one country to assist an LDC with a soft loan in order to minimise its debt burden may be offset by a loan on hard terms by another, or by rapid growth of short-term export credit.

In the earlier years the volume of bilateral resource transfer increased briskly because of the impetus given by setting up of new assistance programmes in countries like Germany, Italy, Japan and the Scandinavian countries. None of these donors had special links with a particular group of LDCs. Australia and Sweden became DCA members in 1965, bringing the membership to 15. Also, in 1965 Australia gave all its aid in grants, and Belgium, Norway and Sweden gave 90 per cent in similar manner. A noteworthy feature is that the two countries where grant element declined year after year were those where they once were the largest, namely, the US and France. In case of the US the shift from grants to loans was a reflection of Congressional requirements, as well as the policy of linking assistance more closely to the economic performance of the recipient. For France the primary reason was the change in the magnitude of assistance to Algeria. Since 1961 the combined flows from the 'big four', namely, the US, France, the UK and Germany, remained more or less on a plateau.

The recipient LDCs started showing noteworthy improvements in their planning process. Due to lack of technical expertise and administrative direction, their first attempts often ended in unrealistic targets. They had also failed to take into account the related manpower requirements. A realistic planning exercise is a big help to policy-makers and bilateral donors alike, and the second-generation plans proved to be much more useful. The experience accumulated by LDCs made their plans more realistic, and the planners as well as the implementers became better aware of the issues and the alternatives. This increased the absorptive capacity of the resources. This is not to say that there were no serious shortcomings in the practical, day-to-day implementation. Possibilities of regional groupings were being looked into because markets in several small LDCs were too small to permit production on an effective scale. Until this point in time most of the resources went into financing infrastructure, even the better-off LDCs needed assistance for basic social and economic infrastructure. African LDCs had particularly weak transport infrastructure. There was a time dimension of this investment, once completed, the task of maintaining the infrastructure facilities fell on the LDCs' governments and their budgets, on which demands were usually in excess of the available funds. So, stories of hospitals and schools without adequate equipment, and roads deteriorating for lack of maintenance, soon started making the rounds.

The importance of agriculture slowly grew in assistance programmes in the early 1960s. This was largely due to the importance of food, which in many cases was the controlling factor in the balance of payments of the LDCs, particularly the large ones. The problem which cropped up – both for the donor and the recipient – was how to improve the low-yielding, subsistence agriculture with its inefficiently sized units and old methods. The assistance programmes in the agricultural sector placed considerable emphasis on the diversification of agriculture for improving the diet, and for general strengthening of the farm sector. It was meant to serve as a defence against the economic disturbances created by harvest failures and wide swings in prices. Transformations needed in the agricultural sector were constantly debated in donors' fora as well as multilateral institutions. Also, economic assistance during this period included services of agricultural experts, promotion of large and small irrigation projects and improvements in credit and marketing institutions.

The LDCs themselves tended to identify industrialisation with development, more emphatically in the 1960s than in the 1950s. Although large-scale steel-mills, oil-refineries, cement plants, etc., were given assistance, but this proved to be a difficult area in which to give economic assistance. The difficulties arose from the fact that the industrial sector in the donor countries is largely in private hands.

Geographical Distribution

Looking at the continental distribution of the financial flows, the share of European recipients like Greece and Spain dwindled during this decade. The share of Africa also fell, whereas that of Latin America rose sharply in 1961, and kept at the same level thereafter. The most populous continent, Asia, which comprised 61 per cent of the population of the developing world, increased its share gradually. In 1965 Asia absorbed nearly half of the official development assistance (ODA), which was marginally less than that in 1960. In terms of per capita receipts Asia was, like the preceding decade, on the lower end of the scale. It received $2.8 of official flows, the corresponding amount in Europe, Africa and Latin America were $3.9, $5.2 and $3.5, respectively.

The direction of resource flows is determined by a complex of historical and political factors. Once a pattern becomes established, it is slow to change. For Belgium, France, the Netherlands and the UK the principal determinant of direction was the existence of past links with LDCs, which had special linguistic, monetary or commercial associations. Other countries had no such past links, yet some of them did have their preferences. Thus, Canadian grants and aid went almost entirely to Commonwealth countries and Italian aid to Latin American LDCs and the Mediterranean countries. During this period France took the policy decision to increase assistance to LDCs outside the Franc zone, but the decision was slow in implementation. The widest dispersion was that of Germany, whose programmes covered 90 LDCs, outdoing even the US, whose programmes covered 70 LDCs. In case of donors with small programmes the tendency was to try to concentrate their efforts so as to have an identifiable responsibility and impact.

The cultural and commercial links also had a bearing on the habits of taste and product familiarity. Changes in the patterns established in the colonial period occurred slowly. Lastly, geographical distribution is theoretically related to the stage of development of the LDC. In the pre-industrial phase a country has a very limited absorptive capacity. However, as the infrastructure is built, manpower trained, market broadened and the industrial base established, investment opportunities increase rapidly. At the next stage of development LDC's own savings – supplemented by capital market flows – may suffice to meet the requirements.

Financial Terms

The data relating to the first quinquennium are not available. During the second one the weighted average of interest rates hovered around 3.5 per cent, only dropping to 3 per cent in 1964. The range of average maturity period of bilateral loans during the same period was between 22.2 and 28.4 years.[18] Information on the grace period is less complete; the available data suggest that over 65 per cent of the loans carried grace periods on capital of four years or more. Generally, longer grace periods were granted by donors whose loans were of long maturity. The donors were becoming increasingly conscious of the individual needs of LDCs, and in an effort to mitigate the debt burden were providing a mix of 'hard' and 'soft' terms loans. Second means adopted was the 'two-steps' procedure according to which the borrowing firm repays to the borrowing government on hard terms, but in local currency, then the government repays the donor in accordance with the terms adapted to the overall circumstances of the borrower. A third device, adopted by the UK, was to grant longer grace periods on interest and capital repayments in selected cases.

A DAC committee, established [in July 1965] to recommend the financial terms and conditions to be adopted by the members, required the donors to increase the proportion of assistance given as grants to 80 per cent, loans at interest rates of 3 per cent or less, and at the maturity period of twenty-five years or higher. In 1965 only eight of the fifteen donors met these numerical objectives. Canada and the UK improved their terms and tried to meet the objectives laid out. At this point the situation was as follows: most donors whose terms had been hitherto on the hard side had softened them. On the contrary, some donors whose terms were softer than the DAC average hardened them. Paradoxically the result was an overall hardening because of the relative weights in the operations of the two groups of donors.

ECONOMIC SETTING DURING THE SECOND POST-WAR PERIOD

By this time the world economy had completely recovered and the economic activity had continued to grow over the years, the post-war investment brought forth good returns, particularly in terms of industrial production. This was the first peace-time expansionist period, which lasted till 1957. The causes of the boom were not the pent up demand after the war or the Korean War boom. The economic expansion initially derived its impetus from investment in housing; next came the expansion in expenditure on consumer durables, followed by the automobile boom. Besides, industrial investment became a dominant force. During this upswing a pressure was being built on prices and wages in the industrial economies; there was a significant rise in costs as productivity began to lag behind the rise in wages. The declining rate of increase in average output per man in some industries was due to this fact and full utilisation of capacity was being approached.

In 1957 the rate of economic activity levelled off in the US and Canada, while in Western Europe the level of economic activity was higher, so was the ability to export, as the pressure of Europe's internal boom abated. The three years between 1956 and 1958 were the best years for the bilateral flows of resources from the industrial market economies of LDCs during the decade under review. The upsurge in economic activity naturally influenced the flows. The deterioration in the competitive power of the US led to a sharp drop in exports, and so adverse developments in the balance of payments, which led to a outflow of gold, and a growing rumour of 'dollar weakness'.[19] Production in the industrial market economies reached a plateau in 1958 and 1959, in fact in 1958 it fell by 2½ per cent. This happened for the first time in the post-war period. Investment slackened in most economies. This state of the world economy was also visible in the flow of resources to LDCs. The industrial economies had developed a certain prowess to resist the downward thrust of the business cycle, therefore the recession was of a short duration.

The years 1959 and 1960 saw an upswing in world industrial activity, which led to a sustained expansion of output and real income. This swiftness of rhythm of the world economy could again be percieved in the flow of resources to LDCs from the industrial market economies. Next year they recorded the highest growth rate of the decade, indicating a normal time-lag of one year.

The 1960s opened on a slightly contradictory note. The economic upswing came to a temporary pause in 1961, the reasons for which were: shortage of manpower in some industrial market economies, slackening aggregate demand and a fall in exports. Of all the mature economies the US showed signs of being the most vulnerable to post-war cyclical instability. The contrast between the booming Europe and a lagging US, reinforced by the difference in interest rates, accentuated the flow of capital to a point that brought the dollar under speculative pressure. This event changed the monetary climate. Dollars were attracted to Europe, and despite enormous reserves the US was impelled to take protective action – for the first time in the post-war period.

The period 1962 through 1965 was one of steady growth, and the US nurtured it by a judicious use of fiscal stimuli. The growth in production was widespread and uniform among the industrial regions. The disinflationary monetary and fiscal policies affected both the demand and supply sides. A diminution in price pressure was not always achieved, and when it was, it was at the cost of a slackening in the expansion of production. Yet the forces of economic expansion had gained strength and become broadly based, and in the international financial market there were fewer strains. In this economic setting the resource flows to LDCs could have been at a brisk pace, but they were not. It is easier for capital to flow to developing world when the industrialised economies are expanding than when they are not. Viewed from this angle, the time-span between 1962 and 1965 was an opportune one, though the opportunity was missed due to lack of political will.

During 1956 the value and volume of international trade touched a record level and was 11 per cent higher than 1955 level. Since there was a small increase in the general price level, the increase in volume was slightly less than proportional. The 1957–8 levelling-off of the industrial activity affected trade. Besides, the Suez Canal crisis introduced a disturbing element in the second half of 1956. World exports suffered a sharp decline in 1958 and the prices fell by 3 per cent. Prices fell again by 2 per cent in 1959. But in 1960 world trade recorded an increase. The unit value of world exports in primary commodities fell between 1956 and 1960, while that of manufactured products remained by and large stationary. The volume of world exports both in primary and manufactured goods recorded impressive rises, it was much higher for manufactured goods, as Table 4.6 shows:

TABLE 4.6   *Value and volume of world exports 1956–65*

Year	Value of world exports (in billions of $ FOB)	Unit value of world exports 1953 = 100		Volume of world exports 1953 = 100	
		P	M	P	M
1956	101.2 (10.8)	n.a.	103	n.a.	138
1957	109.7 (8.3)	101	104	126	149
1958	105.7 (−3.7)	96	103	124	149
1959	113.6 (7.4)	93	103	134	164
1960	126.1 (11.0)	93	105	144	183
1961	131.9 (4.5)	91	105.5	152	195
1962	139.0 (5.3)	90	105	158	208
1963	151.7 (9.1)	92.5	105	168	226
1964	169.8 (11.9)	95	107	178	254
1965	184.0 (8.3)	95	109	186	279

P = primary products; M = manufactured goods.

SOURCE   *International Trade* (Geneva: GATT, various volumes.)

As already mentioned, output in the industrial market economies rose faster after 1962; so did their imports. Relatively, the US and Canada recorded faster growth than the EEC and Japan. The heightened pace of world trade reflected essentially three major developments: (1) the quickening rhythm of manufacturing output in industrial economies; (2) changes in the market situation of certain foodstuffs; and (3) the increased import capacity of LDCs. The unit value of primary products as well as manufactured goods recorded a small rise between 1961 and 1965. The volume of trade in primary commodities also rose after 1962 at rates close to those in the preceding years. Because of the recovery in prices there was faster growth in export earnings of the LDCs. The slower growth in volume of trade in primary commodities as compared with manufactures reflected the continued trend in the international demand for the two commodity groups. Table 4.6 shows their widely divergent growth rates for the period under review. Despite a large number of erratic and conflicting influences,[20] world trade maintained its upward trend in 1965 for the third successive year.

Pattern of Imports of the Creditor Countries

The reason why this issue is being spotlighted, has already been dealt with. The initial projections of Western Europe's import requirements of foodstuffs, fuels, and industrial raw materials from LDCs between 1955 and 1960 were found to be on the low side. This was due to the fact that the growth of GDP in Europe was faster than projected. The marginal propensity to import primary goods at GDP growth rate of 2.4 per cent was calculated at 0.55, but it was found to be 0.7 at GDP growth rate of 4.4 per cent. In volume terms the marginal propensity to import primary goods was found to be 1.2 per cent. Besides, there was an increase in the marginal propensity to import ores and metals. The main reason for the unexpectedly rapid growth in imports of food-stuffs, beverages and tobacco, was that the income elasticity of demand proved to be far higher than assumed.[21] These elasticities were influenced by import liberalisation, reduction of excise and price developments. Many of the primary producing LDCs presented a less than happy picture because of the weakening of the prices of raw materials and beverages since mid-1955. This was largely due to increased competition from substitutes and rapidly expanding output. There was a downward pressure on agriculture and mineral exports prices, and the flattening out of industrial output in 1957–8 accelerated the downward movement. On the other hand, the export prices of manufactured goods, which had been rising since 1955, failed to decline.

The export earnings of LDCs continued to be determined largely by the demand for primary commodities and base metals in the industrial market economies. But since the early 1960s there has been a certain

TABLE 4.7 *Imports of industrial areas from the developing countries, 1956–65*

Year	Value in billions of $ FOB		Percentage of world imports
1956*	20.9		35.1
1957*	21.1	(0.9)	33.4
1958*	20.0	(−6·0)	33.6
1959	18.3		16.1
1960	19.3	(5.4)	15.3
1961	19.3	(0.0)	14.7
1962	20.3	(5.1)	14.6
1963	22.3	(9.8)	14.7
1964	24.4	(9.4)	14.4
1965	25.8	(5.7)	14.0

SOURCE *International Trade* (Geneva: GATT, various volumes).

*The data for these years are not comparable to the rest of the years because they are for non-industrial areas. This GATT classification included LDCs and Australia, New Zealand and South Africa.

diversification of the exports of LDCs, both by commodities and by geographical distribution. Exports of manufactures by LDCs rose more rapidly than those of primary commodities between 1962 and 1965. The first Development Decade fixed a target of 4 per cent for the export growth of LDCs, on the basis of certain assumptions and extrapolation of the past trends. However, between 1960 and 1965 the volume of exports went up by 6 per cent; in value terms they soared by 6.4 per cent. The imports of LDCs were projected to increase by 6.5 per cent over this period, the *ex post* figure was 5 per cent. The result was that LDCs had a comfortable balance-of-payments position in 1965; they achieved a small surplus of $700 million at 1960 prices.

This came to pass despite a continued decline in the prices of beverages and industrial raw materials. The terms of trade of non-oil LDCs fell, and those of industrialised market economies improved almost by the same margin.

As regards the market share of world trade by country groups, LDCs formed 27.7 per cent of the market of the industrialised economies in 1956, 25.5 per cent in 1960 and 21.1 per cent in 1965. Thus the importance of LDCs declined, which was because of the fact that the

TABLE 4.8   *Trends in the terms of trade, 1956–65 (1970 = 100)*

Year	Beverage prices	Agricultural raw materials	Terms of trade Non-oil LDCs	Industrial countries
1956	n.a.	n.a.	118.5	99.5
1957	77.3	73.6	113.4	99.4
1958	76.8	61.4	109.7	104.1
1959	64.8	68.0	110.4	105.8
1960	60.4	71.1	109.1	106.2
1961	56.8	66.2	108.8	107.5
1962	55.5	63.5	107.8	108.6
1963	54.1	64.9	106.9	109.2
1964	62.4	65.0	109.5	108.5
1965	56.6	63.1	109.9	109.0

SOURCE   *International Financial Statistics, Supplement on Price Statistics*, Series no. 2 (Washington, DC: IMF, 1981).

trade between the industrialised economies increased by about the same proportion. On the other hand, the share of size of LDCs' export market in the industrialised world remained by and large constant; they exported 73.3 per cent of their total exports to them in 1956, 72.2 per cent in 1960 and 71.6 per cent in 1965.[21] This is a period when the LDCs missed out an opportunity to expand their export marked in the industrial market economies.

The changing conditions of supply and demand resulted in widely diverging movements in the volume of trade in different primary commodities. Some of the largest increases in the quantity of exports occurred in the case of commodities with falling prices, such as sugar and cocoa. On the whole the value of trade in primary products, and in agriculture in particular, did not increase much over this period. The much faster growth in value terms in exports of manufactures relative to primary products reflected, to some extent, the divergent price movements. As already noted, though the balance-of-payments position of LDCs *en masse* was not unhealthy in 1965, yet a large number of them had inadequate reserves. Some started feeling the debt-servicing burden a little too heavy, so they applied import restrictions. During 1964 and 1965 this defensive measure was taken by Brazil, Colombia, Uruguay, Syria, UAR, Burma, Sri Lanka (then Ceylon), Morocco and Sudan.

THE THIRD POST-WAR DECADE: 1966–75

The sag in the bilateral resource flows, which started in 1962, continued through the mid-1960s. The Pearson Commission Report,[22] published towards the end of the first Development Decade, laments that:

> The experience gained in the last two decades bears out the promise – and the premise – of the efforts that have been made. Economic growth in many of the developing countries has proceeded at faster rates than the industrialized countries ever enjoyed at a similar stage in their own history. . . . However, international support for development is now flagging. In some of the rich countries its feasibility, even its purpose, is in question. This climate surrounding foreign aid programmes is heavy with disillusion and distrust. This is not true everywhere. Indeed, there are countries in which the opposite is true.

This report drummed up public support for development assistance, particularly in Europe and Canada. It saw development as a set of responsibilities, in an essentially bipolar world of developing and developed countries, concerned with mobilising resources for economic growth, which should be subject of 'a continuing review of performance' not dominated by the immediate economic and political interests of either the donors or the recipients.[23] Table 4.9 puts out the net annual disbursement of bilateral flows to LDCs and the multilateral institutions for the period under consideration:

The small increase in 1966 was due to the expansion of programmes of several small donors. The four largest donors – the US, France, the UK and Germany – which accounted for 80 per cent of the total flows, virtually stayed stationary. In 1967 the Official Development Association (ODA) increased by $7\frac{1}{2}$ per cent, the largest since 1961. In June next year Switzerland joined the DAC, bringing the membership to sixteen. In keeping with the trend, 1968 and 1969 proved to be lean years, the latter being the leanest of the decade. The decline stemmed from the virtual stagnation or fall in the flows from the three largest donors – the US, France and the UK – who were afflicted by the international financial crises and by domestic inflationary pressure. The smaller donors did reasonably well, but they experienced difficulty in making disbursements in keeping with appropriations because of their rapidly expanding programmes. However, the fall in the grant element of aid was insubstantial.

TABLE 4.9   *Bilateral flows (net disbursement) 1966–75 (in millions of US$)*

Year	Grants and grant-like flows	Long-term development lending	Total	Percentage change over last year
1966	3 802.3 (63.7)	2 163.8 (36.3)	5 966.1	3.5
1967	3 675.6 (57.3)	2 738.1 (42.7)	6 413.7	7.5
1968	3 418.0 (51.9)	3 168.1 (48.1)	6 586.1	2.7
1969	3 250.2 (58.3)	2 324.1 (41.7)	5 574.3	− 15.3
1970	3 309.3 (59.4)	2 357.4 (40.6)	5 666.7	16.5
1971	3 634.2 (56.6)	2 786.7 (43.4)	6 420.9	13.3
1972	4 369.7 (64.6)	2 396.8 (35.4)	6 766.5	5.4
1973	4 460.3 (62.7)	2 649.3 (37.3)	7 109.6	5.0
1974	5 335.9 (64.6)	2 921.2 (35.4)	8 257.1	16.1
1975	6 268.0 (63.9)	3 547.1 (36.1)	9 815.3	18.9

SOURCES   *Development Co-operation Review* (Paris: OECD, various issues).
The figures in parentheses = percentages of the total.

A word about aid tying, which till this point in time was an accepted practice. The dilemma of the donors was: they wished to minimise the drain on their balance of payments, also, they did not approve of the idea that other donors benefit from economic assistance given by them. On the recipients' side the evidence was clear that tying practices led to a loss in the real volume of aid supplied, and the overall efficiency of development assistance suffered. The air was rife with arguments relating to cost and benefit of this restrictive measure. At this point identifiable tied contributions accounted for nearly 60 per cent of gross disbursement. It should, however, be noted that over 40 per cent of the tied aid was in the form of grants, and so did not impose an increased repayment burden on LDCs. Aid tying essentially originated in American minds, since the US faced chronic balance-of-payments problems in the 1960s. As the US procurement controls became more and more stringent, other donors began to follow suit. To be sure, the DAC conceded the negative contributions of aid tying and explored ways to reduce its scope. Yet, for the time being, no significant formal steps were taken towards the relaxation of tying restrictions. The world moved on.

The Pearson Commission Report[24] exhorted a basic reexamination of the aid policies. Also, donors felt increasingly obliged to participate in the UN system's strategy for the second Development Decade and integrate themselves with it. In September 1970, majority of them agreed to untie bilateral developmental loans, and the LDCs became free to use them on the basis of competitive international trading.

During the second quinquennium the net flow of resources remained virtually stagnant, their real value declined because of inflation and exchange-rate fluctuations. In 1971 there was a spurt, again to stagnate in the next two years. In nominal terms 1974 and 1975 proved to be better. In 1972 New Zealand became the seventeenth member of the DAC. The recurrent stagnation in the flows manifested 'donor fatigue'. Much was also heard about the disillusionment in LDCs with external help, and a determination to get along without it. This was summed up as 'the crisis of development'. The allegation was that the industrial world is no longer interested in economic assistance, which was found to be valid at least for the volume and terms of the US aid.[25] However, the decline in the percentage of GNP disbursement by Germany and Japan was more due to conjunctural difficulties than to any decline in public support of aid. Nearly all donors, except the US, underwent a series of organisational and policy changes designed to improve the quality and quantity of aid.

The LDCs were disgruntled because they thought that the concessional economic assistance was being offered as charity, and it was not dignified to accept it, or they resented the strings that were thought to be inevitably attached to it, or because they sometimes found that it distorted their developmental priorities.[26] Many LDCs made it clear that they prefered an independent position, with development needs financed from their export proceeds or commercial finance over which they had full control. This is the reason why they started entering the international capital market.

In its second effort to streamline the terms and conditions of resource flows, the DAC published (in October 1972) the Recommendations on Terms and Conditions of Aid,[27] under which the donors were coaxed to maintain an average grant element of at least 84 per cent. Of the seventeen donors, twelve complied with the recommendations in 1973, eleven again complied in 1974.

An outstanding feature of this period is that aid burden became more broadly shared. While the commitments of the US fell, several DAC members improved their contributions, the important ones were, Canada, Denmark, the Netherlands, Norway and Sweden.

Geographical Distribution

The pattern of utilisation of external resources changed during this decade, it was better integrated into the development efforts of the recipients. The single-function projects were related to community development. The approach adopted was holistic. Assistance for development was carried out within the framework of a national plan in which the interrelation of projects to other developments could be seen. Multinational projects were another novel feature of this period. Such projects involving the small countries of South-East Asia, Africa or Central America, were based largely upon the efforts to create a market large enough to permit economies of scale to operate. Large river basin related schemes, e.g. Indus or Mekong, were the outcome of this line of thinking.

As for the direction of flows, the old emphases not only continued but became more specific. The donors could now be clearly divided into three groups: the first one which allocated on the basis of historical and political links, e.g. Australia, Belgium, the Netherlands, Portugal and the UK. The second group lacked such links, yet it had come to a decision about the LDCs of its choice, or the 'first choice' countries; the Scandinavian countries, Canada and Japan fell into this category. The third group was the US, Germany, Austria and Switzerland, whose allocations were widespread in many regions of the world. Some recipients had a privileged status in the aid programme of a certain donor. These special ties were based on military alliances, strategic location or mutual economic interests, or more than one of these at the same time. In cases where preferential treatment was missing, aid tended to be provided in greater quantity and on softer terms to countries with low per capita income. Relatively less ODA was provided to countries having access to the capital market.

During the beginning of the decade under consideration, slightly less than half of the net ODA went to Asia. India alone absorbed nearly one-fifth of the total volume, but its share fell soon. Africa accounted for less than one-fourth – two-thirds of which went to the Sahelian countries. Latin America absorbed one-sixth of the total. Among countries, after India, the biggest recipients were Pakistan, South Vietnam, South Korea, Brazil and Turkey, in that order. Towards the end of the decade the share of Asia was almost the same – that is, slightly less than half. India again was the biggest recipient, followed by Indonesia, Pakistan, Israel, Bangladesh and the Philippines. The share of Africa increased somewhat to nearly one-third, with Egypt drawing the maximum attention of the donors, followed by Réunion, Morocco, Algeria and Zaïre, in that order. Latin America absorbed one-eighth of the total.

Financial Terms

During the first quinquennium of the decade the US commitments amounted to over two-thirds of the total; therefore overall terms were dominated by the US terms. Until 1968 the grant element remained around 75 per cent. Average interest rates fell from 3.8 per cent to 3.6 per cent, average maturities rose from 24 to 26 years, and the average grace period increased from 5.5 to 6 years. This improved the financial terms. In the 1970s, however, US domination declined. Also, the ODA was being redistributed in favour of the low-income LDCs, away from the high-income LDCs. Several donors, as indicated, showed more adaptability to the needs of the individual LDCs; for example, they appeared ready to contribute to the financing of so-called local costs. The recommendations made by the DAC regarding 'terms target' in 1972 did have an impact, as seen in Table 4.10.

TABLE 4.10   *Financial terms, 1970–5*

	1970	*1971*	*1972*	*1973*	*1974*	*1975*
Percentage of grants in total	63.4	58.7	63.1	65.5	65.4	69.3
Overall grant element of the total ODA (%)	84.1	82.2	84.1	86.9	86.0	88.6
Maturity (years)	30.2	29.1	29.5	32.6	28.9	32.6
Interest rates (%)	2.8	2.8	2.8	2.5	2.6	2.5
Grace period (years)	7.3	7.1	7.8	8.6	7.7	9.1

SOURCES   Development Co-operation Review (Paris: OECD, various issues).

In 1975 the DAC members even exceeded the 1972 recommendations, and the financial terms were at their softest. Not all the DAC members, however, complied. Japan remained an exception because its overall concessionality level remained below the 84 per cent grant-element target. The financial terms on commitments to LLDCs complied with the recommendations for all the DAC members, the only exception in this regard was Finland.

ECONOMIC SETTING DURING THE THIRD POST-WAR DECADE

The period following 1966 was one in which the world economy was put to severe tests and had to make adjustments. Industrial production decelerated because of (1) limits imposed by capacity shortage; (2) weakening in the underlying forces of expansion; and (3) the disinflationary measures taken earlier. In many industrial market economies inflation persisted and crises in foreign exchange markets kept recurring because of the balance-of-payments disequilibria. Financial instability was exacerbated by delay in applying corrective measures, and, when applied, these measures had markedly adverse effects on growth and employment. Failure to make timely shift in the fiscal policy was widespread; the belated stabilisation measures took the form of more stringent monetary policy than would otherwise have been called for. The outcome of all this was a sluggishness in the international economy, which became pervasive and persistent. The weakening of commodity prices resulted in strain in the balance-of-payments situation of many primary producing LDCs. International monetary and financial co-operation was strained to its limit. The multilateral financial institutions and national monetary authorities acted in concert to support the system and the UK and the US took comprehensive measures to redress their balance of payments. Good harvests and the reflationary policies pursued by some industrial economies led to a turnaround in the cyclical situation in 1968. But it did not influence the bilateral flows to LDCs, and the quinquennium is justifiably noted for being a stagnant period. The financial turmoil of this period told heavily on the ODA to LDCs.

The turnaround in 1968 was ephemeral, and the world economy slid back into recession in 1969 and 1970. The ODA flows were seen at their briskest in 1970, meaning thereby a lagged reaction. The domestic price increases first in the US and then in the other industrial economies spilled over much more strongly than in the past, via foreign trade. The higher costs of imports affected the terms of trade of the LDCs and led to a current account deficit. But there was an overall balance-of-payments surplus because of the renewed surge of ODA in 1970.

In 1970 the relationships between the key currencies was out of joint; added to this was inflation and the succession of currency crises, which led to yield–induced flows of short-term capital. In December 1971 major currencies were realigned. The instability continued, the US and the Canadian economies went into recession, inflation in the industrial economies accelerated and so did the deficits of the US. It should be recalled that deficits in the US were continuing since the 1960s, which meant an excess of dollars with its trading partners, notably Germany and Japan.

Two exogenous factors enhanced the upward pressure on prices. In

1972 there was a poor harvest in a number of countries which caused foodgrain shortages. Second, the Yom Kippur War of 1973, followed by the fourfold increase in oil prices. These shocks worked their interrelated effect on investment, trade and financial flows. It is widely held that the oil-shock exacerbated inflation and caused recession. The explanation is as follows: imported oil – or energy in general – is a third factor in the production function. Therefore an increase in oil's relative price will cause an adverse shift in the aggregate supply curve that produces higher price level and lower output. There are several studies which computed the fall in productivity growth and reduction in real income.[28]

The disinflationary policies were continued in 1974, even after the demand began to recede and industrial production began to slacken. The consequence was reduction in industrial capacity utilisation and, correspondingly, unemployment. Investment showed few signs of recovery in the US in 1975, and prices continued to rise at a rate high by historical standards. In other market economies, there were few signs of recovery; inflation persisted and governments were more tolerent of high levels of unemployment than at any time in the post-war period. As may be visualised, the ODA flows, under such circumstances, stagnated. The nominal increase in 1974 and 1975 was swamped by inflation and currency value realignments.

The performance of the world economy was reflected in trade, at times with lags. As seen in Table 4.11, trade did better than the world production, particularly in 1969 and 1970, because of (1) the unexpected strength of the US import demand; (2) sharp price hikes, which inflated trade in value terms; (3) large increases in the invisible earnings of countries heavily dependent on such earnings, which enabled them to increase their commodity imports more than their exports; and (4) the substantial increase in world liquidity, reflecting the US deficits, the introduction of SDRs and the multiplier effect of the Eurodollar market.

Error enters these estimates because of the distortions introduced in the process of translating trade values expressed in national currencies into US dollars, while currencies fluctuate, which leads to a loss of precision in all price indices and measures of unit value. In 1971 the dollar value of world trade increased by almost 11 per cent. The year 1973 is noted for a strong investment and production boom of brief duration, record trade expansion, the demise of the fixed exchange-rate system and an adoption of managed floating. This was stimulated by a superabundance of national and international liquidity. The dollar

TABLE 4.11   *Value and volume of world exports 1966–75*

Year	Value of world exports (in billions) of $ FOB)	Unit value of world exports (1960 = 100) A	MF	M	Volume of world exports (1960 = 100) A	MF	M
1966	204 (10.2)	101	113	104	130	140	171
1967	215 (5.4)	100	109	106	130	153	181
1968	240 (11.6)	101	110	107	133	173	205
1969	273 (13.8)	104	115	108	139	181	238
1970	312 (14.3)	108	121	117	149	198	254
1971	351 (12.5)	114	135	124	151	197	273
1972	416 (18.5)	127	146	134	163	208	302
1973	576 (38.5)	199	194	156	152	230	347
1974	836 (45.1)	248	480	193	149	209	370
1975	878 (4.8)	282	489	217	165	199	360

A = Agricultural products
MF = Minerals and fuels
M = Manufactures
SOURCE   *International Trade* (Geneva: GATT, various issues).

value of exports increased by 45 per cent in 1974, and the unit value by some 40 per cent. This must be interpreted with caution, because inflation occurred in the export prices of the exporting countries. The recession which hit the world in 1975 was the deepest so far in the post-war period, total world production declined by 2 per cent, that in the industrial countries by 6 per cent. But the value of world exports recorded a small gain.

Pattern of Imports of Creditor Countries

In 1966 the non-oil LDCs had a balance-of-payments surplus of $450 million, but it was limited to a few in the Far East, where external receipts expanded in connection with the hostilities in Vietnam. The exports of the LDCs accelerated more in the second quinquennium of the 1960s than those of the industrial countries. The reasons were: First, because of the significant demand of the industrial economies for raw materials, particularly for ores. Second, the impact of the growing exports of manufactures from LDCs began to be felt. These exports were concentrated in a few product groups, but they were gradually diversifying. Third, a number of middle-income LDCs were drawn into

TABLE 4.12 *Import of industrial areas from the non-oil developing countries, 1966–75*

Year	Value in billions of $ FOB		Percentage of world imports
1966	27.4*		13.4*
1967	28.7*		13.4*
1968	20.6		8.7
1969	na		na
1970	26.5		8.5
1971	27.3	(3.0)	7.9
1972	33.1	(21.2)	8.0
1973	47.7	(44.1)	8.3
1974	67.2	(40.8)	8.0
1975	66.9	(−0.4)	7.8

*Also includes oil-exporting countries.
Figures in parentheses = growth over the previous year.
SOURCE *International Trade* (Geneva: GATT, various issues).

the expanding markets of the industrial countries and gained from the boom in commodity imports.

Though the volume of developed market economy imports from LDCs increased by 5 per cent in 1971 – below the long-term average – the subsequent upsurge raised the average 1971–3 rate of increase to 12 per cent a year. The expansion was greater, over 20 per cent a year, in the case of the manufactured goods. Manufacturing production in the industrial market economies rose with a steep rate, before levelling-off in 1974. The resultant increase in the input requirements, and in income, was reinforced in varying degree by policies favouring imports from LDCs. The dominance of the major items remained; three categories of imports (petroleum, beverages and non-ferrous metals) continued to account for half the total. Another four categories (ores, fruits and vegetables, fibre and sugar) brought the share to two-thirds. The recession in the industrial market economies started influencing their imports from LDCs, which declined for the second time in 1975 since the war.[29] The fall was marginal in value terms, but 8 per cent in volume. The industrial market economies' exports to LDCs rose in value terms by 7 per cent, resulting mainly from the increase of 60 per cent in exports in OPEC in 1975. The corresponding figure was 80 per cent in 1974.

Table 4.13 shows the changes in terms of trade of the two country groups. The prices of beverages and agricultural raw materials increased substantially between 1966 and 1974, though they registered a recession-induced fall in 1975. The terms of trade of the non-oil LDCs remained virtually stationary, until 1975 when they registered a fall. This was not due to the improvement in the terms of trade of the industrialised countries, because their terms of trade also remained virtually stationary till 1973, and in the aftermath of the oil-shock fell in 1974, but recovered in 1975. The fall of 17 points between 1973 and 1975 in the terms of trade of LDCs can be attributed to a rise in the unit value of oil, which went up from 29 to 100 during this period.

TABLE 4.13 *Trends in the terms of trade, 1966–75 (1975 = 100)*

| | | | Terms of trade | |
Year	Beverage prices	Agricultural raw materials	Non-oil LDCs	Industrial countries
1966	59.0	64.7	110.4	110.2
1967	59.1	58.8	108.9	111.6
1968	59.6	57.3	112.6	111.0
1969	61.8	60.8	115.5	111.9
1970	69.9	55.4	116.8	111.4
1971	64.5	55.1	109.4	111.0
1972	70.6	72.1	108.5	112.5
1973	87.1	129.2	116.7	110.7
1974	104.0	124.6	111.2	97.7
1975	100.0	100.0	100.0	100.0

SOURCE *International Financial Statistics, Supplement on Price Statistics*, Series No. 2 (Washington, DC: IMF, 1981).

As regards the market shares of the world trade by country groups, the developed market economies exported 20.9 per cent of their exports to LDCs in 1966, 18.4 per cent in 1970 and 24.0 per cent in 1975. This means that the LDC markets became more important to the industrial economies. The mutual trade of the industrial economies fell by about the same proportion. On the other hand, the developing countries exported 72.5 per cent of their exports to industrial countries in 1966, 74.0 per cent in 1970 and 70.2 per cent in 1975. Thus the importance of the western economies declined for the LDCs; their mutual trade recorded an increase by the same proportion. This implies that their trade pattern of LDCs became diversified.[30]

The Impact of Economic Fluctuations on the Liquid Resources of the LDCs

The growth capacity in LDCs is sensitive to the external environment because their ratio of exports to total production is almost twice as high as that in the developed countries. An important exogenous factor is weather; the poor harvest of 1972 coincided with rise in demand, sending prices up. There was a rapid rise in the export unit value, and so notable expansion in export earnings. Since most LDCs exercise exchange controls the effect was accumulation of international reserves. In aggregate they increased by 43 per cent in 1972 and 23 per cent in 1973. The average increase between 1966 and 1971 was 9 per cent.

TABLE 4.14 *Total reserves of non-oil developing countries, 1966–75 (in million of SDRs)*

Year	Amount
1966	11 280
1967	12 001
1968	14 006
1969	15 360
1970	16 874
1971	17 778
1972	25 343
1973	31 216
1974	31 682
1975	30 913

($1.16 = 1 SDR)

SOURCE *International Financial Statistics* (Washington DC: IMF, 1982).

The flush reserve position was short-lived. For some LDCs poor harvests necessitated larger imports of cereals, whose prices trebled between 1971 and 1974. Next the oil prices soared and those of commodities weakened. These developments adversely affected the liquidity position of certain LDCs. The terms of trade of LDCs began eroding in 1974, and the cyclical downturn in the industrial countries soon started influencing the current accounts of LDCs (see Table 4.13). There was a loss of buoyancy in their export markets and a need to maintain essential imports, which raised the current account deficit even further in 1975. Their need for external resources remained high, many non-oil LDCs had already strained their debt-servicing capacity, and confronted an enlarged deficit in the current account. The deficits rose from $11 billion in 1973 to $37 billion in 1974, they further deteriorated to $47 billion in 1975.[31] Despite nominal increases in the flow of the IDA, the non-oil LDCs were forced to borrow abroad in 1974 and 1975, or in some cases draw down their reserves. They had to do this in a period when prices of manufactured goods were rising (Table 4.11). By the end of 1975 the volume of imports into LDCs were shrinking under external financial strains.

The statistics relating to the reserves of non-oil developing countries indicates something striking; rather than draw down their reserves to a low level to finance the deficits the developing countries borrowed abroad to add to their reserves.[32]

THE CONTEMPORARY PERIOD: 1976–83

After two years of progress in nominal terms, bilateral flows recorded a set-back in 1976, for the first time in the 1970s. The ODA contributions of seven donors fell due to accidental factors, such as, bunching of expenditures out of 1975–6 appropriations in the case of Australia, or unexpected disbursement delays in case of Canada and Japan. Severe restrictive budgetary policies affected the contributions of Germany and New Zealand. The American performance remained relatively stable. During the conference on International Economic Co-operation in 1976 in Paris, Japan, the Netherlands, the Nordic countries and Switzerland expressed their determination to raise their ODA levels.

This was the period when it was being increasingly realised that North–South co-operation is a non-zero-sum game. The DAC flows, in nominal terms, were trending upwards, as shown in Table 4.15. This cause was aided by the two Brandt Commission Reports.[33] Notwithstanding the flaws, they were the most comprehensive and robust account of the North–South issues. The sluggish performance of 1979 was due to a decline in the US disbursement by $1 billion, because of the delayed action on contributions by the Congress. In 1981 the dollar appreciated markedly against most members' currencies – on average 14 per cent. Therefore, adjusted both for price fluctuations and for exchange rate, there was a meagre rise in the ODA volume. The outstanding feature of 1981 was an impressive rise in the ODA/GNP

TABLE 4.15 *Bilateral flows (net disbursement), 1976–83 (in millions of US$)*

Year	Grants and grant-like flows	Long-term development lending	Total	Percentage change over last year
1976	6 541.9 (68.9)	2 962.5 (31.1)	9 504.6	− 3.2
1977	7 202.7 (71.4)	2 881.1 (28.6)	10 083.8	6.1
1978	9 402.8 (71.6)	3 720.6 (28.4)	13 123.4	30.1
1979	11 285.4 (70.9)	4 628.4 (29.1)	15 913.8	21.3
1980	13 656.2 (77.6)	3 948.6 (22.4)	17 604.8	10.6
1981	13 184.3 (72.1)	5 098.4 (27.9)	18 282.7	3.9
1982	13 421.0 (72.5)	5 122.0 (27.5)	18 543.0	1.3
1983	14 126.0 (76.2)	4 403.0 (23.8)	18 529.0	− 0.03

SOURCE *Development Co-operation Review* (Paris: OECD, various issues).
The figures in parentheses = the percentage of the total.

ratio of the Netherlands, which reached 1.08. The erratic effect of the exchange rate continued in 1982, when the ODA volume stayed virtually stationary. Countries whose ODA had grown slowly in the earlier periods, adopted larger volume targets in the 1980s, this group included Finland, France, Italy, Japan and Germany. On the contrary, some countries slowed down, because they had either reached, or come close to their volume targets. This group included Denmark, the Netherlands, Norway and Sweden. According to 1982 data this country group remains the highest donor in terms of ODA/GNP ratio; the Netherlands again reached its 1981 performance, and the average for the four for 1982 was 0.95 per cent. Budgetary constraints arising in the late 1970s account for the slowing down in the growth of ODA from Canada, New Zealand and the UK. For the US the rate of growth of ODA was slower than that of GNP, so the ODA/GNP ratio remained at 0.23.

In nominal terms the ODA level in 1983 was slightly less than in 1982, but in real terms it dipped below the level of the preceding year. The fall can be ascribed to a marked decline in development lending. This led to a fall in the ODA/GNP ratio of the DAC countries from 0.38 per cent in 1982 to 0.36 per cent in 1983. A wide disparity is visible in the performance of the individual donors. Between 1982 and 1983, nine of them increased their disbursements in real terms. Switzerland, Japan, Finland and Canada recorded increases of more than 10 per cent. To offset these increases were the declines recorded by Austria, the Netherlands, Sweden, Australia and the United States. In terms of the ODA/GNP ratio Norway (1.6 per cent), the Netherlands (0.91 per cent) and Sweden (0.85 per cent) top the donor list, whereas Austria (0.23 per cent) remains at the bottom and is closely followed by the United States (0.24 per cent).

Let us not lose sight of the woods while looking at the trees. Therefore, for a better perspective, I propose to look back at the recent past years. If biannual averages are taken for the volume of ODA between 1977–78 and 1982–3, we observe an average annual growth rate of 4.8 per cent in real terms. This rate is more rapid than the growth rate of combined GNP of the DAC countries over this period. Yet, this rate clearly suggests a slowing down in the recent past, because the same biannual average for the years 1976–7 to 1981–2 comes to 5.3 per cent. Another feature which emerges from this examination is that the four Nordic donors, namely Norway, Sweden, Denmark and the Netherlands, contributed 12 per cent to the growth in ODA over this period. This level is more than twice as high as their combined share in the GNP of the DAC countries. This country group reached the ODA/GNP target of 0.7 per cent during the 1970s, and has remained above this level ever since. In terms of volume, the large donors are Japan, France, Germany, Italy and the United States; these five countries accounted for 79 per cent of the combined DAC GNP but provided 88 per cent of the growth in ODA during the 1977–8 to 1982–3 period. The United States, the largest donor among DAC countries, has not recorded wide fluctuations in disbursement during this period; the bilateral assistance grew at a moderate pace throughout the period and has accelerated a little since 1980. France, the second largest DAC donor, is the only country among the five major donors which has attained the 0.7 per cent target. During the period under review, both France and Japan maintained a high (22 +) average growth rate of contribution to the ODA coffer.

Geographical Distribution

Once the world economy picked up from the 1975 recession, the volume of ODA rose, but the volume of geographical distribution was not always in line with the needs of a particular country or country group. If the non-oil LDCs are divided into two main groups: low-income and middle-income countries, with the former group comprising LDCs having per capita income below $265 (in 1975), the share of ODA to this group declined marginally. It was 50 per cent in 1970, but

45 per cent in 1976. Though the DAC members collectively raised their share to low-income countries, it was offset by the cessation of US aid to Vietnam. If aid per capita is taken into account, it would seem that the low-income LDCs received less. Their ODA receipts as a group amounted to $5.5 per capita in 1976, compared with $8.6 for the middle-income LDCs.[34] On the other hand, in case of the ODA as a share of the GNP, the low-income LDCs were higher than the middle-income ones. This share was 3.7 per cent for the former group in 1976, while 1 per cent for the latter group. Similarly ODA made a much greater contribution to financing the imports of the low-income LDCs than that of middle-income ones, 28.5 per cent versus 4.2 per cent.

The averages mentioned in the preceding paragraph should not be read too closely, because the crux of satisfactory distribution lies in the need and absorptive capacity of an LDC. Also, there are limits to drawing on external resources for stimulating domestic investment and saving. This limit is determined by the stage of growth of the LDC and by other financial variables. The poorer an LDC the more difficult it would be to service new debt,[35] this acts as a deterent in many cases.

Slowly rising aid levels to LLDCs became a major feature of aid flows during this sub-period. This country group received 4.5 per cent of the total in 1976, 17.7 per cent in 1979 and 20.5 per cent in 1982. For the other country groups the division was as follows:

LDC groups	Per capita income in 1980	Proportion of total ODA	
		1979	1982
		%	%
Least-developed countries	According to the UN definition	17.7	20.5
China and India	$240 & $290	4.7	6.8
Other low-income countries	Below $600	27.7	22.3
Lower middle-income countries	$600 to $1200	14.9	13.8
Upper middle-income countries	Above $1200	18.4	15.7

N.B. Totals do not add up to 100 because large portions of resources remained unallocated and unspecified during both the years.

Among the least-developed countries (LLDCs) the Sahelan countries of sub-Saharan Africa reflected a special problem; this was recognised by the donor countries and agencies. With 11 per cent of the total developing country population this region accounted for 40 per cent of the total increase in allocation since 1978. The aid reliance ratio[36] of this country group is high and rising. In 1980–1 it reached 17.1 per cent. For the other low-income countries this ratio was 7.8 per cent. Efforts to India and China increased substantially, essentially because China was recognised as an LDC in 1980 by the DAC, and added to the list of recipients. The other groups of LDCs recorded small declines in their shares.

According to the 1981 data Asia, having 70 per cent of the developing country population received 28.6 per cent of the total ODA, making it 1.1 per cent of their GNP. Latin America, having 10.8 per cent of the population, received 10.5 per cent of the ODA, it was 0.4 per cent of their GNP. In the populous, low-income countries of Asia, namely, Bangladesh, India, Indonesia and Pakistan, aid receipts have declined. India suffers from the large-country effect. Besides, many donors view the Indian economy as a resilient one, and so believe that it should rely on less concessional types of flows. Yet it remains the largest aid recipient in absolute terms, notwithstanding the fact that its share of total ODA dropped from 10.6 per cent to 7.5 per cent between 1976 and 1981. The declining share of Indonesia is a reflection of its increases in foreign exchange receipts from oil. Pakistan's needs were reduced by massive remittances from the Gulf states. The effect of a decline in non-project aid for Bangladesh was partly offset by higher project aid. Latin America's ODA share has remained stable around 10 per cent. Among the low-income countries of this region, Bolivia registered above-average increases, notably from Japan and Germany. Haiti, the only LLDC of the region, registered an aid increase significantly below the average for LLDCs.

If for a fuller perspective one looks at a longer period, say, 1977–83, one again finds that the observations already made are confirmed. Over this period there has been a sharp increase in the volume of assistance to LLDCs, it grew at an annual average rate of 5.8 per cent in real terms. In particular, the sub-Saharan countries absorbed 40 per cent of the increases in bilateral assistance. This was largely because of the realisation that economic situation in these countries is nothing short of dire emergency. A fall was observed in the proportion of receipt by the low income countries in Asia, like India and Pakistan. The upper-middle-income developing countries are still significant recipients of bilateral assistance.

Financial Terms

In February 1978 the DAC made a third set of recommendations for the financial terms, which was readily adopted by the members. It was proposed that in order to achieve further softening of financial terms the grant element should be 86 per cent on average; the softest possible terms were recommended for the LLDCs, with average grant element at 90 per cent. The financial terms for the period under review were as shown in Table 4.16.

TABLE 4.16 *Financial terms, 1976–83*

	1976	1977	1978	1979	1980	1981	1982	1983
Grant as share of ODA commitments (%)	69.6	72.1	73.4	76.6	75.2	75.2	76.9	79.7
Interest rates (%)	2.6	2.7	2.6	2.6	2.8	2.6	2.8	2.9
Maturity (years)	32.8	32.2	32.5	31.2	29.8	29.1	29.8	28.4
Grace period (years)	9.0	10.8	8.9	8.5	8.8	10.1	8.5	8.2
Grant element (%)	62.3	61.5	61.5	61.0	59.2	58.2	58.3	56.6
Grant element of total ODA commitments	88.5	89.3	89.8	90.9	89.9	89.6	90.4	91.2

The financial terms softened. In 1976 over two-thirds of ODA commitments by the DAC countries were outright grants; in 1982 this rose to over three-quarters. The terms of loans hardened a tiny bit, though they remained effectively shielded from the general rise in the world interest rates during these years. The concessionality, as measured by the grant element using the standard discount rate of 10 per cent, remained very high, varying between 89 and 91 per cent. Australia, New Zealand, Norway and Sweden, extend virtually the totality of their ODA in grant form. Only two donors, Austria and Japan, commit more aid in the form of loans than in the form of grants. All DAC members, other than Austria and Japan, met the terms target. Ten DAC members extend aid to LLDCs in grant form only. The DAC average for grant element for LLDCs was 94 per cent in 1982. Italy and Japan did not comply with the sub-target of terms for LLDCs.

ECONOMIC SETTING DURING THE CONTEMPORARY PERIOD

The recovery that set in in 1976 was a hesitant one, because of the lack of fixed investment. The economic conditions took a turn for the better in 1977, but the two years following the recession were the leanest years from the point of view of bilateral resource flows to LDCs, they recorded a fall even in nominal terms in 1976, perhaps a result of the 1975 recession. The recovery continued in 1978, but historically high levels of unemployment persisted, though inflation continued to subside. Three years after the trough of the recession there was 11 per cent capacity underutilisation in the industrial economies.

Like 1973, 1979 turned out to be another eventful year. The internationally co-ordinated measures taken in 1978 for calming the foreign exchange markets, fructified the next year. Stagflation (inflation + unemployment) persisted in the industrial market economies. Also during the same year OPEC put into operation a complex system under which the official export prices of oil ranged from $18 to $23 a barrel, compared with a weighted average of $13 a barrel. This occurred when the oil market was bullish. In the US interest rates rose at historically high levels because of the fiscal and monetary policies, and the high rates were quickly transmitted to Euro-currency markets. How these developments proved to be detrimental to LDCs, we shall see later. Recession began to set in in the developed market economies in the second half of 1979; the second recession in one decade. This recession was not quite as deep as the 1975 one, but it was, for sure, a broad one, and the growth of output slowed markedly in 1980 in the industrial market economies. This coincided with oil prices touching the $30 mark. A notable source of uncertainty and international concern during 1980–1 was the prevalance of very high rates of interest, in nominal and real terms. These interest rates resulted from the interaction of firmer monetary restraint in a number of industrial countries with the momentum of inflation. The resource flows to LDCs picked up during 1978–80, both in real and nominal terms. Again, in 1981 the GNP growth rate of industrial countries dipped to less than 1 per cent, for the second time in succession, and the resource flow to LDCs was of disappointing proportion. An encouraging fact was that monetary expansion was restrained and the inflationary surge abated; this was conducive to stable prices. The aid flows levelled off in 1981–2. Sluggish economies can be reluctant donors.

Over the years various rigidities and structural imbalances had become entrenched in the industrial economies. To name a few: wage bargaining, price-setting, government subsidies, protection of ailing industries, structural unemployment heavy burden of transfer payments. These rigidities were also reflected in the fiscal policies, and large deficits became prevalent. The deficits had an adverse direct effect on prices and costs, and hindered the effectiveness of monetary restraint in various ways.

The anti-inflationary measures taken by the major industrial countries led to demand contraction, which in turn curtailed growth of production. The deflationary effect of such policies was vividly visible till 1982, for example, for the first time in the post-war years the developing countries did not grow, the production actually contracted in 1982 by 0.7 per cent. In the industrial countries as well as the newly industrialising countries (NICs) unemployment reached record levels. During the first quarter of 1983, the international economy, led by the United States, started moving out of the recession. West European countries were slow movers in this respect. At this point a high-performing LDC, Mexico, defaulted on its international financial obligations, and several other Latin American countries were at the brink. This created turbulence in the international financial and monetary markets and dampened the capital market flows to developing countries. A monotomic decline in the terms of trade of non-oil LDCs since 1977 created debt-service problems for several LDCs, and many of them found themselves painted in a corner.

The recovery which reluctantly began in 1983, gained momentum in 1984. The fast movers were the United States and the NICs. The EEC countries remained lethargic. World production expanded at a rate of 2 per cent in 1983, the forecast for 1984 was 4 per cent. It should be noted that these are moderate for a recovery period. To accommodate the debt service payments, the Latin American economies were forced to go on austerity programmes which deflated economic activity. The demands for primary commodities and oil were weak, therefore numerous developing countries experienced payments difficulties. Various sub-groups among the developing countries were plagued by their own problems, for example, the Latin American had a high debt-service ratio, the sub-Saharan were reeling under a drought, and those in South and South-East Asia found that their growth and investment rates in 1984 were lower than their averages for the 1970s.

In 1976 the value of world trade rose by 13 per cent, the corresponding increase in volume was 11 per cent. The recovery in industrial economies stimulated imports more than exports. As mentioned earlier, the two distorting statistical effects should be borne in mind: those caused by high rates of inflation and fluctuations in exchange rates. Besides, the statistical change in dollar unit value is a composite of

TABLE 4.17 *Value and volume of world exports 1976–83*

Year	Value of world exports (in billions of $ FOB)	Unit value of world exports (1963 = 100)			Volume of world exports (1963 = 100)		
		A	MF	M	A	MF	M
1976	991 (12.8)	230	510	212	163	184	328
1977	1 125 (13.5)	255	550	232	166	188	344
1978	1 303 (15.8)	262	563	266	183	193	364
1979	1 635 (25.5)	300	780	303	196	201	382
1980	1 985 (21.4)	330	1 200	337	202	183	398
1981	1 970 (− 1.0)	315	1 320	352	208	162	416
1982	1 842 (− 5.2)	288	1 232	314	209	153	410
1983	1 807 (− 1.9)	283	1 140	300	211	152	429

A = Agricultural products.
MF = Minerals and fuels.
M = Manufactures.
The figures in parentheses = the percentage increase over the previous year.
SOURCE   *International Trade* (Geneva: GATT, various issues).

domestic prices of goods entering world trade and the exchange rate of the dollar. So the trade estimates were subject to a considerably wide margin of error.

In 1978 world trade increased by 16 per cent in dollar terms, the corresponding rise in volume terms was 6 per cent. Increases in 1979–80 were particularly sharp, due essentially to the accelerated rise in dollar unit values, from 10 per cent in 1978 to 18 per cent in 1979. The dollar unit values of petroleum recorded the steepest rise of some 45 per cent, while those of other primary products and manufactures rose by 14 per cent. It should be noted that the growth in the value of world trade in the 1970s, particularly since 1975, was determined more by the rise in dollar unit values than by increase in volume, which was the case for the 1960s.

Until 1975 the spirit of the Rome Communiqué[37] was observed by most countries in restraining their intensification of trade restrictions, despite enlarged current account deficits and recessions.[38] Output in industrial countries had stagnated, while in LDCs industrial capacity, production and exports continued to rise. Import absorption in a stagnant market created friction and so demand for protection intensified in the industrial market economies. By 1977 protectionistic pressures became a dreaded reality. In the 1970s the world economy remained on a lower long-run growth path, when the cyclical downswing was imposed upon it, the result was minimum growth in production and then trade. World trade stagnated in 1981; on value basis it declined by 1 per cent.

After a recession-induced decline, world trade in primary commodities increased by 14 per cent in dollar value in 1976, also the prices recovered. This applies more to raw materials of agricultural origin, which benefited from the recovery of manufacturing activity in the industrial economies. There was a further substantial rise in the prices of the non-fuel primary products in 1978. Unit values of manufactures also continued to rise; they increased by more than a fifth in 1978, mainly due to rising costs. The export prices of petroleum went up by 75 per cent in 1980, well above the increase for other primary commodities (14 per cent) and manufactures (11 per cent). The dollar appreciated by 19 per cent in 1980, the European currencies relatively depreciated; consequently export unit values of agricultural products and manufactures actually declined in 1981. Reflecting the demand pattern, volume of manufactures rose twice as much as that of agricultural products in world trade, during the period under review.

The volume of world trade recovered by about 2 per cent in 1983. For the fourth consecutive year, trade in minerals declined, led by an 8 per cent fall in the volume of crude petroleum exports. This brought trade in crude petroleum to its lowest level since 1970. Trade in agricultural products rose in volume by 1 per cent, this was far below the average rates of growth achieved in the 1960s and 1970s, and reflected the fact that the volume of exports of several food products and agricultural raw materials declined sharply in 1983. This was coupled with a marginal decline in the unit value of agricultural exports. World trade in manufactured products, after a fall in 1982, recovered by 4 per cent in 1983 in volume terms, though its unit value continued to fall for the third consecutive year.

The non-oil developing countries registered an impressive increase in their exports during 1983 and 1984. This performance can be considered good when compared with that of their own past, and when compared with the general trend in the world trade. Manufactured exports were the prime movers. Their traditional exports, like textiles and clothing, kept a low profile. It was observed in 1982 that the non-oil developing countries were increasing their share of the market in the industrial economies, and this trend was further confirmed in 1983. It was due to a strong import demand in the United States because of the recovery. The volume of imports of this group of countries stagnated, in fact in the heavily indebted LDCs it declined. This led to an improved balance of payments position for the non-oil developing countries.

Pattern of Imports of Creditor Countries

For the reasons given in the preceding section, exports of LDCs rose by 21 per cent in 1976, the increase was both in value and volume. By and large the domestic economies of the non-oil LDCs were less affected by the 1975 recession.

The price buoyancy and the cyclical recovery of import demand in industrial economies contributed to renewal of growth in export earnings of LDCs. Therefore despite slackness in bilateral flows in 1976–7 the reserves of LDCs recorded impressive gains for the two years. The fact that during this upturn, imports of the non-oil LDCs lagged behind their exports, had a lot to do with the flush reserve position. It is at this point that the economic environment in the industrial countries became frustrating to the aspirations of LDCs, for their economies were dependent on market-access to the industrial countries.

The impressive increases in exports of non-oil LDCs [Table 4.18] up to 1980, were largely due to higher prices. In terms of volume the growth showed a decline. The dollar value of exports of non-oil LDCs rose by 2 per cent in 1981 owing to an increase in volume, as the dollar

TABLE 4.18 *Imports of industrial countries from non-oil developing countries, 1976–83*

Year	Value in billions of $ FOB		Percentage of world trade
1976	81	(21.1)	8.1
1977	92	(13.6)	8.2
1978	106	(15.2)	8.1
1979	131	(23.6)	8.0
1980	160	(22.1)	8.1
1981	163	(1.9)	8.3
1982	157	(−3.7)	8.5
1983	166	(5.7)	9.2

SOURCE *International Trade* (Geneva: GATT, various issues).

The figures in parentheses = growth over the previous year.

nit value declined. Export earnings of many LDCs declined because of
. fall in the export prices of non-fuel primary commodities. The dollar
alue of manufactured exports from LDCs increased by 10 per cent,
lue to higher volume.

As brought out in Chapter 3, due to a steep rise in the price of
everages the terms of trade of non-oil LDCs recovered in 1977,
lowever, thereafter they were to shift adversely. It became difficult to
naintain earlier growths rates and growth of investment, yet many
.DCs maintained them remarkably well. In this they were assisted by
xpansion of exports, especially by the NICs, better agriculture har-
ests, and financial support provided directly or indirectly through the
urpluses of the oil-exporting countries made this feasible. First, a low-
rowth path, and, second, the sluggishness in the industrial market
conomies took their toll and affected the growth pattern of the non-oil
.DCs. Their real output increased by 2.5 per cent in 1981, compared
vith 5 per cent in each of the preceding years, and 6.5 per cent in 1978.
This shows how the LDCs have become integrated in the world
conomy over the last three decades. The two major linkages are the
xports of LDCs to the industrial economies and the terms of trade,
vhich weakened due to deterioration in demand.

TABLE 4.19 *Trends in the terms of trade, 1976–80 (1975 = 100)*

			Terms of trade	
Year	Beverage prices	Agricultural raw materials	Non-oil LDCs	Industrial economies
976	191.7	124.2	105.3	99.2
977	332.0	128.2	114.7	97.9
978	240.9	137.9	107.9	100.5
979	254.9	168.2	106.6	97.7
980	223.8	175.1	100.7	90.1

ource *International Financial Statistics, Supplement on Price Statistics*, Series No. 2
Washington, DC: IMF, 1981). This series ends in 1980.

The Impact of Economic Fluctuations on the Liquid Resources of the LDCs

The gains in reserves in 1976 (34 per cent) and 1977 (18 per cent),
nentioned earlier, were impressive and fairly widespread – three-

fourths of the oil-importing LDCs of Asia and those of Wester
Hemisphere registered gains. Subsequent developments were far fror
happy. Exogenous factors like: higher energy costs and interest rate:
recession and subsequent stagnation in exports, affected individu:
LDCs in different ways, but gave an adverse turn to their terms c
trade. High rates of inflation in the industrial economies increased thei
import costs, depleting foreign exchange reserves. Under these pres
sures their current account deficits steadily mounted, from $32 billio
in 1976 to $99 billion in 1981, it fell marginally to $97 billion in 198:
As a policy measure LDCs ceased to accumulate reserves to meet th
increased financial requirements. In the past they had borrowed t
maintain an adequate level of reserves, but during the latter half of th
1970s and thereafter their reserves fell in real terms. Large deficit
forced many of them to borrow from the financial markets at a tim
when the interest rates were at their historically high levels. Thi
economic milieu proved to be a daunting one for LDCs.

AN OVERALL VIEW OF THE RESOURCE FLOWS FROM THE DAC COUNTRIES

A long-term decline has been observed in the ODA/GNP ratio of th
DAC countries over the years:

	%		%
1960	0.54	1979	0.35
1965	0.44	1980	0.38
1970	0.34	1981	0.35
1975	0.36	1982	0.38
		1983	0.36

This does not imply a decline in ODA disbursements in absolute term
because the economies of the donor countries were growing; it doc
imply that the growth rate of ODA has been less than that of the GNF
of the donor economies. The DAC has had some influence over th
volume of ODA, and it has had more influence over the quality of ai
and its division and distribution among the recipients. In many DA(
countries authorities have found it increasingly difficult to convince th
governments that increasing ODA should take precedence over th
indigenous claims on the national resources. It is a politically sensitiv
issue. Therefore the DAC has not succeeded in persuading its member
to increase economic assistance as a proportion of GNP. As seen fror

the above data, the ODA/GNP ratio has fallen since the establishment of the Committee. Over the 1970s the ratio remained close to 0.35 per cent. In 1982 it rose to 0.38 per cent; this can be accounted for, in part, by a bunching of contributions to multilateral development agencies. It is a meritorious achievement because it occurred in a period of severe budgetary stresses in many donor countries.

According to the figures presented in this chapter, in 1946 the dimension of the resources flowing to LDCs from the industrial market economies was $1.7 billion, while the corresponding figure for 1983 is $18 529 million. There is a bit of money illusion here, because these figures are in current dollars. In constant dollars they would appear as follows:

ODA volume in real terms (1975 = 100) (in millions of $)	
1953	5 263.2
1955	5 719.9
1960	7 692.4
1965	10 251.1
1970	8 840.4
1971	9 655.5
1972	9 849.3
1973	9 686.1
1974	9 205.2
1975	9 815.3
1976	8 932.9
1977	8 860.9
1978	10 748.1
1979	11 540.1
1980	11 996.1

N.B. Series deflated by the US wholesale prices, using IMF tape data. The US wholesale prices series begins in 1953 and ends in 1980.

The above data are in terms of real dollars, adjusted for inflation but not for, it is important to state, exchange-rate fluctuations. They show that in real terms ODA doubled between 1953 and 1965, there was a fall in the late 1960s and the 1970s. The DAC aid rose again in 1978 after a long spell of virtual stagnation, to stagnate again. Recent trend in the volume of ODA, in real terms, gives a dispirited impression that the bilateral development assistance is a crumbling, over-the-hill business.

From this mass of data and factual information can one come to some succinct conclusions? How much does the economic climate in the industrial economies influence the flow of resources to LDCs? Is the buoyant economic climate or surging world trade a necessary and sufficient condition for easy flow of financial resources at concessional terms to LDCs? Let us look for the answers in the preceding sections. Out of eight periods of upswing in the flow of bilateral resources during the last thirty-five years, the economic activity was buoyant five times, while thrice the world economy was in the doldrums. On the other hand, out of six times the resource flows stagnated or declined, the world economy was at a plateau or in a downswing five times. The inference is that the brisk pace of the world economy may contribute to a higher rate of resource flow to LDCs, though it is neither necessary nor a sufficient condition. It is easier to share the booty when the circumstances are bountiful. However, a sluggish economic climate in the industrial world almost always serves to reduce the flows.

Out of eight periods of upsurge the world trade was brisk four times, grew at a moderate pace twice and nearly stagnant twice. Out of six periods of decline, four times the rhythm of the world trade was found to be high, once moderate and once low. Which goes to prove that the rhythm of the world trade is not a determinant of the rate of resource flows. The volume of international trade is poorly correlated with the volume of ODA.

THE FLOW OF CONCESSIONAL ECONOMIC ASSISTANCE TO LDCs FROM OPEC COUNTRIES

ENTER OPEC

A novel feature of the ODA in 1970s was the emergence of a new donor group, the Organisation of Petroleum Exporting Countries (OPEC). It is depicted in the media as a *nouveau riche* country group. Judged by the relevant socio-economic indicators, these countries, though rich in terms of liquidity, are at an early stage of economic development. None of them has an industrial base, they are food-deficit countries, some import all of their foodgrains requirement. With the possible exception of Indonesia, none of them has a major export other than oil. The

OPEC countries project an image of excessive wealth because of two facts: (1) The high per capita income of four of them because of tiny populations, and (2) the production of oil and the income therefrom is way above their financial needs, so five of them (Kuwait, Libya, Qatar, Saudi Arabia and UAE) have been able to accumulate large liquid assets.

The first fact should be taken to mean that these countries are rich for the time being, and that their wealth is not based on recurrent production from an industrial and/or agricultural base. Regarding the second, there is an age-old economic dictum that liquidity is not wealth. The resources that the OPEC countries are transferring into liquidity are depletable, so if one were to take a long-run view, it is making them poor not rich. The OPEC wealth is, apparently, based on a capital asset: a pool of oil in the ground, which is a non-reproducible natural resource. The size of existing stock cannot increase through time. It can only decrease.[39] This is true even of recyclable materials.

Financial resource flow from OPEC is a novel historical phenomenon, inasmuch as it represents a transfer of resources from some LDCs to others. An unprecedented situation emerged after the first round of oil price hikes, the increments in the world savings were being realised but the ownership of the assets had geographically shifted to some developing countries – that is, OPEC. The result was that the assets to be recycled had changed hands. Although LDCs gained in absolute terms, they did not gain in relative terms.[40]

The aid burden is heavier on an OPEC donor than is prima facie apparent, because it is given from oil revenues which are, in fact, part income and part capital. These revenues are the monetary realisation of an asset. The benefits to recipients are also greater than apparent, because OPEC grants and loans, for evident reasons, are provided untied.[41] In fact OPEC aid is used to finance the purchases of goods and services from the industrial economies.

There are wide divergences in the individual donor performances. Countries with limited absorptive capacity at the time of oil price hike, generally provided a greater (though falling) share of their national incomes than those with large populations and with domestic development programmes, which absorbed a good part of extra foreign exchange earnings.[42] Most of the OPEC aid originated from those countries which had large balance-of-payments surpluses, namely, Kuwait, Libya, Saudi Arabia and the UAE. Two other countries, Qatar and Iran, have run small aid programmes; so has Iraq. The programmes of the other six members has less significance. The status of major donors can only be given to the first-named four countries. Kuwait has come to acquire a unique position among OPEC members in building up a strong capability for the management of economic aid programmes. It chalked out small but highly professional programmes of technical and financial assistance. Beginning early, in 1961, the Kuwait Fund for Arab Economic Development financed projects which met fairly rigid standards of economic returns.[43]

A QUESTION OF MOTIVATION

A marked geographic concentration of OPEC aid portends to its political motivation. First, all the four major donors use financial resources to support the so-called 'front-line states', namely, Egypt (before withdrawal in 1978), Jordan, Syria and the Palestine Liberation Organisation. Other Arab and Islamic states have benefited from this line of motivation. Second, national security is a driving motive. Saudi Arabian aid to Somalia, Oman and particularly to North Yemen, comes under this category. Large amounts are given to North Yemen so as to keep the balance of stability, which is upset by the Marxist-leaning South Yemen.[44] The OPEC donors, particularly Saudi Arabia, also used aid as a means to support ideological and religious issues. In support of Islam the Arab states, the fringe Muslim states and India, which is a secular country with large Muslim population, get financial assistance. Also, to combat the spread of Communism these donors extend financial assistance. To add up, there are three predominant motives: the Arab conflict with Israel, regional security and the ideological and religious factors. These motives dominated the pre-1973 Arab aid thinking.

Attitudes in this regard are slow to change, though there was a change after 1973. The rest of the LDCs – particularly LLDCs – were not completely neglected by OPEC, but they received scant attention, far too inadequate to compensate for the higher outlays of imported oil. OPEC believes that it is not logical to expect them to do so.[45] Latin America and the Caribbean received little economic assistance until recently. Asian non-Muslim states were another area of neglect. Also, the non-Muslim African states were ignored on the same count. Diversification started around 1980, when the OPEC aid became broad-based. Political factors as well as sound economic rationale led to this thinking. Arab donors became concerned about promoting the Third World solidarity and winning diplomatic support in the internaional fora. Besides, OPEC made common cause with other LDCs in several international issues like technology transfer, tariff reductions and control over transnational corporations. These factors helped broaden the base of OPEC assistance.

THE OPEC AID RECORD

The volume and structure of the flow of concessional economic assistance from OPEC can be neatly divided into two periods. Inasmuch as 1973 was a watershed, we shall analyse the aid performance in two parts: before and after 1973.

The Pre-1973 Period

Though little noticed, the financial co-operation between OPEC and other LDCs had begun soon after the creation of OPEC in 1960. The pioneer in this regard was the Kuwait Fund for Arab Economic Development, organised in 1961. Its operations were modest by today's standards. Between 1961 and 1973 it committed $450 million in forty-one loans to twelve Arab countries, half of the capital was directed to Egypt, Sudan and Tunisia. Other aid institutions sprang up in the early 1970s; for example, the Abu Dhabi Fund for Arab Economic Development was launched in 1971, and the Arab Fund for Social and Economic Development was established in 1968, it became operational in 1972. It is a regional institution and even has non-OPEC members. During this period it remained active in granting project loans on concessional terms to Arab states.[46] Resource flows during this period were not uniquely channelled through the financial institutions; this was to be a characteristic of the second period. In the late 1960s major donors began to extend substantial grants to Egypt, Jordan and Syria as a straight budgetary support. Unlike these bilateral flows the financial institutions' operations were wider and in the form of loans.[47]

There is a data gap here. No time series are available for the bilateral resource flows during the 1960s. The OECD Secretariat has prepared estimates for the three years between 1970 and 1973. For 1970 and 1971 the totals were $369 and $452 million, respectively. The level reached in 1972 was almost twice as high, $704 million. As a proportion of total bilateral resources received by LDCs, it was 2 per cent for 1970, 2.1 per cent in 1971 and 2.8 per cent in 1972.

Beyond 1973

Before the first round of oil price hikes the bilateral flows were not insubstantial, but it enabled OPEC to invigorate its aid efforts. The political will and the institutional base was already in existence. The scope of aid in terms of objectives, spread and scale, broadened during this period. Bilateral assistance was far greater than OPEC resources going to multilateral institutions; between 1973 and 1977 81 per cent of it went as bilateral. The reason for this is the same as in the case of the DAC, bilateral resource flows afford the donor more political leverage and manipulative control. The lending operations of the OPEC financial institutions increased sharply after mid-1970s, since by then the institutional machinery found itself in the right gear. These institutions became responsible for distributing all non-concessional and some concessional flows. The OPEC Fund for International Development started its operations in August 1976. Its cumulative commitments at the end of 1981 were $452.1 million.[48] Total disbursement in 1982 was $706.2 million, of which $341.2 million were grants. Eighty per cent of the total went to LLDCs.[49] Other active multilateral development finance institutions are: the Saudi Fund for Development, the Arab Fund for Economic and Social Development, the Arab Bank for Economic Development of Africa and the Islamic Development Bank. From the point of view of the authorised capital the OPEC Fund for International Development is the largest.

A word about the OPEC data: there are two sources of comprehensive data, the United Nations Conference on Trade and Development (UNCTAD) and the Organisation for Economic Co-operation and Development (OECD). The two series display differences in aggregates and details owing to differences in reporting practices. Yet the disparity is relatively small. The ODA statistics for OPEC include bilateral assistance, flows from various OPEC funds and multilateral financial institutions. The data used here are the revised data published by the OECD, following increased statistical co-operation with the Finance Ministries of Kuwait, Saudi Arabia and the UAE. Statistics of the three main donors and Venezuela are now entirely based on official records, but those for Algeria, Iraq, Libya and Qatar are still based on secondary sources and the OECD Secretariat estimates. A functional subdivision of OPEC members has been made into three sub-groups: the Gulf states (Kuwait, Qatar, Saudi Arabia and the UAE); other Arab states (Algeria, Iraq and Libya) and non-Arab donors (Iran, Nigeria and Venezuela). The nominal and real values of the resource flows have been set out in Table 4.20.

TABLE 4.20 *Bilateral flows from OPEC countries, 1973–83*

Year	Gulf states	Other Arab states	Non-Arab states	Total		At constant prices (1981 = 100)
1973	1 875	251	25	2 133	(202)	4 158
1974	3 479	617	483	4 579	(115)	8 076
1975	5 086	515	638	6 239	(36)	6 239
1976	4 775	379	944	6 098	(− 2)	9 047
1977	5 619	205	341	6 138	(− 0.0)	8 334
1978	7 425	352	353	8 130	(34)	9 702
1979	6 466	1 233	117	7 816	(− 4)	8 271
1980	8 261	1 360	68	9 689	(24)	9 399
1981	7 877	538	50	8 465	(− 23)	8 466
1982	6 536	171	96	6 803	(− 19)	6 998
1983	5 034	146	315	5 495	(− 19)	NA

N.B. Figures in parentheses = percentage annual change.
SOURCE *Development Co-operation, 1983 Review* (Paris: OECD, various issues).

Of the three sub-groups the Gulf states are the largest donors, both in relative and absolute terms. The ODA/GNP ratios of the three sub-groups are as follows:

Year	Gulf states	Other Arab states	Non-Arab states	Total
1973	12.8	1.2	0.04	2.25
1975	8.6	1.3	0.60	2.92
1980	4.5	1.3	0.03	1.84
1982	3.0	0.2	0.04	1.22
1983	3.0	0.1	0.13	1.05

Although three ODA/GNP ratio of the Gulf states has declined over the years it does not mean a fall in absolute amount, because the income of this sub-group rose with a steep rate. Flows show no trend whatsoever; the same applies to real flows, but the years between 1976 and 1981 can be called high-performance years, though with rises and declines.

During the first period very little was given with long-term economic development of the recipient in mind, and there were essentially three donors, namely, Kuwait, Libya and Saudi Arabia. In the second period, first, the quantum of assistance increased greatly. Second, ten out of thirteen OPEC members started seriously participating in the efforts. In 1974 OPEC became the second-largest donor group, providing $4.6 billion, a little over half of the flows from the DAC countries. High levels of commitments and disbursements continued in 1975, the nominal (not real) level as well as the ODA/GNP ratio increased. In fact that the different bilateral and multilateral financial development institutions became operational or stepped up their activity, had a lot to do with this.[50] At the same time the composition of assistance changed; there was a sharp rise in the project commitments as compared to general support and oil credits.

An interesting feature was the emergence of jointly sponsored projects by OPEC and non-OPEC sources of finance. In 1976 some sixty projects were being jointly financed, and fifteen were on the drawing-board. Initiative for this came either from the World Bank or bilateral donors. The principles involved were two: 'parallel financing' whereby each participant finances a distinct part of the project, and 'joint financing' in which the various lenders share in agreed proportion in the common project. The second form remained restricted to Arab institutions only. These institutions felt manpower bottlenecks, so they made use of the appraisal experiences of the World Bank and some DAC members. After a fall, OPEC flows rose in 1978, both in real as well as nominal terms, but nose-dived in 1979. This was a period when OPEC surpluses were dwindling and Iran completely withdrew. Iraq, however, went against the grain and quintupled its disbursement in 1979, and thus became the third-largest OPEC donor, after Saudi Arabia and Kuwait. OPEC aid declined in 1981 and slumped in 1982. The decline in the ODA/GNP ratio which began in 1979, continued till 1983. In real terms 1982 saw the lowest annual level since 1975. This development is related to the substantial decline in oil revenues. The decrease in demand for oil in 1982 contributed to reduction in selling and spot prices of oil. Also, falling prices did not stop the decreasing trending in rising.[51] The second adverse factor was the war between Iran and Iraq, which eliminated these countries from the donor list, and curtailed the aid-giving capacity of the Gulf states.

The largest fall occurred in the disbursements of Saudi Arabia. The same was the story of UAE, the third-largest OPEC donor; their net disbursement declined for the third successive year in 1981. Another decline in 1982 need surprise none, because of the budget constraints. On the other hand, Kuwait, the second-largest donor, increased its disbursements for the third successive year. Among the non-Arab donors, Venezuela's disbursement rose substantially in 1982, but that of Nigeria fell sharply, after an exceptionally good performance in 1981.

Owing to flattening of oil production, deterioration in balance of payments and budget constraints, the bilateral assistance from OPEC countries further declined in 1983. The decline started in 1981 and has been continuing ever since; the 1983 level of OPEC economic assistance is about a half that for 1980. Despite declining oil revenues Kuwait and Saudi Arabia provided the bulk of resources, which was in keeping with tradition. Other Arab countries' contributions recorded a sharp fall, the net disbursements from Iraq being negative. Offsetting this trend were the non-Arab donors, who recorded a rise because of contributions by Venezuela and the return of Iran after four years of net negative contributions, which means that repayments exceeded disbursements.

To set the record straight it needs to be pointed out that the Gulf states accounted for nearly 95 per cent of the total OPEC ODA in 1981, as compared to 85 per cent in 1980, with Saudi Arabia alone extending 74 per cent. Saudi Arabia has remained the most generous donor since the inception of the OPEC programme, followed by Kuwait. In the total scheme of ODA from OPEC countries occupies a significant position; in 1983 the ODA extended by the DAC countries was $18.5 billion, while that by OPEC members was $5.5 billion.

The short-term prospects for OPEC assistance to LDCs do not seem to be good because the oil demand of the industrial countries was flat in 1983, and it declined in 1984. Besides, the non-OPEC oil production has been rising and OPEC will have to bear the financial brunt of it. Neither of the factors depressing OPEC oil demand will go away quickly. The present ambience of austerity may have to last well into the 1980s.

Geographical Distribution

During the five-year period 1973–8 Africa received almost a half (48.5 per cent) of the total OPEC disbursements; this was due to Egypt, the largest OPEC recipient. Other Muslim African recipients were Sudan, Mauritania, Somalia and Morocco. West Asia, which included Arab mid-East, Pakistan and Afghanistan, was the second-largest recipient, 27 per cent. Disbursements to South and South-East Asia were relatively small – only 17.2 per cent, largely to India. Latin America and the Caribbean continued to be neglected. OPEC's inclination is easy to see; of the twenty largest recipients all except India and Thailand were Muslim countries. Of these, eleven were Arab countries, and received 65 per cent of OPEC's bilateral flows during the quinquennium under review. The largest four recipients were Egypt, Syria, Pakistan and Jordan, in that order. Some of these resources, indeed, went to the poorest countries of the world. Of the twenty under review, ten had per capita income below $300. But this happened because some of the Muslim countries also happened to be poor, not because of a conscious policy objective to assist the poorest.[52] This was to change, albeit slowly.

The Arab boycott of Egypt in 1978 did not bring about geographical diversification. Syria and Jordan became the two largest recipients the next year. A large proportion of the flows benefited Gaza, the West Bank and the Palestinians, the so-called 'confrontation states'; in 1979 they received almost 60 per cent of OPEC flows. Changes in disbursements among various country groups were as shown below:

LDC groups	Per capita income in 1980	Proportion of total ODA 1979	1982
		%	%
LLDCs	According to the UN definition	8.9	16.2
China and India	$240 & $290	0.5	−1.7
Other low-income countries	Below $600	4.2	1.8
Lower middle-income countries	$600 to $1200	23.1	18.5
Upper middle-income countries	Above $1200	29.9	27.9

N.B. Totals do not add up to 100 because during both years large portions of resources remained unallocated and unspecified.

The above statistics show that the importance of LLDCs is on the increase in the minds of policy-makers. India and China received small amounts; in 1982 the net transfer to them was negative. The share of low-income countries fell because of exclusion of Egypt from the list of OPEC beneficiaries.

In 1982 almost half (43.2 per cent) of the resources went to the Middle East; Africa received 16.6 per cent whereas Latin America continued to be neglected, these LDCs received 1.8 per cent of the total. There was a reverse flow (−0.22 per cent) from the South Asian LDCs.

The allocations of OPEC economic assistance did not show many changes in 1983, and the Arab countries continued to receive 85 per cent of it. The share of non-Arab countries in Africa increased marginally to 10 per cent, while those of non-Arab Asian countries fell substantially. In 1983 OPEC began to give assistance to China, while flows to India still continued to be negative. Another notable feature is that in 1983 the share of the LLDCs doubled its 1981 level. Overall the allocation shows a wider geographical spread and more in favour of the poorer developing countries. By 1983, OPEC had given assistance to 84 LDCs. Also, senior OPEC leaders repeatedly expressed their concern regarding the poorer LDCs and stated that LLDCs and the other low income LDCs are more eligible for economic assistance from them.

As for the sectoral distribution the share of agriculture increased; assistance for mineral resource development began, while the importance of infrastructural development declined. Aid for education, health and tourism development remained small. Economic assistance was provided to local development banks. Sectoral distribution continued to be dominated by non-project assistance, largely in the form of general support assistance. Project assistance primarily concentrated on the transport, storage and communication sectors.

Financial Terms

As already seen, OPEC flows are more in the form of non-project aid; another important channel is co-financing. A third is the balance-of-payments support to LDCs, many of them needing it after their balance of payments started worsening during this period. There is a data gap regarding the financial terms for the first period. From the available information it appears that the terms hardened in 1975 and became harder than those of the DAC. The concessionality or grant element was almost equal in 1973: 85 per cent for OPEC while 88 per cent for the DAC. In 1974 the corresponding figure was 74 per cent, and in 1975 65 per cent. During both the years the hardest terms were often extended to the poorest LDCs, and the softer terms were offered to the richer ones having per capita income above $1 000. The reason was a sharp fall in the share of grants in the total commitments, which declined from 74 per cent in 1973, to 58 per cent in 1974 and further down to 38 per cent in 1975. Iran's loans to India and Pakistan had particularly low concessionality, and affected the averages. Both countries at that point in time had per capita income below $200. The financial terms of other OPEC members were better. The grace period was 5.2 years in 1973; it fell to 4.5 years in 1975. Interest fell from 3.3 per cent to 2.4 per cent over the same period, while the grant element remained around 40 per cent.

The grant element improved over the years and reached 88 per cent in 1978, but fell to 80 per cent the next year, the fall was again caused by a sharp decline of grants in total commitments. The grant element also fell marginally, from 51 per cent to 50.2 per cent. The disquietening feature mentioned in the last paragraph continued, harder terms (51 per cent grant element) were offered to low-income countries, whereas the commitments made to the middle-income countries were on softer terms (80 per cent grant element). This incongruity was due to general support assistance grants to the so-called 'confrontation states', which belonged to lower-middle income groups. The special donor–recipient relationship explains the fact that the grant element of the higher-income LDCs was relatively higher. There was a marked improvement in overall concessionality from 79 per cent in 1979 to 89 per cent in 1980; this was due to an improvement in the grant element. Financial terms after 1980 have not been published by any authoritative source. The grant element of the overall ODA commitments from the OPEC and the DAC countries for the last four years for which the data are available are compared below:

	OPEC	DAC
1978	79.1	89.9
1979	68.3	90.9
1980	77.0	89.9
1981	73.0	89.6

Thus OPEC aid goes at relatively stiffer terms than that from the DAC countries.

THE FLOW OF CONCESSIONAL ECONOMIC ASSISTANCE TO LDCs FROM THE CENTRALLY PLANNED ECONOMIES

THE INCEPTION

Economic relations between the Centrally Planned Economies (CPEs)[53] and LDCs are new in comparison to those with industrial market economies. Although a beginning was made in 1954, real developments did not start till early 1960. During the years following the war several new states were born in Africa and Asia; after it became clear that

Communist parties in these countries could not come into power the USSR thought of cultivating economic relations with them. Prior to 1954 the Soviet Union's national economy was not strong enough to offer assistance to LDCs; the same was true of other CPEs. Even when the programme was initiated these economies could not embark on extensive activities in all fields of economic assistance.

TRADE AND AID

The genesis of foreign assistance should be traced back to the transformation in the foreign trade policies, notably that of the Soviet Union, which began in the early 1950s. Since trade and aid, in this case, have a close nexus, let us briefly look at the dimensions of trade between the two country groups. The expansion in absolute terms has been fast. Starting from virtually zero in the 1950s, the turnover of trade virtually doubled every four years, up to 1963. The growth did slow down thereafter, but in absolute terms the rise was substantial. The statistics below show that as a percentage of the total the share of trade between the two groups is still miniscule. Relatively, East–South trade is far smaller than West–South trade. Trade of the CPEs is, by and large, evenly distributed among the three continents of the developing world; during the last decade Asia accounted for 40 per cent of the trade turnover, while Africa and Latin America for 30 per cent each.[54] The major trading partners in the developing world are: Argentina and Brazil in Latin America; Algeria, Egypt (before the break-up), Ghana and Sudan in Africa; and Afghanistan, India, Iraq, Malaysia and Pakistan in Asia.

On balance this trade relationship has somewhat benefited LDCs, because had bilateral trade not started the CPEs could not possibly have offered economic assistance in the form of development credits. Second, given the endemic and chronic shortage of foreign exchange in most LDCs, this bilateralism added to the import capacity of the LDCs, which, in turn, underwrote an expansion of their exports. The special payment agreements reduced the burden of debt-servicing, since repayments could be made in terms of exports, domestic currency or out of the aid-financed projects, which saves scarce convertible foreign exchange. However, the questions arise, can we quantify these gains? Can the expansion of trade *per se* be called a gain? Probably not. It is more a matter of terms of trade and the net increase in exports.[55] On the other hand, the CPEs cannot deny economic advantages to themselves;

TABLE 4.21   *Trade of LDCs with CPEs, 1963–83*

| | Export of LDCs to CPEs | | Export of CPEs to LDCs | |
	Value in billions of $ FOB	Percentage of total	Value in billions of $ FOB	Percentage of total
1963	1.70	1.1	2.80	1.8
1968	2.25	0.9	4.18	1.7
1970	3.10	1.0	5.51	1.6
1975	8.25	0.9	13.30	1.5
1980	21.00	1.0	31.00	1.6
1981	22.00	1.1	37.00	1.9
1982	20.10	1.1	29.10	1.6
1983	20.80	1.2	28.20	1.6

SOURCE   *International Trade* (Geneva: GATT various issues).

that is, apart from the political leverage aid affords. Development assistance promotes expansion of foreign trade of the CPEs, including higher imports from the credit-receiving LDCs, and an assurance of steady supply of commodites at stable terms of trade. During the 1970s the orientation of CPEs' aid was increasingly turned from the promotion of import-substituting production to stimulating export-oriented output in LDCs. This had a focus on creating complementarities in the production structure of LDCs, furthering export links. These exports were destined for the CPEs' markets.[56]

THE AID PHILOSOPHY

Nobody, certainly not the donors, has any illusions about the cardinal objectives of bilateral economic assistance. It is not philanthropic and the donors make no bones about it. It is considered an indispensable condition for the expansion of foreign trade. The policy-line in the CPEs is that real economic co-operation consists in creating mutually advantageous trading conditions. Or, to put it bluntly, economic assistance is a way to commercial penetration.[57] The policy-makers believe that economic assistance should be "mutually advantageous" and should make a direct contribution to the recipient's economic growth; therefore it has to be project-oriented. Among the projects, those in the industrial sector are considered of vital importance. It may also be used for infrastructural projects, like irrigation and road-building. Their assistance comes mostly in the form of medium- and long-term credit; outright grants are rare. What is meant by 'mutually advantageous'? The supply of capital equipment helps accelerate the growth of the LDC, concurrently the sale provides a market for the donor. By charging low interest the donor avoids making a dent in the national income. All the economic assistance is tied to the projects for which it is made, and the credits granted can never be used in a third country.

A QUESTION OF MOTIVATION

After Stalin's death in 1953, the Kremlin's policy towards LDCs changed dramatically. They saw in the LDCs economically weak and politically uncommitted regimes, having strong national and anti-colonial sentiments. The Kremlin thought that they were susceptible to Soviet influence.[58] The 'cold war' proved to be supportive to this line of logic. Even in LDCs which were linked to the West by alliances there were groups who resented these pacts. But the governments always defended their policies by saying that withdrawing from the pact means being deprived of economic assistance. Soviet bloc assistance became a means of strengthening neutralist tendencies, particularly in these LDCs. The same basic motives, coupled with the geopolitical strategic interests, are the prime movers of the aid programmes of the CPEs.

Gradually economic relations with LDCs came to be an integral part of the overall political strategy, and in the 1950s they tried to cultivate trade relations with LDCs with political objectives in mind. Comparatively, bilateral assistance from the CPEs is more closely linked to trading operations than that from the DAC countries. Trade as well as aid follow the swings of the political pendulum. Strained political relations lead to sharp contraction in trade and bilateral economic assistance, and vice versa.[59]

The second rationale, which has assumed considerable importance for the CPEs, is the supply of raw materials from the LDCs. It is vital for continued economic expansion of the CPEs. There are two reasons why they prefer to purchase them directly from the producing LDCs, rather than procuring them through the commodity market: (1) They can enter into long-term supply agreements and therefore count on these supplies while drawing up their own raw material plans, and (2) payments can be made by means of bilateral agreements on a barter footing, so that valuable foreign exchange can be saved.

The CPEs stepped up their economic assistance in the late 1950s, and started appearing in competition with the western donors. This led to some changes in the DAC aid policy, and neutrality or non-alignment became acceptable. The LDCs were no longer expected to show immediate appreciation and gratitude for aid in their foreign policies.[60]

Since the CPEs are characterised by full employment, the opportunity cost of resource transfer is considerable. That economic assistance to LDCs is stimulating the indigenous demand is not a valid argument, because in CPEs the growth-limiting factors are usually on the supply side. The internal rates of return in CPEs are still high; besides they are chronically short of capital. Therefore, investing in LDCs at low rates of interest means a substantial cost to CPEs in terms of domestic projects forgone.

THE AID RECORD OF THE CPEs

The First Period: 1954–70

The first definitive study documenting the volume of economic assistance to LDCs, was published by Weltwirtschafts Archiv,[61] Hamburg, in 1960. Assistance in small trickles had started between the 1953 and 1956 period.[62] It went to a small number of LDCs on an experimental basis. Until 1958–9 the full scope of their efforts did not become clearly defined. Until 1960 the CPEs did not give any grants, and argued that grants are not compatible with the economic interests of LDCs.[63] Credits to LDCs were granted on sound economic reasoning. Evidently, at this point the deciding factor was how much strain the aid programme was going to put on the donor non-market economies [NMEs].

There is an inevitable problem relating to the data. There has been a long-drawn controversy about the earlier data, because no competent authority has published it. The Soviet government published no figures for international consumption. The Council of Mutual Economic Assistance (COMECON) in Moscow also does not publish economic assistance-related figures.[64] At the beginning of 1966 the Institute of World Economics of the Socialist System, attached to the USSR Academy of Science published aid figures; they substantially revised these figures next year. In 1967 the Economic Studies Department of

TABLE 4.22 *Bilateral flows from CPEs (net disbursement),*
1954–70 (in millions of $)

	Annual averages		
	1954–60	*1961–5*	*1966–70*
USSR	340	332	427
Eastern European			
countries	80	253	369
Total	420	585	796

Gleaned by the author from the *World Economic Survey, 1974*, part I (New York, UN), p. 195–7.

the USSR Ministry of Foreign Trade published a different set of data. Secrecy around military aid is understandable, but around economic aid is hardly defensible. However, the controversy shrouding the data has been dispelled by the UN, which compiled the data from the following sources: Bank of International Settlements, *Press Review* (Basle); *Biulleten inostrannoi kommercheskoi informatsii* (Moscow) *East–West Commerce Bulletin* (London); and other official and unofficial sources. The coverage provided by the UN is fairly complete: there is substantial agreement between them and Soviet economists.

The Soviet Union remained by far the largest creditor in the first period, accounting for 73 per cent of the total flows, during the subsequent periods its share fell to 54 per cent. Among the East European countries Czechoslovakia was the largest donor, followed closely by the GDR. To be sure, compared to the DAC flows these flows are on the low side, but with per capita income similar to that of Italy in 1965 the USSR made a far greater contribution.[65]

Geographical Distribution

The economic assistance flows were restricted to a few LDCs. India, Indonesia and Egypt absorbed among them 50 per cent of the total. Among the developing world India was the largest trading partner of the USSR during this period, and Egypt occupied second position. Ten LDCs absorbed 82 per cent of the flows. In some cases bilateral economic assistance from the NMEs made a major contribution to economic development; for example, in Afghanistan 60 per cent of all foreign assistance for implementing the 1956–61 five-year plan came from the USSR and Czechoslovakia. The NMEs financed 33 per cent of Egypt's 1960–5 plan and 17 per cent of the public sector investment in industry and the energy sector in India's third five-year plan (1961–6).[66] Thus viewed, the geographical distribution was far from wide; it was restricted to LDCs with which the CPEs had trade ties, with particular attention to Egypt and India.

During this period the NMEs, particularly the USSR, were criticised for emphasising 'impact type' projects; that is, projects which can be rapidly completed and leave a big impression on the local population. Examples cited are: a bakery complex and paved streets in Kabul, a hotel in Burma and the Asian Games stadium in Jakarta. But such projects were relatively few, the bulk of the assistance was channelled into basic industrial facilities and infrastructure.[67]

Financial Terms

Unlike the other two donor groups CPEs did not give grants. There was a practice of 'gift exchanges' in the 1950s, which meant that the CPEs and the LDCs exchanged a package of goods of pre-specified value. Normally the LDC would gift its major export commodity. The expression 'gift' was a misnomer. Aid was provided in the form of loans, though the interest and payment terms were softer than those of the international capital market. In the loan agreements the amount was mentioned in the currency of the donor and the recipient as well as in the gold equivalent of the creditor's currency, so as to insure against devaluation.

During the 1950s the majority of loans extended by the USSR carried an interest rate of 2.5 per cent, while the East European countries charged between 3 and 4 per cent. The larger Soviet loans were generally repayable in equal annual instalments over a period of fifteen years, reckoned from the year in which the credit is utilised. Interest was payable one year after this date. The smaller loans were repayable in shorter terms, say seven years.[68] The payments were made in kind, in terms of raw materials or part of the output of the proposed plant, e.g. part of the output of Bhilai steel works in India was to be delivered to the USSR as repayment. Where these means were not feasible, repayments were made in hard currency. The grant element in this kind of loan was estimated between 25 per cent and 45 per cent.

The state trading agencies of the NMEs provided short- and medium-term commercial credits, with maturities up to eight years and interest rates ranging between 4 and 8 per cent, and a grant element ranging between 11 and 21 per cent. All aid flows took the form of inter-governmental credit lines. Loans from the Eastern European countries were on somewhat harder terms, since many of these countries provided larger parts of their flows through commercial credits.[69]

The Second Period: 1971–83

Resource flows gathered considerable momentum during the first quinquennium of the Second Development Decade. They rose steadily up to 1972, then dropped off to a trough in 1975, largely due to halving in the Soviet contribution. Among the East Europeans, large commitments were made by Czechoslovakia and Romania. As in the past, exclusively bilateral credits were extended for the purchase of capital equipment and the necessary expert services, and the credits were tied to procurements. The disbursements picked up in 1976, but they did not reach the pre-fall level of 1974, until 1978. The experience gained in carrying out economic assistance projects made the CPEs flexible. They started the practice of participative projects, in which several CPEs joined hands. Also, tripartite co-operation became frequent, involving CPEs, LDCs and organisations in the industrial economies; such projects could be found in Algeria, Egypt, Iran, India and Morocco. For example, India produces equipment for steel mills originally built by the USSR in other LDCs.

After a lean spell the net disbursements of the USSR rose from $953 million in 1978 to $1 403 in 1979, an increase of over 36 per cent; in relation to percentage of GNP it rose from 0.10 to 0.13 per cent. The net disbursement of the six East European CPEs rose by a smaller proportion. The average for the six masks large differences in performance of individual donors. In 1979 the GDR provided almost half of the total amount, while Hungary, Poland and Romania followed, in that order. Again, 1980 was a year of substantial rises by the USSR, and the East European CPEs. However, thereafter, the volume has stagnated; in fact fallen in real terms. This was accompanied by increasing concentration on a small number of recipients. The ODA/GNP ratio remained unchanged at 0.14 per cent until 1983. As usual the USSR provided three-quarters of the net disbursement; this is likely to continue, given the difficulties faced by the East European donors. Among them the disparities continue and the GDR continues to remain the largest donor, although its net disbursement fell by 10 per cent in 1982. Together they accounted for 14 per cent of the CPEs commitment in 1982, twice the 1979 level.

A comparison of the USSR's aid performance was made with that of

TABLE 4.23 *Bilateral flows from CPEs (net disbursement), 1970–83 (in millions of $)*

Year	USSR	Eastern Europe	Total		Net disbursement as percentage of GNP USSR	Eastern Europe
1970	754	207	961		0.15	0.10
1971	1 008	254	1 262	(31.3)	0.20	0.11
1972	1 173	214	1 387	(9.9)	0.20	0.09
1973	1 132	226	1 358	(−2.0)	0.17	0.08
1974	1 055	211	1 266	(−8.7)	0.15	0.07
1975	517	225	742	(−41.4)	0.07	0.07
1976	782	280	1 062	(43.1)	0.10	0.08
1977	847	250	1 097	(3.3)	0.10	0.07
1978	953	337	1 290	(21.5)	0.10	0.09
1979	1 403	358	1 761	(36.5)	0.13	0.09
1980	1 664	489	2 153	(22.3)	0.15	0.12
1981	1 841	570	2 411	(11.9)	0.14	0.14
1982	1 850	557	2 407	(−0.2)	0.14	0.14
1983	2 449	490	2 939	(22.2)	0.19	0.12

SOURCE   *Development Co-operation: 1982 Review and 1983 Review* (Paris: OECD, 1983).
N.B. Figures in parentheses = percentage annual change.

Italy for the first period. At the end of the second period, in 1983, the USSR provided 0.19 per cent of its GNP, as against 0.24 per cent for Italy. In absolute terms the USSR was higher than Italy, which disbursed $824 million.

The bilateral flows showed a sharp upward trend during 1983, yet the ODA/GNP ratio for the CPEs remained 0.17 per cent, lower than the most parsimonious DAC donor for that year Austria (0.23 per cent). The increase in flows can be ascribed to the USSR, in relation to GNP it touched a level of 0.19 per cent, which is an all time high. To offset the increase by the USSR, there was a fall in contributions by the six East European Countries, whose ODA/GNP ratio fell to 0.12 per cent. The reason for the decline was that the assistance from Poland, Romania and Hungary was almost negligible. This trend further increased the share of the USSR to 85 per cent of the total bilateral flows from the CPEs.

Flows to Developing Non-market Economies

Over the years six developing non-market economies have come into being: Cuba, Kampuchea, Korea (PDR), Laos, Vietnam and, lastly, Afghanistan. During the 1970s the volume of financial resources granted to these economies exceeded that to developing market economies. It was not a novel trend, even during the 1950s and 1960s, socialist states received thrice as much as the other LDCs. The trend became stronger in the 1970s. The data indicate that between 1970 and 1973, these countries accounted for 70 per cent of the CPEs resource flows, between 1974 and 1977 75 per cent, in 1978 82 per cent and during 1979 70 per cent. Flows to non-market developing economies accounted for 88 per cent of the total in 1982, as against 84.7 per cent in 1981. About half the Eastern European aid during the second half of the 1970s went to Cuba and Vietnam, with the latter being the largest single recipient of the East European aid. The bulk of CPEs' assistance to this sub-group of countries takes the form of commodity grants; however, project assistance picked up some momentum during 1981. The non-Communist LDCs, as a result, have received a declining share.

Flows to non-market economies declined further, they accounted for 80 per cent of the total in 1983. Cuba, Mongolia and Vietnam, which are full members of the Council for Mutual Economic Assistance (CMEA), remained the principal recipients. Another important recipient, largely from the USSR, was Afghanistan. The statistics convincingly prove that the NMEs have adopted their six developing brethren and channel an overwhelmingly large part of their bilateral economic assistance to this sub-group of LDCs. Apparently the choice has been made entirely on the basis of the political ideology of the recipients. This trend is well established and likely to continue in the future.

Geographical Distribution

Although bulk of the resources were going to the non-market developing economies, yet the distribution was wide until 1975. During this quinquennium new credits were offered to 42 LDCs, of which 22 were in Africa, 12 in Asia and 8 in Latin America. The LDCs of North Africa and West Asia were the major recipients, with each area's share accounting for about one-fourth of the total. The developing countries of South and South-East Asia were offered 16 per cent of the total, while the countries of sub-Saharan Africa received 13 per cent. During this period the bulk of the allocations were concentrated on a small number of LDCs. Seven of the 42 LDCs obtained about two-thirds of the total. During the second part of the decade the flow to developing market economies was reduced to a trickle, as already indicated. Main recipients among the non-socialist LDCs were: Turkey, Syria, Pakistan and India. In Latin America, Nicaragua, which had already received a first grant in 1980, became a significant recipient for political reasons.

Financial Terms

Traditionally the terms of the CPEs have been hard. Grant element (excluding Cuba and Vietnam) decreased from 33 per cent in 1973 to 31 per cent in 1974, due to hardening of terms. Generally loans carry a grant element of 23 to 37 per cent and are tied to specific projects. All the credits of the East European countries were not only tied but also were extended on non-concessional terms. For this reason the repayments on previous credits were high in relation to new gross disbursements.

The terms offered to non-market developing countries are much softer than those to other LDCs. Financial terms are determined by the links the recepient has with donor. In 1982, the grant element for the non-market developing economies was 66 per cent.

5 International Capital Market and the Developing Countries

INTRODUCTION

After the Second World War, down to the late 1960s, large parts of the financial resource flow to LDCs came from bilateral and multilateral sources. Capital market finances were limited to export credits and direct foreign investment. The domestic bias was still a norm in the early 1960s among English, French and US banks. Only a small number of them had international networks; the rest concentrated on their traditional home markets, passively responding to the needs of their corporate clients for trade finance and foreign exchange. In the late 1960s the scene started changing; the banks started becoming more international than national in response to a series of pressures: (1) economic stagnation at home; (2) the need to be competitive with foreign banks; and (3) the growing desire to increase the breadth of the banks' funding base and reduce overall capital costs by tapping the international money market.[1] From this time on, the international business of banks expanded unprecedently fast. This was accompanied by far-reaching changes in the structure of banking. This took place when the Euromarkets were poised for a take-off. The pace was spurred to a breakneck one due to the 'telex banking'. The macroeconomic implications of these developments were: (1) the financial markets worked as an efficient mechanism for allocating world savings, including those of the newly affluent OPEC countries, to economically productive projects in the creditworthy countries, and (2) financial markets made an indispensable contribution in the recycling process and the financing of the deficits of many countries including LDCs. Between 1973 and 1975 trade deficits of the oil-importing LDCs increased 3.3 times in real terms, as measured in relation to their GNP.

137

The deficit of the low-income countries increased 2.2 times in real terms over the same period.[2] They were less affected because oil formed a smaller part of their total imports. ODA flows were low during this period; however, multinational institutions and depletion of reserves helped.

Recycling by transnational banks was one of the prime factors behind the spectacular increase in the commercial bank lending to LDCs. Flows from the capital market were $6.99 billion in 1970, $33.92 billion in 1980 and $44.30 billion in 1983. Flows from the capital market accounted for 18 per cent of the total external financial inflows into LDCs in 1970, the corresponding figure for 1980 is 33 while for 1983 it is 45. This rapid growth in volume in nominal terms became a cause of concern because this capital was on shorter maturity and harder terms than the ODA. In what follows we shall analyse the trends in resources flows from the various segments of the international capital market, namely, the bank sector, bond markets, export credits and direct investment.

THE COMMERCIAL BANK LENDINGS

At the end of the 1950s the convertibility among the major currencies was fully restored, which facilitated commercial transnational flows. Apart from the reasons given above, this was a part of the general diversification of the banking business, which also proved to be profitable. Earnings from international operations accounted for a major part of increase in total earnings for large US banks.[3] By the end of the 1970s top-ranking transnational banks were earning 30 to 40 per cent of their total profits from their international operations.[4] The exposure of banks to LDCs increased, and the fact that many of them were able to tap the financial market on a large scale proves their ability to maintain relatively high rates of growth and imports. This, in turn, provided stimulus to the OECD economies by way of export multiplier.

Growth of the International Financial Market

Restoration of the international financial market after the war was imperative because first capital and technology were needed for the rehabilitation of Europe, then, for the growth of the newly independent states of Asia and Africa. Smoothly functioning financial market encourages foreign trade and investment, which enhances the efficiency of the world economy. The multilateral financial institutions and the transnational banks made a significant contribution in re-establishing the flows of funds into and out of the international capital market. For example, the financial institutions siphoned resources from New York, London, and Tokyo financial markets to LDCs. The internationally oriented commercial banks helped the transnational corporations and formed financial consortia to assist LDCs. Commercial banks, which already had some semblance of an international network, extended short-term credits to finance international trade, and later on they were to play a greater role. These instititions, plus the major insurance companies, brokerage firms and offshore mutual funds, provided confidence for the rebirth of modern financial markets.[5] As the markets grew in size and depth, the number and complexity of instruments used increased. Interest differentials in different markets stimulated world-wide arbitrage operations. This growth soon became a mixed blessing. On one hand, these markets helped allocate the productive resources. On the other hand, integration of markets exposed individual nations to massive international capital flows and balance-of-payments disturbances.

The Borrowers and the Lenders

Several LDCs were eager to borrow, for developmental purposes. Second, the oil-price hike of 1974 raised their import bill by $11 billion, and during the second round in 1979 raised it by $12 billion.[6] Third, inflation was reducing the burden of previous debt which tempted them to borrow more. Fourth, there were several newly industrialising, highly creditworthy LDCs in the market. Presuming that the export markets would continue to grow with the past trend, and the interest rates would move within the range of historical experience, these LDCs borrowed heavily from the capital market.[7] Fifth, the banks were awash in a flood of Eurocurrency and eagerly sought borrowers. Besides, they were attracted by the profitability of these operations and by the notion of increasing their assets and the return on shareholders' equity.

A negative perspective of the commercial market lending is that it weakened the economies of LDCs because of its commercial, non-concessional, terms. It is argued that these lendings permitted imprudent delays in the macroeconomic adjustment process in LDCs, which later on proved to be pernicious.[8] A parallel assertion is that private banks cannot attach macroeconomic conditions to their loans like the

public institutions, such as, the International Monetary Fund (IMF)
Over the last two decades many LDCs played to the gallery, adopted
populist economic policies and in the process committed gross macroeconomic errors. The result was that those economies soon became
basket cases and the authorities darted to the IMF, seeking a salvage
operation. Critics argue that the LDCs at times approached the capital
market only to avoid the discipline of macroeconomic conditions they
knew the IMF would impose.

The Genesis of the Eurocurrency Market

A striking institutional phenomenon of the last two decades in the
international financial market is the growth of the Eurocurrency
market. The term Eurocurrency or Euromarket refers to all international money and capital markets on which currencies held outside
their countries of origin are traded.[9] In the last two decades or so
this became a world-spanning market, with banking competition truly
international. The growth of this market was aided by Regulation Q,
which stipulated maximum interest rate limits on domestc time deposits
in the US. Maximum US interest rates have been usually lower than
those prevailing on the Euromarket, where they are determined by the
forces of demand and supply. As regards the size of the Eurocurrency
markets, in 1960 it was $2 billion; it rose to $70 billion in 1970.
According to the data published in the *World Financial Markets* of the
Morgan Guaranty Trust Company, in its various issues, the size of the
market grew as follows:

Billons of $		Billons of $	
1973	315	1980	1 559
1975	489	1981	1 924
1978	950	1982	2 140
1979	1 233	1983	2 253
		1984 (Sept.)	2 321

It has become a gigantic financial system, which respects no national
borders. This market came into its own in the 1960s, when the bankers
started mobilising excess dollars held in banks outside the US as a
result of the US deficits during that period. Severe credit crisis in the US
in the mid-1960s further stimulated the Euromarket, when, following
the collapse of the Penn Central, the American banks were forced to
borrow dollars abroad through their overseas branches to meet the
insatiable demand of their customers in the US. After the financial

crisis was over the market did not wither away; in fact it came to acquire a remarkable resilience and grew with a brisk pace. The Euromarket is, in large part, an inter-bank market.

The world is aware of the hazard that the Eurocurrency market has no 'lenders of last resort'. Unofficially the Bank of England keeps an eye on its operations. It is generally believed that in case of a débâcle each national financial system would be rescued by its central bank, but this is a moot issue. The support of central banks cannot be taken for granted. The Euromarket has its vices and virtues: its vices are that it is over-extended, under-controlled and exceedingly volatile. Its biggest virtue, unarguably, is that it works. In its short life-span, it has withstood several hurricanes: the Polish crisis in 1981, the Mexican crisis in 1982 and general Latin American crisis thereafter. After each one of these, some market observers prophesised débâcle, but despite periodic waves of near panic and numerous reschedulings, collapse has still remained a part of the fantasy world.

Eurocurrency Credits to Developing Countries

During the 1970s a shift from traditional to non-traditional sources of finance took place, it is sometimes called the 'privatisation' of the debt structure of LDCs. A few LDCs gingerly entered the Euromarket in late the 1960s; Ivory Coast was probably the first to raise $10 million in 1968. Borrowing really began in 1971, when several LDCs unexpectedly entered the market, which caused consternation among conservative banks. In 1972 and 1973 borrowings increased with a steep rate, as seen in Table 5.1:

From 1974 onwards the rate of increase in borrowing became relatively sedate. The sharp increase in 1978 was due to balance-of-payments-induced borrowings of LDCs. The sharp fall in 1980 was anticipated by market observers, given the uncertainty surrounding the market at the end of 1979. Banks became more conscious of creditworthiness of the borrowing LDCs, and borrowers became cautious on their part. Preference for sounder borrowers explains why spreads on prime credits remained under downward pressure. The LDCs which raised large amounts in 1979 included those from Latin America and Malaysia and Korea, which made 1979 the year of peak borrowing. In mid-1981 the rate of new commitments picked up, yet the 1979 level was not reached. In mid-1982 Mexico declared that it could not meet its international financial obligations, and Brazil also started having problems with repayments, which made lending policies restrictive,

TABLE 5.1 *Volume of Eurocurrency bank credits to developing countries*

Year	Amount in millions of $	Percentage change over last year
1971	1 475	—
1972	2 475	67.8
1973	7 257	194.4
1974	8 142	12.2
1975	11 164	37.1
1976	15 017	34.5
1977	20 976	39.7
1978	37 300	77.8
1979	47 964	28.6
1980	35 054	− 26.9
1981	45 239	29.1
1982	41 246	− 8.8
1983	32 883	− 20.4

SOURCE   *World Financial Markets* (New York: Morgan Guaranty Trust Co., various issues).

though not indiscriminately so, because even after this there were some LDCs which could borrow at paper-thin spreads. The deceleration in 1980 reflected the slowing down of international lending by European banks, it was largely because these banks had invested heavily in East European countries and were having repayment problems. However, American, British and Canadian banks continued expansion. The Japanese banks, which had substantially reduced their activities in 1980, once again began participating in 1981. The Mexican default and the repayment agonies of other Latin American LDCs took their toll. The capital market became wary — if not down right apprehensive — which resulted in a 20 per cent decline in lending to LDCs in 1983.

Financial Terms

The syndicated Eurocredits, usually, are for the most part 'roll-over' credits, whose price to the borrower has three components: (1) an interest rate altered every three, six, nine or twelve months, in line with the current short-term interest rates, usually the LIBOR (London Inter-Bank Offered Rate on Eurodollar), (2) a premium or spread which is usually fixed for the life of the loan, over the floating interest rate, and (3) various fees called the 'front load'. The roll-over period is chosen by the borrower bearing in mind the interest rates. For the lending bank, LIBOR means the cost of the funds, and the other two profits made on the loan. LIBOR follows the short-term interest rates in the US.[11] It should be noted that there has never been a single LIBOR computed at some central point for all the banks.

Terms in Euromarket were easy till 1973. They significantly hardened in 1974; that is, spreads widened and maturities shortened. This was the beginning of a trend, and the terms went on hardening till 1981. The average effective interest rates rose from 7 per cent to 18 per cent. There was a two-year interlude (1978–9) which saw a 'borrowers' market', in which most borrowers were able to negotiate thin spreads. Since the beginning of 1980 LDCs faced again stiff terms; also the LIBOR rose to a high average level, around 18 per cent; therefore many LDCs opted not to enter the financial market. The high LIBOR especially affected the non-prime borrowers, who found themselves in an even tighter bind, because they had to accept higher spreads on their loans.[12] In 1981 the non-oil LDCs, on average, paid a spread twice as high as borrowers from the industrial market economies. There has been a decline in the interest rates since mid-1982.

Despite the hardening of terms Euromarkets went on becoming competitive and borrowers became skillful in exploiting the competitive tendencies of banks. These conditions were the result of the fact that, beginning in 1977 through 1980, the market had an excessively high level of liquidity due to inflation and accommodative monetary policies. Banks saw Euromarkets as an incremental, handy way to invest the excess liquidity. In the future the Euromarkets would remain competitive; however, the emphasis would change.[13] For the creditworthy borrowers the spreads would remain paper thin, but for the poorer risks they would widen. Some LDCs may not get anything even at high margins.

VARIABLE INTEREST RATES

The bulk of credits obtained by LDCs from the capital markets were at variable interest rates [VIRs]. As indicated in the preceding section the base rate for the variable interest rates is LIBOR, which has been particularly volatile since 1977. Until that time, for most of the period, LIBOR was below the inflation rates in the industrial countries, so the borrowing LDCs benefited from a negative interest rate, as seen below:

| Year | Interest rates (per cent per annum) | | |
	LIBOR (3-month)	Inflation rate in OECD	Real interest rates
1976	5.6	6.7	−1.1
1977	6.2	7.0	−0.8
1978	8.8	5.5	3.3
1979	12.1	9.5	2.6
1980	14.2	13.2	1.0
1981	16.8	8.8	8.0
1982	13.2	5.8	7.4
1983	9.6	4.4	5.2
1984 (1st half)	10.7	5.8	4.9

SOURCE *Midland Bank Review*, London, Winter, 1984, p. 18.

In the last several years interest rates for all maturities have reached historic levels in the US. From 1981 to mid-1984 the *real* interest rate averaged 6.3 per cent more than the inflation rate, compared with an average of only 1.5 per cent more in the previous fifteen years. The explanations for the surge includes: large budget deficits, tight monetary policy, improved prospects for profits and investment and financial deregulation. High interest rates increased the cost of financial resources to LDCs which relied heavily on the capital market. Interest payments of non-oil developing countries – at $31 billion in 1980 – doubled between 1978 and 1980. They rose to $55 billion in 1981 and $59 billion in 1982. Every one percentage point decline in the LIBOR rates, after a year, reduces the flow of interest payments of non-oil developing countries by roughly $4 billion. One consequence of the rapid growth in debt service – particularly in interest payments – has been that in recent years an ever larger proportion of new borrowing had to be used to service outstanding debts.

Where the Money Went

Euromarket flows affected a substantial amount of short- and medium-term transfer of resources to LDCs. The real value of net transfers depends upon such elements as interest rates and inflation rates of currencies in which the loans were denominated. These transfers helped LDCs maintain short-term growth, despite balance-of-payments deficits generated by the oil-price hike and recession. The investments made with the help of these resources are expected to help long-term growth. A close examination of the purpose to which these resources were put reveals that the net magnitude of the additional debt was substantially less than that indicated by the gross figures, because a great deal of Eurocredits were mere substitutes for other types of financing in an *ex ante* and *ex post* sense. By *ex post* substitution we are replacing an existing obligation with a Eurocredit to improve the debt profile. The Philippines was the first LDC to do this. *Ex ante* substitution, implies choosing Eurocredits instead of other kinds of commercial financing, e.g. suppliers' credit or portfolio investments. To the extent substitution has improved the debt profile, particularly the maturities, it is beneficial to the borrowers.[14] It has been found that Eurocredits have substituted not only for other types of foreign borrowings, but also for domestic borrowings.

Access to International Capital Markets

A few large debtors dominate the capital markets. It is the NICs which are most active in the international capital market and corralled three-fourths of the capital going to LDCs in 1980. The middle-income countries (MICs) get less than a quarter, while the low-income countries (LICs) get an insignificant amount.

	%
NICs	73.7
MICs	21.0
LICs	2.6

SOURCE *Development Co-operation, 1981 Review* (Paris: OECD, 1982).

Turning to LDCs, which have dominated the international capital market over the years, during 1975 the largest two borrowers were Mexico and Brazil, accounting for 19.7 per cent and 17.8 per cent of the total bank borrowings, respectively. The first five borrowers (which included Indonesia, Algeria and Iran) accounted for 59.4 per cent of the total borrowings, while the first ten accounted for 78.3.[15] The position of total liability of the first ten LDCs in June 1981 and June 1983 was as shown in Table 5.2:

TABLE 5.2   *Concentration of borrowing*

	Millions of dollars 1981	1983	Percentage of total LDC borrowings 1981	1983
1. Mexico	46 604	65 483	10.6	12.3
2. Brazil	46 382	62 778	10.5	11.8
3. Venezuela	24 472	26 765	5.6	5.0
4. Argentina	23 025	25 451	5.3	4.8
5. Korea	17 954	22 731	4.1	4.3
6. Yugoslavia	10 530	9 552	2.4	1.8
7. Philippines	9 852	13 339	2.2	2.5
8. Chile	8 754	10 946	2.0	2.1
9. Greece	8 637	11 159	1.9	2.1
10. Algeria	8 331	7 125	1.9	1.3

SOURCE   *The Maturity Distribution of International Bank Lending* (Basle: Bank of International Settlements, July 1982 and Dec 1983 issues).

As seen above, between 1981 and 1983 the concentration has increased marginally. The largest two borrowers accounted for 21.1 per cent of the total liabilities in 1981 and 24.1 per cent in 1983. The first five accounted for 36.1 per cent and 38.2 per cent during the two periods. A large number of LDCs now have an access to the capital market; the present number of LDCs participating in the market is 74; that is, if we consider only those which have borrowed in excess of $100 million.[16] Indeed, there are major differences among them in the scale of liabilities.

Trends in Bank Exposure

The US banks were the first and most active in lending to LDCs. While their share has fallen over 10 per cent since 1975, the offsetting increases have been widely distributed, with no banking group increasing its share by more than 2 per cent. In 1980 the market shares were as follows: the US banks 28.3 per cent, French banks 22.7 per cent, British banks 23.4 per cent and Luxemburg banks 15.8 per cent.[17] In 1981 there was a recovery in lending (Table 5.1); one of the reasons for this was higher market participation by Arab banks. (More about them later.) In the wake of the debt crisis in 1982 the bankers started reviewing their strategy, and the smaller ones became understandably sober and started pulling out. It is not yet clear whether this decline is the establishment of a trend. The European banks all but abandoned the field to the US and Japanese banks after 1980. These banks lost no time in expanding their operations, the Bank of Tokyo heads the *Institutional Investor*'s ranking of lead managers for syndicated credits for the first half of 1983, followed by the Chase Manhattan Bank and Citicorp.[18]

In the first flush of the OPEC surpluses the Arab financial institutions got muscled out. Western banks took on the recycling job with great gusto, and the IMF lent a hand. When the real price of oil dropped, the Arab surpluses dwindled. By 1980 the situation changed again, the oil price and the surpluses rose and a new phase of recycling started. This time the western as well as Arab banks agreed that the Arab banks play a greater role. Also, at this time the spreads were much less attractive than in the mid-1970s. Although Arab banks started playing a noticeable role in 1977, their operations gained momentum after 1980. One of the quickest ways to build rapidly was through international syndication and several of these banks worked their way into the upper ranks of international lists by virtue of their placing power. Under the market conditions described above they found it easy to expand their operations. A shift was observed in their operations from an initial period of heavy emphasis on lending to OECD and Islamic countries to LDCs. The proportion of lendings going to different country groups is shown below:

	1976	1980
1. Non-oil LDCs	3.0	32.0
2. OPEC/Islamic LDCs	43.6	38.4
3. OECD	43.9	24.0
4. CPEs	9.5	5.6
Total	100.0	100.0

SOURCE *Amex Bank Review* (Sept 1981).

The non-oil LDCs' share of Arab bank credits rose substantially. Their activity as lead managers also accelerated in 1980–1. No one in international banking circles disputes that the Arab banks have been working hard to make their presence felt. In a short time-span they achieved what other banks have achieved over a longer period.[19] Of late a large quantum of Arab credits have started finding their way to various parts of the developing world, including Latin America and Asia–Pacific.[20] In mid-1982 the Arab banks became less active due to the reduced buoyancy of the Arab capital markets following the lower oil prices as well as stagnation in the demand for oil.

The Maturing Relationship

The new relationship between the private capital market and LDCs has expanded fast; the opportunities and the risks which exist in the relationship are being questioned in many quarters. How important is the relationship? Will it endure? Will it expand or contract? Are LDCs inherently weak borrowers? Will they repay? Is it going to lead to an apocalypse today or an apocalypse tomorrow? Whether the stability of the international banking system has been endangered by loans to LDCs, has been endlessly debated in the literature.[21] Let us face it squarely. Mistakes of indiscreet borrowings and imprudent lendings have been made. For many years banks lent on risks which were thought to be dubious, and did so merely because their competitors did so. A lemming-like mentality was observed among the bankers. Till the end of 1981 the bankers, for example, were queueing up to lend to Mexico at rates $\frac{1}{4}$ per cent over their loans to Western Europe.[22] The largest borrowing LDCs, on the other hand, absurdly took money for wealth. Mexico would have been a wealthier country today had it borrowed $40 billion instead of $80.

The three Latin American cases, namely, Brazil, Mexico and Argentina, can potentially deal fatal blows to the well-integrated capital market. Naturally, Santa Claus will not head their way again. This is not to say that there would be an abrupt pause to LDC lending.[23] After the twin crises of 1982 international lending is still considered attractive.[24] However, what it does mean is that, in the past, LDC lending was influenced by the fashion of the day and based on inadequate data. Bankers will be choosier in future. The well-performing LDCs will continue to have high creditworthiness, the concentration in borrowing would decline, and lending in the developing world will become broad-based. Since spreads in the 1980s are thinner than in the 1970s the profitability will become a source of concern. A recent survey shows that the bankers expect their international lending and earnings to go on growing faster than their other business in the coming five years, although less rapidly, perhaps, than in the last five years.[25] A large number of banks found their international transactions profitable, more profitable than their domestic lending; they would find abstaining from it difficult.[26]

The large money-centre bank today seems to be in a better shape, with stronger balance sheets and rising profits. The Latin American countries have been demoted from a crisis to a problem status by the transnational banks. They no longer feel to be on the brink of disaster but face the future with optimism.[27] Many of the largest banks have also bolstered the banking system by raising fresh capital, which has made their balance sheets sturdier. Every cloud has a silver lining.

BOND MARKETS

The external bond markets consist of two types of bonds, namely, foreign and international. These are two more instruments used by LDCs to raise capital. They are defined as bonds issued by a borrower who is of a nationality other than the country of the capital market in which the bonds are issued. Foreign banks are issued in one national market; these issues are usually underwritten and sold by a group of banks of the market country and are denominated in that country's currency. International bonds are those which are underwritten and sold in various national markets simultaneously, usually through international syndicates of banks.

Bonds are an attractive source of finance for LDCs. Their maturities are relatively long, their interest rates, unlike Eurocredits, are normally fixed for the lifetime of the credit, and they are free of procurement restrictions and 'conditionality'. This being said, only a small number of LDCs possess sufficient creditworthiness to appear regularly on the bond market. As their economies grow and diversify, the LDCs pass through various stages of creditworthiness on the bond markets. LDCs with low growth rates have no access, even those with uneven growth pattern have little access. Second, LDCs with moderate per capita income growth rates (2.5 per cent +), and having a well-performing export sector as well as domestic savings for investment, have good access – the better the economic performance the broader the access. Third, LDCs with a high rate of growth, and a booming export sector assume continued access at reasonable terms.[28]

THE FIRST PERIOD: 1960–72

During the first quinquennium, LDCs' borrowing on the external bond[29] market was minor, almost spotty. There was an institutional reluctance and the LDCs for their part were shy because of lack of familiarity with the market, limited information and the restraints which the market placed on the end-use of the finance. The volume of borrowings was small compared to the market size and to the total resource inflow into LDCs. Also, for the small amount borrowed, there was a large interest differential between the market rates and LDC rates. Only three LDCs appeared in the market in 1960, their number reached twelve in 1970. The main borrowers were Mexico, Israel and Argentina. It generally took a long time to overcome the legal complications involved in issuing bonds and securing acceptance of the lending public and investors.

For the first period separate data for foreign and international bonds are not available; it is jointly available in the form of foreign bonds, which does not cause major loss of information.

In absolute terms the amount borrowed through these instruments rose almost monotonically up to 1968; the market share, however, hovered around 7 per cent of all issues. The large increase between 1966 and 1968 was due to greater availability of liquidity and the increased

TABLE 5.3   *External bond issues of LDCs,*
1960–72 (millions of $)

Year	Amount	Percentage of external issues of all countries
1960	73.1	5.7
1961	91.6	5.4
1962	93.2	5.5
1963	89.6	4.3
1964	228.2	8.8
1965	237.1	7.3
1966	278.0	7.4
1967	445.2	9.2
1968	532.4	7.0
1969	388.9	6.3
1970	345.3	5.8
1971*	134.0	1.7
1972*	588.0	5.2

SOURCE *Development Assistance, 1971 Review* (Paris: OECD, 1972), p. 92, for data up to 1970).
Borrowings in International Capital Markets (World bank), various issues for the two years marked by *.

technical capacity of the financial institutions. Because of high interest rates in the bond market in 1969 it was not possible for LDCs to keep up the tempo.[30] The tight monetary policies in the US and the revaluation of the D-mark made the bond markets a reluctant contributor of long-term resources to LDCs. Although eleven LDCs floated issues, the 1971 level remained the lowest for this period. For the first time India appeared on the list with a small issue by a private firm. In 1972 the LDCs sustained a major increase.

In the early 1960s the large US capital market was the primary source of funds. However, by the end of the period it was surpassed by Switzerland, Germany and the Netherlands in the number of issues. The balance-of-payments problems of the US in the 1960s was a big factor causing the decline of the importance of the US market. It is worthy of note that the international bond market, which is largely outside government controls, had a relatively low share of the LDC bonds.

The Relative Insignificance of External Bond Markets

As seen in Table 5.3 the market share of LDCs has always remained small. On the other hand, this has been almost an equally unimportant source of external resources to them, because it has remained a minuscule part of the total external resources received by them. Bond issues for the period of 1960–4 were only 0.3 per cent of the net financial inflows to LDCs. In the late 1960s they accounted for 2 per cent of the total, only to fall in 1970–1 to 0.8 per cent again. As noted earlier there was a surge in issues in 1972 which raised this proportion to 3 per cent.[31] This goes to prove the marginal importance of the bond issues as a source of external resources to LDCs.

For a tiny sub-group of LDCs bonds did prove to be relatively important. The truth stays that the majority of LDCs never ventured into the external bond market. Only for four LDCs, namely, Mexico, Argentina, Malaysia and Panama, did foreign issues amount to some 10 per cent of total external finances. The bond-issuing LDCs generally had higher creditworthiness and so, also, received larger flows from the capital market and direct investment. The non-issuers had most of their external resources coming in as ODA.[31] For the period under consideration Mexico was by far the largest single borrower; with over $1 billion. It accounted for nearly one-third of all LDC bonds and has been a consistent issuer in the market. Mexico issued three times the volume of bonds issued by Argentina, the second-largest issuer, which accounted for 10 per cent of all LDC issues. Five of the eight issuers were Latin American LDCs. This region accounted for two-thirds of all issues by LDCs. As for the remaining issues, both in volume and number they were evenly spread among all regions, with issues for Malaysia, the Philippines and Singapore putting East Asia into second place. The Middle East was next.

Financial Terms

Data in this regard were scanty. From what were available, Hawkins *et al.* have prepared Table 5.4 below. It is based on a sample of issues in each market. The average interest rates were the highest in Germany, the UK and the international market. This does not represent cross-market differences in yields, because it may be the influence of the time at which the issues were made. The average maturities were, by and large, identical, with Switzerland having the longest maturities. With respect to the grace period Switzerland again offered the most lenient terms. Thus, transnational differences are inconsiderable.

TABLE 5.4   *Financial terms*

| | US 1963–8 | | UK 1963–8 | Switzerland 1966–73 | | Germany 1968–9 | International 1966–73 | |
	G	P	G	G	P	G	G	P
Average maturity years	14.0	20.0	12.2	15.0	15.5	10.0	11.7	14.7
Average grace years	2.0	6.0	2.6	5.3	6.1	3	3.7	3.8
Interest (%)	6.55	6	7.47	7.17	6.75	7.63	7.5	7.8

N.B. G = government bonds and P = private bonds.

THE SECOND PERIOD: 1973–83

Because of better availability of statistics, the transparency for this period has improved, so we can see the two segments of the external bond market separately. Although the value of this long-term, fixed-interest-rate finance for LDCs cannot be exaggerated, yet bond markets remained secondary to Euromarkets. The amounts raised by LDCs on external bond market during this period were as shown in Table 5.5.

Total external bond issues of LDCs were around 8 per cent of the total issues in 1973, they declined sharply in 1974–5. The major sources of portfolio flows were the US, Germany, France and Canada, in that order. During the three years (1973–5) thirty-four LDCs succeeded in launching bond issues on the two markets.[33] Three LDCs, namely, Israel, Mexico and Spain, accounted for two-thirds of total annual borrowings. Other LDCs which were relatively better off, or possessed some potential wealth in the form of mineral resources, placed modest issues, averaging $30 million each. In the ensuing years the volume of new issues rebounded vigorously, reaching over 13 per cent in 1978.

TABLE 5.5   *External bond markets, 1973–83*

	International bond		Foreign bond		Total external bond	
1973	471.9	(10.0)	282.5	(5.3)	762.4	(7.7)
1974	96.2	(2.1)	233.8	(3.0)	330.0	(2.6)
1975	240.5	(2.3)	305.0	(2.5)	545.5	(2.4)
1976	1 046.4	(6.8)	587.1	(3.1)	1 633.5	(4.9)
1977	2 473.4	(12.7)	1 328.5	(8.0)	3 801.9	(10.4)
1978	2 919.3	(18.3)	1 940.0	(9.0)	4 859.3	(13.7)
1979	1 691.9	(9.4)	1 242.6	(6.4)	2 934.5	(7.9)
1980	1 019.4	(5.8)	534.1	(2.9)	1 553.5	(4.4)
1981	2 945.3	(9.4)	878.0	(4.3)	3 823.3	(12.2)
1982	3 155.8	(6.3)	450.9	(1.8)	3 606.7	(7.2)
1983	1 659.8	(3.3)	549.4	(2.0)	2 209.2	(4.4)

SOURCE *Financial Market trends* Paris: OECD, Feb 1980 for data up to 1979, thereafter from OECD, *Financial Statistics*, monthly, part I, various issues.
N.B. Figures in parentheses = percentage of the total market borrowings.

Years 1977–8 were the years of high borrowings from these two markets. These markets follow the Euromarket trend. The reason in both the cases was large balance-of-payments deficits of LDCs. The depressed market conditions of 1979 were largely responsibile for a drop in new issues. Adverse market conditions dampened the borrowing pitch; besides, the market concentrated on better risks. LDC issues picked up in 1981, but the twin-crisis (Brazil–Mexico) told heavily on the LDC issues and they went into a sharp decline in the following two years. In this the trend is similar to the Euromarkets again.

Access of LDCs to External Bond Markets

Although the external bond market was the source of 0.74 per cent of the external resources in 1975, 1.4 per cent in 1980 and 2.1 per cent in 1982, and had limited significance to LDCs, the issue of improving the access of LDCs to both segments of the market was constantly debated in the international fora. The number of LDCs' issues has increased over the years, yet borrowing activity is highly concentrated in a small number of high-income LDCs, and those having oil and mineral resources. Brazil, Mexico and Israel were in the market almost every year, followed by Korea and the Philippines, which borrowed frequently.

The bond markets are importants to LDCs because: (1) it is a demonstration of the creditworthiness of the LDCs to the investment community; (2) unlike Eurocredits, the interest rate is fixed for the life of the loan, which is to the LDC's advantage; and (3) maturities are relatively long, in the vicinity of ten years. The international capital market's perception of an LDC as creditworthy is the ultimate acid test; it generates confidence in the soundness of the economy and its managers.

It was for these reasons that the matters relating to the improvement in LDCs' access to external bond markets were under consideration in the IMF–IBRD Development Committee Working Group on Access to Capital Markets in early 1975. The Group defined the problems and proposed that the industrial economies should consider relaxing existing restrictions against LDCs by:

– waiving for LDC borrowers the requirement of prior authorisation for issues of securities;
– enacting legislation to permit institutional investors to acquire a somewhat larger share of LDC securities in their portfolios;
– simplifying registration and disclosure requirements for LDC borrowers.

Whether the regulations can be relaxed is a moot question, because they may be needed for keeping good order in the financial market. Besides, judgement of the market regarding creditworthiness is more important than access through favourable legislation. The recent decline in the relative position of LDCs is due to growing current account deficits,[34] which adversely affects investors.

Relative Significance of the Two Segments of the External Bond Market

Until 1965 there were more LDC issues on the foreign markets, but the situation took a turn in the 1970s, and the international bond market became a more important source of finance. There was an interruption in 1974 and 1975, when relatively unsettled financial market conditions did not favour new issues. Of the two, why is the foreign market less accessible? The basic reason is that foreign bond markets are a virtual extension of the domestic bond markets; therefore, are subject to regulation by national financial authorities. This implies that the domestic policy considerations play a role and at times LDC borrowing is limited to issues by the IBRD and the regional development banks. Of late, these institutions have started acting as intermediaries for the middle- and low-income LDCs. One market which does not have such restrictions is the US. After the mid-1970s in many industrial economies the markets were pre-empted by government borrowers due to budget crunches; this happened at the expense of the domestic borrowers and LDCs. Sovereign risk also plays a role in the foreign markets. Investors in the foreign markets have been found to be conservative, while the prudential regulations make matters more complex.[35]

The outlook of investors in the international bond market is less conservative, more international and sophisticated. The LDCs find operating easier because investors are receptive of lesser-known entities and not overly risk-adverse. Besides there exists a relative freedom from stringent financial regulations. Also LDCs have benefited from change in the market attitude, e.g. during the latter part of the period under review the Japanese market became rather favourable to LDC borrowers. The Swiss market, over the years, has become increasingly international. These two markets have therefore become more important to LDC issuers, and they account for relatively larger market shares. It is worth noting that the Swiss market for franc bonds is formally foreign in character, but its *modus operandi* gives it an appearance of an international market, which facilitates LDCs' borrowings. In the Japanese market it was the conscious policy of the government to promote LDC issues; a consensus was obtained with the financial participants to this end.

Financial Terms

Again, for the initial years, the statistics relating to issue conditions are scratchy. Different foreign markets have different terms and in the international market the terms depend on the currency in which the bonds are denominated. The terms that an individual LDC faces is a matter of its creditworthiness rather than the market conditions. As a rule they get harder terms than the industrial country borrowers, their maturities are shorter and yields higher. The yields on the D-mark denominated bonds were some 1.5 per cent higher for LDCs in the early 1970s; in 1976–8 this differential was 0.6 per cent and has not changed despite stiffer market conditions.[36] As opposed to this an increase in yield differential occurred in dollar-denominated bonds; it rose to 2 per cent, against 1 to 1½ per cent in the past, with the result that LDC issues were crowded out of this market in 1979. On the Swiss market LDCs generally pay 1 per cent higher, which has not fluctuated over the years. In the yen-denominated bond market LDCs generally pay the market rates; they do not have to pay any premiums. Only in exceptional cases is there a deviation of ¼ to ½ per cent, and no noticeable difference in maturities. Presently the Swiss and the Japanese markets offer the best terms to LDCs, also the access to these two bond markets is trouble-free.

THE REVERSAL OF CAPITAL CURRENTS – NEGATIVE FLOWS TO THE LDCs

The watershed for the capital market lending to LDCs can be dated from mid-1982. There was a well-publicised decline in new lending which, to be sure, represented the shock reaction of a market place to a widespread collapse of confidence in LDC lending as a viable activity. Although the debt service and liquidity position of LDCs have improved since then, the net flow of liquidity has remained negative. Overall, the net outflow of funds from 24 major LDC borrowers, in the first half of 1984, totalled $19.6 billion.

The statistics published by the Bank of International Settlements show that there has been a remarkable growth in deposits of non-oil LDCs with international banks during 1984. The $18.5 billion increase

(in billions of $)

Year	Repayments	Net capital inflow	Change in credit commitments	Total net flows
1982 (1st half)	− 24.4	+ 15.3	+ 1.3	− 7.8
(2nd half)	− 19.8	+ 10.6	− 12.1	− 21.3
1983 (1st half)	− 17.0	+ 2.9	− 1.8	− 15.9
(2nd half)	+ 18.4	+ 11.8	+ 1.8	− 4.9
1984 (1st half)	− 21.2	+ 5.0	− 3.4	− 19.6

SOURCE   *Amex Bank Review*, London, American Express Bank; 27 March 1985, p. 30.

in their deposits is the largest yearly expansion yet recorded. LDCs in Asia and Latin America chalked up the most significant increase by replenishing their depleted reserves out of their trade surpluses. The non-oil LDCs' deposits with the international banks was about five times as much as banks' lending to these countries in 1984. This country group was a big supplier of money to the banking system. During the same period there was a large increase in capital market lending to the United States, which helped finance its massive current account deficit. So, one can imagine where the resources made available by LDCs went. This is a good example of the new capital currents. With its robust economy thirsting for finance, its huge federal budget wallowing in red ink, the United States became a net debtor in 1985. It should be recalled that since 1914 the United States had remained a large supplier of financial resources to the international banking system.

EXPORT CREDITS

When a foreign buyer of exported goods and services is allowed to defer payment, export credit results. These credits are granted to finance capital goods, and are supported by the private sector. They may take the form of (1) suppliers' credit, extended by the exporter, who then rearranges his own refinancing, or (2) buyers' credit, where the exporter's bank or other financial institutions lend to the buyer or his bank the finance needed for the purchase. These credits are provided in the exporter's currency. They, indeed, promote exports, but to LDCs they are the least expensive type of financial resources available, after perhaps the ODA. The interest rates are fixed and subsidised within the limits prescribed by the Arrangement on Guidelines for Officially Supported Export Credit Guarantees (ECG), to which all industrial countries adhere. These are large and medium sized loans by which the industrial countries persuade the buyer LDCs to purchase from them rather than from their competitors. These credits serve as a financial sweetener, and sometimes keep even shoddy exporters in business.

A third category of export credit is called the 'official export credits', which are directly extended to exporters or foreign buyers by the government of the exporting country. One common factor in all the three kinds is the assumption of the credit risk inherent in extending finance to foreign buyers by the government. This is generally done indirectly through an official institution. These institutions are members of the Berne Union (International Union of Credit and Investment Insurers), where these institutions exchange information regarding creditworthiness and try to harmonise the policies. The scope and degree of credit coverage available is identical in most industrial economies.[37]

Growth of Export Finance to Developing Countries

The seeds for the birth of export credits lie in the post-Second World War capital goods market. Exports were made on credit because of the wide-spread shortage of international liquidity and convertible currencies. These credits were the basic instrument of trade financing among non-dollar countries. Initially these credits were negotiated for two to three years to cover short-term fluctuations. In spite of clear agreements the exporter countries found themselves obliged to delay repayments in order to facilitate smooth flow of exports, and the intended short-term credits became unintended medium-term credits. This situation soon became institutionalised into organised financing systems for medium-term suppliers' credit. The pressure on the supplier to provide both goods and capital, or to arrange for the financing of his sales, frequently led to an over-emphasis on the credit factor by buyers who, lacking ready liquidity, might be willing to ignore higher prices or inferior quality in an attempt to secure more advantageous credit terms. Gradually, as the sellers' market of the immediately post-Second World War period developed into buyers' market of the 1950s, and credits became more easily available.[38]

During the two post-Second World War decades the growth rate of world trade was the fastest ever, and concurrently extending export credits to LDCs became an integral part of the growing volume of world trade. During this period the proportion of trade in engineering and capital goods grew at a brisk rate. According to a study done by the GATT[39] the share of trade in these goods in world exports rose from 19.1 per cent in 1955 to 57.8 per cent in 1966. Exports of these goods to LDCs increased from $6.1 billion to $13.3 billion over the same period. More than 95 per cent of these exports originated in the industrial market economies. That apart, there is evidence to show that the growth of credits was at a faster rate than the growth of exports of capital goods. This was partly due to the nature of goods exported. Other reasons were: the pressure from LDCs for larger credits on extended terms, and growing competition among the industrial countries to capture the LDC markets. Many LDCs had accumulated foreign exchange reserves during the war; these were depleted by the late 1950s. As their demand for capital goods exceeded the size of their budgets the requests for better and extended terms increased.

LDCs needed financing for the replacement of obsolete equipment, expansion of existing industrial base and the creation of new industrial units. Since the supply of ODA or resources from the multilateral institutions were limited, the buyer LDCs sought to cover part of their capital outlays with financing arrangements with their suppliers. The suppliers found it possible to comply with the demands made by LDCs because of the gradual liberalisation of exchange controls, which enabled them to extend credit for long periods.

Export Credits and Development Finance

The dividing-line between export credits and development finance gradually became indistinct. Attempts have been made to define the two clearly, but there is no agreement regarding when export credits are only a means of financing exports and when they become an investment for development. As already noted, export credits have grown fast in volume and the interest rates have stubbornly lagged behind those in the capital market. Progressively they have become intertwined with development finance. In the absence of precise quantitative measurements, definitions and motivation, it is difficult to separate the two. With growing competition among national export credit institutions, and their seeming overlap with the work of the agencies for development, a technocratic search for a formula to separate the two is foredoomed. Attempts to draw a neat line between the two end up concluding that the agencies of development finance (the bankers of the poor) and the national export credit agencies (the bankers of the rich) are increasingly coming closer, and becoming dependent upon one another.[40]

Another practice which has pushed the export credits into the field of development finance is that of guaranteeing part of the local cost in the export finance package. This move was initiated by the European bankers in the 1960s, and then followed up by American bankers to meet foreign competition.

The Berne Union

The International Union of Credit and Investment Insurers is popularly known as the Berne Union. As export financing and its techniques developed, *pari passu*, a need was felt to maintain orderly and standardised conditions of competition in the capital goods trade, which led to the creation of the Berne Union in 1934. It was an organisation of private and public institutions for export credit insurance; in its attempts to co-ordinate export credit activities it makes frequent recommendations to its members regarding the terms and conditions of export credit. It was the understanding that departures from the recommendations would be informed to the Union. Initially it was assumed that the exporter would bear part (10 to 20 per cent) of the risk himself and the buyer would make a down-payment of 15 to 20 per cent, prior to the delivery. Also it was assumed that the Union would be kept posted of all the credits which are provided for more than five years, but by the end of the 1950s they became so frequent, that the five-year limit had to be abandoned. Longer repayment periods were granted *de facto*, by adopting late starting-points from which to count the repayment period.

The Union continued its co-ordinating job until the 1960s. Thereafter, the departures from commonly adopted standards became common despite a clear definition of the starting-point. Another problem was the increasing scale of official export financing. This made the terms dependent upon the government's policies. In such a climate, adhering to the Union's recommendations needed more inter-governmental co-operation and co-ordination.

Flow of Export Credits between 1950 and 1969

First, a word about the quality of statistics, which are compiled by two sources: the OECD and the IBRD. The OECD data are compiled from the creditor countries who are members of the Group on Export Credit Guarantees (ECG), while the IBRD data is based on reports from the debtor countries. For as long a period as possible, the OECD data have been used in this work, because they depict flow of export credits to LDCs alone. It should be clarified at the outset that, for the initial years, only incomplete information is available. Also, during earlier years many transactions remained unrecorded and formed a part of the 'errors and omission' in the balance of payments.

TABLE 5.6 *Net flow of export credit to LDCs, 1956–69 (in millions of $)*

1950–5* (annual average)	200
1956	483.3
1957	490.7
1958	229.9
1959	424.1
1960	570.9
1961	698.5
1962	657.8
1963	666.7
1964	941.4
1965	825.0
1966	1 214.8
1967	1 052.5
1968**	1 596.0
1969**	2 047.0

SOURCES *Between 1950 and 1955, from *Financing for Industrial Development, Export Credit Systems and Institutions* (Economic and Social Council, UN, CE/C.5/26, Mar 1963). Others from *IMF Staff Papers* (Mar 1970), which in turn has culled it from the OECD data.
**Development Co-operation Review, 1971* (Paris: OECD, 1972).

The first definitive study of export credit flows to developing countries was done by the IMF,[41] from which most of the above statistical data orginate. The annual average flow was $200 million betweeen 1950 and 1955. During the mid-1950s, the European exporters started pressurising their governments to provide export credit insurance for a period in excess of five years. They cited the long-term project and equipment loans given by the Export–Import Bank of the US. These were official export credits, granted directly to LDC buyers, enabling American exporters to sell on terms which Europeans could only match if they could obtain long-term export credits. The European exporters increased lobbying in 1957 when the UK expanded the volume of the long-term financial assistance granted through the machinery provided for in section 3 of the Export Guarantee Act of 1949.[42]

Looking at the numerical perspective of the net flow of guaranteed export credits over this period, during 1956–9 they averaged $400 million per annum and the US was the main supplier. In 1960 and 1961 they rose sharply, only to dip somewhat the following two years. There was a trend towards longer maturity periods, over half of the guaranteed net export credits during 1962 were extended for more than five years, compared with less than half in 1961 and 26 per cent in 1960, and less than 5 per cent in 1959. This ratio recorded a fall in 1963, at 40 per cent.[43]

The importance of export credits grew with industrialisation in LDCs. After 1964 the rate of growth in export credits was faster, they reached $1 596 million in 1968 and $2 047 in 1969. Taking a medium-term perspective, between 1956 and 1968, Japan was the most important source. It was followed by Germany, France, Italy, and the UK, in that order. These five countries among them accounted for over four-fifths of the cumulative credits.[44] They were followed by Switzerland, Belgium and the US. The reason why Japan was at the top is that Japan had the biggest share in export financing of ships, particularly to the 'flag of convenience' countries. The US lagged behind essentially because these facilities existed in the private sector in Europe and Japan during the inter-war period, whereas the US programme was organised by the Export–Import Bank, which was born in 1961, and was an official organ of the US government. The major recipient LDCs during this period were: Mexico, Argentina, Korea, Brazil, India, Iran and Yugoslavia, in that order.

Flow of Export Credits between 1970 and 1983

The quality of statistical data available for the second period is more reliable and comprehensive. Also, for this period we have the breakdowns of official and private export credits. As documented in Table 5.7, the faster growth pace of credit expansion in the second quinquennium of the 1960s continued into the 1970s. After 1975 they acquired a significant place in the total financial flows to the LDCs.

Official export credits have grown since the late 1950s, when the US was virtually their sole supplier. Aggregate statistics for them, however, are available only after 1970. Yet they serve to demonstrate a particularly rapid expansion of this form of export financing: from $59 million in 1970 to $245 million in 1982. The two categories of export finance added up to over $12 billion in 1978, which was, for the first time, equal to ODA flows from the DAC, whose growth was slowing. The principal recipients were such rapidly industrialising LDCs as Korea, Brazil, Mexico, Taiwan, Yugoslavia, Greece and the Philippines.

Table 5.7 sets out the net volume of export credits – that is, after deducting service payments in respect of earlier lendings. On a gross basis some $15 billion of new export credits were extended in 1975, twice as high as the 1972 level.[45] On the gross level the period between 1972 and 1975 was one of decline. Yet exports to LDCs were well-maintained, so it can be inferred that LDCs found alternative means of financing their imports. An apparent alternative was funds from the Euromarkets, which, though more expensive, may have been preferred because of the greater liberty in choosing the source of imports, and relative simplicity and convenience as compared with export credits. Table 5.1 also supports this statement.

There was a spurt in 1975, both in real and nominal terms, for the

TABLE 5.7   *Net flow of export credits to LDCs, 1970–83 (in billions of $)*

	Private export credits	Official export credits	Total	In constant prices (1981 = 100)	Percentage share in total inflows
1970	2.09	0.59	2.68	6.91	14.1
1971	2.71	0.71	3.42	8.3	16.2
1972	1.44	0.75	2.19	4.78	9.4
1973	1.15	1.18	2.33	4.54	7.3
1974	2.40	0.86	3.26	5.75	9.0
1975	4.42	1.22	5.64	8.82	10.3
1976	7.22	1.39	8.61	12.07	14.8
1977	9.11	1.48	10.59	14.54	14.9
1978	10.22	2.15	12.37	14.77	14.9
1979	9.49	1.72	11.21	11.86	13.1
1980	12.20	2.46	14.66	14.22	15.3
1981	10.59	2.76	13.35	13.35	12.9
1982	7.09	2.45	11.54	11.79	9.0
1983	5.50	2.10	7.60	NA	7.6

SOURCE *Development Co-operation, 1982 Review* and *1983 Review* (Paris: OECD, various tables).

following reasons: (1) there was a widening gap between the stagnating export earnings of LDCs and the sharply increased import bill for essential commodities, including food and oil; (2) imports of capital goods by relatively poor OPEC countries like Indonesia, Algeria and Nigeria stepped up; (3) due to prevailing high interest rates the terms of export finance seemed extra favourable. The major sources were: Germany, the US, France, Italy and Japan, in that order.

During the second quinquennium, export credits recorded and maintained a high level, particularly up to 1981. They also recovered in their proportion of total resource inflows. OPEC countries received almost half of the total, and the middle-income and newly industrialising countries accounted for a large part of the rest. The officially supported credits peaked in 1980 (Table 5.7), with a drop in subsequent years; a large part of the decline can be attributed to the UK. Expressed in constant prices they more than doubled during the 1970s; their annual growth rate was 5.3 per cent on average. After 1980, a monotonic decline set in. Exporters in the developed countries have taken to relying more heavily on banks, which increasingly are sharing the risk and efforts involved in bidding for export orders and contracts.[46] The debt crisis has also taken its toll and the export credit agencies are being urged by their governments to trim their services to exporters. During recent years the main source countries were: France, Germany, Italy, Japan, the UK and the US; together they accounted for three-quarters of the total. As regards the geograpical concentration, 37 per cent went to NICs, 25 per cent to the MICs and 18 per cent to the LICs.

There are reasons to believe that a growing proportion of the manufactured exports to LDCs are covered by export credits. In 1973 and 1974, while the exports of manufactures from industrial to developing countries were $59.5 billion and $95.8 billion, respectively, the proportion of export credit as a percentage of manufactured exports was 5.8 and 5.3 per cent respectively. Let us now see the recent figures:

	Exports of manufactures to non-oil LDCs	*Export credits as percentage of manufactured exports*
	$ *billion*	%
1978	95.8	13.8
1979	120.1	9.3
1980	144.6	10.7
1981	151.0	8.9

SOURCE   Exports statistics come from *International Trade* (GATT, various issues).

Whether this rapid growth in export credits indicates growing mercantilism in the developed market economies, remains a moot question.

Financial Terms

All industrial countries provide financial support to their exports on a medium- or long-term basis. The US, Japan, Canada, and Australia finance part of export credit directly through official institutions. Usually the commercial banking structure is used far more for this purpose, with the governments subsidising the difference between the market rates of interest and the fixed rate of interest. These efforts particularly intensified after 1973–4, sometimes at substantial budgetary costs. This quickened the process, begun in the early 1960s, of insulating export credit terms from those of the domestic and international money markets. It needs to be pointed out that export credits are on fixed interest and the rate of interest is below that of the market for similar maturities. In the 1970s, when inflation was high, the competition for the export of capital goods became keener, and accusations and counter-accusations among various export credit agencies of offering better terms became rampant. As a reconciliatory measure something referred to as 'The International Agreement on Officially Supported Export Credits' came into being, which was responsible for the 'Gentleman's Agreement' regarding the terms of export credits.[47]

Another controversial point was regarding the grace or maturity period. Payments normally commenced six months after the 'starting-point', which was the time point when the buyer receives the completed plant or the finished goods. In the case of capital goods there was an unavoidable grace period – that is, the period between the signing of contract and manufacturing and final delivery. This can take two or more years. From what time point the maturity period has to be counted and what has to be the grace period: understanding regarding these has changed frequently and been a cause of confusion as well as tension among the export credit agencies of different industrial countries. There was an agreement reached in this regard in July 1980, which was replaced by one in October 1981, which in turn was replaced by one in July 1982.[48] According to the last agreement the minimum interest rates were fixed at 10 per cent for the relatively poor countries, that is, those LDCs who are eligible for IDA credits, having per capita income below \$750. For the countries with per capita income in intermediate range the interest rate has been fixed at 10.85–11.35 per cent. For countries having per capita income of $4 000 and above it was fixed at 12.15–12.40 per cent. This agreement also enlisted the countries falling in each category to avoid more disputes and confusions. Talks relating to the new interest-rate regime broke down in April 1983, because of serious differences within the EEC, and the Community and the US and Japan. The Community countries are pressing for the present range of officially supported credit rates of 10 per cent to 12.4 per cent, to be reduced by between 0.5 per cent and 2 per cent. This proposal was rejected by the US and Japan. The Japanese, meanwhile, demanded a reduction in the 'penalty' they pay for having low market rates of interest.[49]

FOREIGN DIRECT INVESTMENT

Foreign direct investment is essentially a package deal comprising long-term finance, technological know-how, managerial expertise and marketing experience. There are different effects of foreign direct investment (FDI), sometimes referred to as 'the spillover'. It may have a two-way effect; it may influence the industrial structure of the host economy as well as the performance of the investing economy. It is claimed that one of the most significant contributions of foreign investment is likely to come from the externalities created by it, but few empirical estimates are available because they are difficult to quantify. Inasmuch as FDI brings in advanced technology, the technological efficiency of the host LDC is enhanced. Development of forward- and backward-linkages promote industrialisation. Singapore, Taiwan and the Republic of Korea are good examples of this potential of the FDI. If labour productivity is taken as a measure of technical efficiency, it can be demonstrated, with the help of regression analysis, that FDI has a positive correlation with the technical efficiency in the industrial sector of the host LDC.[50] There had been a divergence of views on the role of FDI in LDCs. There are some who hold that in a milieu when the ODA is not rising in real terms, and the needs of LDCs are pressing, FDI is the way out essentially because they are non-debt-creating assets. Entrepreneurial investment can bridge several gaps, such as the balance of payments gap, the saving gap, the resource gap, and so on.

The other side of the coin is that the investing transnational corporations, in the process of organising their operations beyond their national framework, may become centres of economic power. This may lead to an abuse of concentration of power and to conflicts with the policy objectives of the host government. In addition, the complexity of the transnational corporations and the difficulty of clearly perceiving their diverse structures, operations and policies sometimes leave the host country confounded. These arguments have been belaboured in the literature.

There is another school of thought which maintains that FDI is the twentieth-century refinement of the 'imperialistic' powers of the last century, and that it aggravates the development crisis. Holders of this view worry about the foreign ownership of the productive assets in LDCs, dominance over the market, influence over the allocations of resources and distribution of income. The balance-of-payment crises, like the one that occurred in the US, have made the investors wonder, whether, after all the immediate balance-of-payments costs, the game is worth the candle, whatever the long-term benefits.[51] Besides, the overall profitability of the FDI has been questioned by the investors.

According to the classical economic theory FDI was beneficial to both the host LDC and the investor, because the assumption was that the capital flows from relatively capital-abundant to capital-scarce countries, or from countries with low marginal productivity of capital to those with high productivity. Under the classical assumption the host LDC benefited from the entrepreneurial investment to the extent its productivity is higher than what the foreign investor withdraws in the form of profits or dividends.[52] The neoclassical economic theory and the standard development theory both unequivocally suggest that FDI has a positive impact on the host LDC because it dispels the twin constraints of foreign exchange and financial resources.[53] In addition FDI pursues the highest rate of available return, so it must increase world welfare. That apart, the investor stands to gain because the rate of return on FDI is higher than that in the domestic economy.

Although the classical and neoclassical views still influence a good deal of thinking, the fact remains that the presumption that the FDI is in the form of a loan no longer holds good. It is mostly in the form of equity investment, which gives rise to complex analytical problems. These views have not gone unchallenged. The classical theory of distribution of gains between the recipient LDC and the investor has been questioned on several grounds. The analysis has gone beyond the welfare considerations of the two sets of countries. Numerous other related issues have attracted considerable attention, foremost of which has been the balance-of-payments effect of FDI.[54] Singer was the first economist to raise his voice against the classical approach. His well-acclaimed study reached the inference that by and large FDIs have been beneficial to the investing countries, but have had no impact, or at times negative impact, on the host LDC.[55] Singer concluded this primarily through a terms of trade argument, and, second, through asserting that insofar as FDI is not integrated in the LDC economy, it should be treated merely as domestic investment by the investor in an economic sense. This was true till the time of his writing, however, it is no longer wholly correct, particularly in the cases of the NICs and the MICs. He opined that the classical presumption about the mutual benefits can only be reached on the basis of static comparative advantage, which is inappropriate with respect to FDI. What is needed is a dynamic approach; accordingly he showed that a large part of the benefits accruing from rising productivity are appropriated by the investor. It is worth noting that until the time of Singer's writing a large part of FDI was in extractive industries, so little wonder his analysis deals essentially with that scene. Ten years later MacDougall inferred, arguing on lines slightly different from Singer, that FDI may not be in the ultimate self-interest of the LDCs.[56]

There are other serious works which take the opposite view. For example, Balogh and Streeten,[57] and Kemp[58] hold that FDI, if it proceeds at high rates, may be harmful to the investing economy. It is outside the scope of this study to go into the finesse of these arguments and counter-arguments. However, a clear thinker can infer that FDI is far from a zero-sum-game played between the capital-exporting and the recipient countries. It need not be a game of gains of one side representing parallel losses to another. Both may gain or lose. The argument concerning distribution of gains can be interminable. Much of the confusion arises on both sides from a failure to discard a pedagogically convenient framework of ideas in favour of dynamic trade and capital movement theory, in which technological factors play the central role.[59] Without this shift in focus, clarity of vision seems far-fetched.

One important question has so far remained unanswered: Is FDI indispensable for economic growth? An empirical study establishes that on the basis of cross-country data no final solution can be given, either theoretically or statistically.[60] FDI is neither a necessary nor sufficient condition for economic growth – the same is also true of its absence.

The balance-of-payments considerations are important to the investor as well as to the host LDC. No verdict can be given based on straight-laced comparison of inflows and outflows. Numerous other factors have to be taken into account, e.g. an LDC's projection of its short-term and long-term foreign exchange gap, the loan-equity composition of FDI, net import savings or export gains from the contemplated project and indeed the overall contribution to employment, production and technological advance. Therefore, a case by case analysis would be needed, and the upshot would depend upon the variables involved in each concrete factual instance. Most LDCs offer incentives to attract FDI. It is difficult to evaluate the effectiveness of incentives, yet an LDC might lose much of new FDI were it to abolish all its incentives unilaterally. The incentives can be direct or indirect, they can be put in two categories: those that offer commodity protection (e.g. tariffs and quotas on imported competing products), and those that offer factor protection (e.g. tax holidays, investment allowance, subsidies on fix investment). While the first type alters the prices of goods and services bought or sold by the investing firm, the second alters the prices of inputs used by it. The LDCs that wish to attract FDI to serve the domestic market generally offer commodity protection, whereas those LDCs that wish to promote export-oriented investment are more likely to offer the latter type of incentives.

This should serve as a backdrop for what follows.

The First Period: 1946–55

The old problem persists, the data for this period are again far from perfect. The two US studies, subsequently quoted, fail to provide complete time-series. In Table 5.8 the statistics for the US – the largest investor for the period – are consistent and of good-quality. The same

TABLE 5.8   *Foreign direct investment in LDCs, 1946–55*

Year	Amount in millions of $	Percentage change over last year
1946	486	–
1947	1 112	129
1948	1 267	14
1949	1 371	8
1950	1 342	−2
1951	1 580	5
1952	2 527	60
1953	2 290	9
1954	2 269	1
1955	2 149	−5

SOURCE   Computed from Avramovic and Gulhati (1958), op. cit., table III, p. 9.

cannot be said about those of other industrial economies. Table 5.8 comes from Avramovic and Gulhati,[61] who in turn have aggregated statistics from the US Department of Commerce *Survey of Current Business* and various UN publications. For countries other than the US, data are based on the balance of payments, reporting of which became substantial and consistent after 1945.

The European economies were reconstructing. The US became the principal investor country of this sub-period. France and Switzerland followed the US and soon acquired important positions as investors, particularly during the second quinquennium. The Swiss investments were derived not only from its own savings, but also from foreign funds seeking refuge from political instability and stringent foreign exchange laws. Other investing countries, in a small way, were Belgium and Sweden. During this period the FDI were financed through the reinvestment of undistributed profits by as much as three-fourths or more.[62] Only dubious quality figures of reinvestment are available; generally they are understatements because the recorded profit is reduced through depletion or depreciation allowances. Resources were attracted towards LDCs which had acquired a certain level of industrial development and were richly endowed with natural resources. The Latin American LDCs met both these criteria. The following LDCs belonged to this group: Brazil, Chile, Colombia, Mexico and Peru. The second country group which attracted FDI was one having petroleum resources – namely, Venezuela, Saudi Arabia and Iraq. Third, Belgium, France and the UK made investments in their 'dependent territories' particularly in Africa.

Unlike the country groups mentioned above, many of the world's over-populated regions, with underdeveloped manufacturing sectors, recorded a net outflow of private long-term capital. This applied to Ceylon (now Sri Lanka), India, Indonesia and Egypt. The reverse-flows partly represented normal amortisation. The contrast, however, suggests that the FDI was attracted more towards natural resources than to abundant manpower.

There was a change in the sectoral pattern of investment. Railroads and public utilities were given secondary importance to petroleum and other extractive industries. A large increase in the book value of US FDI took place in agriculture (sugar and fruit plantations) and mining and smelting, mostly in Latin America. Large investment in the same sectors was made by the European metropolitan countries in Africa. The growth of transnational corporations (TNCs) led to considerable expansion of FDI; with that the direction of investable funds also changed from the primary to secondary sector. Second, FDI shifted from portfolio investment to direct holdings. Many LDCs encouraged FDI in industries as they realised that their economic structures were unbalanced, and the manufacturing sector was lagging behind.

The annual rate of outflow of the US – the largest investor – fluctuated considerably over the whole period. It began at $486 million in 1946 and reached a peak of $1.73 billion in 1952, mainly in response to the demand for raw materials generated by the Korean War, and fell to $400 million in 1954. On the whole, self-financing was a more important source of addition to the existing stock than new investment.[63]

The Second Period: 1956–70

Despite the recent flood in literature on FDI, and various investigations undertaken by national and international organisations, statistics on the nature and extent of FDI are still far from exhaustive. That is not to say that they are as patchy as those for the first period. There are some persistent definitional problems in measuring foreign investment, particularly when investment takes the form of machinery and capitalised technological contributions. If the distinction is made on the basis of control, such that, if the effective control lies in the hands of the investor, it is foreign investment proper, and where the local entity calls the shots it is mere technology transfer, then there arise difficulties in determining how, and to what extent, control is exercised. A majority share holding is not always necessary for the investor to exercise control.[64] An investor can at times exercise control with an equity share as low as 10 per cent, for example, investments made by the Intercontinental chain of hotels in the LDCs. In such instances there are practical and conceptual difficulties in quantifying FDI.

Apart from these difficulties, there are gaps in the statistics available, from both investor and recipient countries. Most industrial market economies did not publish comprehensive information on the foreign operation of their firms due to business secrecy. The UN Centre on Transnational Corporations attempts to estimate FDI on a worldwide basis, but difficulties of collecting and reconciling information from about 150 member countries explains why its published data tend to be four or five years out-of-date. The OECD collects its own series, which are the most up-to-date. The reliability of these data is not comparable to that of the data for the ODA, which are derived from the official records. Also, there is a marginal difference between the two series: the

TABLE 5.9   *Foreign direct investment in LDCs, 1971–82*

Year	Amount in millions of $	Percentage change over last year
1956	2 350	9
1957	2 724	16
1958	1 970	− 28
1959	1 782	− 10
1960	1 767	− 1
1961	1 829	4
1962	1 495	− 18
1963	1 603	7
1964	1 572	− 2
1965	2 468	57
1966	2 179	38
1967	2 105	− 15
1968	3 043	45
1969	2 910	− 4
1970	3 557	22

SOURCE   *Development Co-operation*, Review, (Paris: OECD 1972 and earlier issues).

one compiled by the OECD and that by the UN Centre on Transnational Corporations.

Due to petroleum the Middle East continued to attract FDI; in fact, 1957 recorded a high level of FDI and it is known as the year of the petroleum boom. At this point there were ten major oil companies operating in Iraq, Iran, Kuwait and Saudi Arabia. In India the investment was traditionally concentrated in plantations, trade and transportation, but during 1956–7 manufacturing became more important. The UK was the largest investor, owning over 80 per cent of the total foreign assets. About three-quarters of the total foreign investment in India in 1956 were derived from retained earnings.[65] FDI in South-East Asia was concentrated in the agricultural sector. Japan entered the foreign exchange market in a small way, beginning with investing in South-East Asia and subsequently in Latin America.

The spurt of 1965 was due to the US investments, which included certain large tax settlements, which were invested as well as payments for the new leases by the petroleum industry. After stagnating in the late 1950s and early 1960s, FDI picked up, though there was no uniform upward trend. Both in terms of their absolute size and the rate of growth over the period under review, FDIs were substantially smaller than the ODA flows to LDCs. At the end of the decade they stood at $3.5 billion. FDI were 78 per cent of the total private capital flows in 1956, 56 per cent in 1960 and 51 per cent in 1970. Credits from the bond markets and export financing expanded at a relatively steady pace. Why was there a slump in FDI between 1958 and 1964? A variety of factors contributed to hold back the level of FDI in LDCs. From the point of view of investors the promise of a return was not enough to compensate for the risk and trouble encountered in LDCs. That is, the economic environment did not inspire confidence among the investors. In addition, inflation and the growing balance-of-payments problem (as in the US) proved to be the other environmental snags.

Initially the TNCs were accorded a high degree of market protection in LDCs, which enabled them to reap monopoly profits. Soon it generated discontent in LDCs, and some of them became schizophrenic in their attitude towards FDI. The resistance by the TNCs was manifested in the form of complete control of subsidiaries, ignoring the local governments, unwillingness to place native staff in high positions and forbidding exports to third countries. The relationship soon became a tense one, with each side becoming doubtful of the other. What made it worse was the fact that the rules of the game were not clearly drawn. This created an environment of antipathy in many LDCs. Besides, in the case of large LDCs, for example, Argentina and India, there was a balance-of-payments-related concern; these LDCs considered FDI acceptable only if the advantages to the economy were clear-cut.

By mid-1960s the TNCs came to be a force to reckon with in the world economy. According to an estimate the total sales of these enterprises, both exports and local, were second in value to the combined GNPs of the US and the USSR in 1966.[66] Much of the FDI was owned by the TNCs. Their pattern of investment had shifted from the extractive industries to manufacturing, therefore industrialising LDCs interested them even more than the developed economies. For example, in 1946 the book value of the US direct investment in Latin America was three times as much as that in Europe. In 1967 the proportion was not far lower.[67] The other change in the pattern was joint enterprises with local firms and jointly owned firms in the third markets, especially in Latin America. The creation of subcontracting enterprises by the US in Mexico, Taiwan and Hong Kong, started in this period.

Investments by Germany, Italy and Japan had substantial growth during this period. The UK and the US had exceptionally high investment levels in 1968 (Table 5.9). The US surpassed the previous record year of 1957. It is not easy to explain the volatility of FDI in the late 1960s. Yet it may be noted that the trends in FDI are often correlated with the pace of expansion and the degree of economic optimism in the industrial market economies. In 1968 the spurt in FDI coincides with the strong growth in the industrial economies. On the other hand, the LDCs recorded over 5 per cent GNP growth in 1967–8, which also may have influenced the mind of the investors.

Latin America, the Caribbean and the oil-producing countries all over the globe stood out as the dominant recipient regions. A third of total FDI went into oil. If plantations and mining is added to it, then nearly half of the total stock of FDI was in sectors which provided raw materials for the industrial economies. A comparison between stocks and flows in the various sectors confirmed the impression that manufacturing was becoming an increasingly attractive field for FDI.[68] Apart from the LDCs US investment in Europe also grew at a rapid rate during this period.

The Third Period: 1971–83

The quality of statistical data available for this period is the least tenuous. A certain amount of uncertainty lingers because reinvested profits are as much as 40 per cent of the FDI, which are not always accurately reported. Also, over the years the nature of FDI has changed from less formal equity investment to management contracts.

As the time changed so did the reality and its perception. Heresies of yesterday become the conventional wisdom of today. Controversies persisted, but the issues changed. The powerful oligopolistic world of TNCs, possessing commercial and economic power, gave way to a competitive world of foreign investors acting as a neutral agent of capital transfer. In the 1950s the growth rate and the volume of FDI was on the low side; during the 1960s the growth rate averaged 4 per cent. During the 1970s it became readily available to LDCs, particularly in the manufacturing sector and to those LDCs which had an open-door policy towards FDI. Some of the major factors in attracting FDI during the 1970s were: not-too-stringent economic climate, and clarity and stability about the rules of the game, so that long-term decisions and forecasts could be made. These factors also led to an ability to plan productive investment projects.[69] To the extent that the new, slightly strict but clear, rules established by the LDCs are likely to

TABLE 5.10   *Foreign direct investment in LDCs, 1971–83*

Year	*Amount in billions of $*	*Percentage changeover last year*	*At constant prices (1981 = 100)*	*Percentage share in total external financial inflows*
1971	3.31	− 10	8.03	15.6
1972	4.23	28	9.23	18.1
1973	4.72	12	9.20	14.7
1974	1.89	− 60	3.33	5.2
1975	11.51	509	17.60	21.2
1976	8.64	− 25	12.82	14.8
1977	9.59	11	13.17	14.2
1978	11.83	37	14.11	14.2
1979	13.42	13	14.20	15.7
1980	10.36	− 22	10.05	10.8
1981	17.24	70	17.24	15.7
1982	11.86	− 35	11.24	12.2
1983	7.80	− 34	NA	7.8

SOURCE   *Development Co-operation, 1982 Review* and *1983 Review* (Paris: OECD, 1983, 1984).

remain in force for a long time to come, they may in fact contribute to an improved investment climate. In fact, it is widely believed that there has been a rise in the receptiveness of LDCs because of political stability and domestic economic reforms, which implied high potential profitability of FDI. Besides, the post-war investment boom in most industrial market economies had reached steeply diminishing marginal returns in the early 1970s, and so capital had to scout for areas of higher marginal returns. In addition, real wage growth accelerated in the early 1970s in most industrial economies, except the US, and did not moderate greatly during the years following the first oil price hike. The result was a rise in labour's share of income (L_w/GNP) and fall in the pre-tax rate of return on corporate capital in many developed economies.[70]

The FDI reached $4.7 billion in 1973, a new high. It was due to sizeable investment by the US and an unprecedented growth in Japanese private investment in the Far East. They fell to $1.9 billion in 1974 because of the heavy disinvestment in the oil industry. Again, because of the heavy investment in the oil industry in other parts of the world, FDIs reached $11.5 billion in 1975. They fell in 1976, but rose again to $13.4 billion in 1979, and fell to $10.36 billion in 1980, which was due to new oil take-overs. A sharp recovery occurred in 1981; the over-valued dollar had something to do with this. The average annual growth rate of 1970–81 was 15.5 per cent at current prices and exchange rate, but just over 5 per cent in real terms. As seen in Table 5.10, the share of FDI in total external resource receipt of LDCs has hovered around 15 per cent for most of the years, without a trend. Yet, it is clear that these flows recorded their strongest growth – over-valued dollar notwithstanding – and peaked in 1981. Thereafter they made a nose dive because returns on these investments fell sharply as a result of the world recession. The FDI-related repayments from non-oil LDCs rose from $3.5 billion in 1973 to $9.5 billion in 1981, before declining sharply to an estimated $6.25 billion in 1983.[71] Expressed as a percentage of exports of goods and services, non-oil LDCs' total repayments on FDI declined gradually over the decade from 3 per cent in 1973 to less than 1.5 per cent in 1983.

Table 5.10 shows that FDIs by and large maintained their level after 1977. It should be noted that the last four of these are recession years. The implementation of previously planned investment provides one explanation. FDI also got a boost during these years because of a flat demand in investors' home countries and a tendency of trade barriers to promote foreign manufacturing as an alternative to exporting. For all appearances FDI has a counter-cyclical trend as a hedge against local competition, which is more fierce.

On the recipient side two-thirds of the flows went to Latin America, and much of the remainder to middle-income countries in other regions. The low-income LDCs attracted little FDI. The division, according to 1980 figures is as follows:

	%
NICs	55.0
MICs	30.9
LICs	6.8

Among the MICs FDI has preferred what is called 'safer locations'.

CHANGING PROFILE OF THE FOREIGN DIRECT INVESTMENT

There are few areas of economic activity in LDCs which have seen so

much experimentation as the FDI. The international debt crisis accelerated the change in the attitude of LDCs towards FDI. Gradually, the
FDI came of age and a constructive network of investment relationships between LDCs and investors has come into being.[72] The stable
pattern of a viable relationship became perceptible during the late
1960s. The subsequent period saw a structural transformation in the
forms of FDI in LDCs. One of the most significant departures from the
past was that the investors ceased to insist on the full ownership of the
investment ventures. The practice of a 'packaged' deal was almost
totally abandoned. New and more functional forms of foreign investment developed. These often comprised a spectrum of complex,
pragmatic and *ad hoc* arrangements, to suit the particular situation.
They can be minority participation, joint ventures, production-sharing
and sub-contracting arrangements, management, technology licens-
ing, marketing contracts, phase-out agreements, turnkey projects, and
myriad other functional forms.[73] The differences between FDI, non-
equity investment, inter-company and foreign trade are increasingly
being blurred. The new form of FDI is without the ownership of capital
by the foreign investor, or at least with a diluted formal ownership.
This allows the host LDC to increase its influence while co-operating
with the transnational corporation or the investing firm from the
industrialised country. In the traditional form FDI was an integrated
unit of ownership–management–technology, in its new form it can be
broken up into separate economic transactions, which in turn can be
negotiated with different firms of the host LDC's choice.

Traditionally, FDI was concentrated in the raw material sector and
the investing firm sought, and had, extensive and exclusive rights to
exploit. The host LDC usually had to be contented with meagre
proceeds from leases or taxes. Since the early 1970s the raw material
sector has been restricted for foreign firms. Some LDCs have gone so
far as cancelling the existing contracts, and nationalising certian
industries or sectors. These contracts have been renegotiated on an
entirely different footing, with the host LDC sharing in the profits.[74]
This has increased the formal power and control of the host LDCs over
FDI in their economies. Yet, there are areas, such as technology,
management or marketing, in which an LDC may be completely
dependent upon the foreign firm. In such cases 'service contracts' are
made with the firm, these contracts allow for minority holding or no
holding by the foreign firm. Generally the conditions agreed upon are
such that the venture is profitable for both, the LDC and the foreign
firm involved, which is reasonable and realistic. Under 'service con-

tracts' the foreign firm operates as a contractor for a national firm or a state institution.[75]

Among LDCs new areas of concentration of FDI have grown up, especially the South-East Asian countries. The potential range of activity for FDI has been extended considerably. FDI has moved out of agricultural production, plantation and extractive industries almost entirely. There has been a long-term shift towards non-fuel minerals and subcontracting in a large range of activities. The recent concentration is in new industries, particularly those using electronics and high technology. It is to be seen whether the new form of FDI is more viable. Indications are that, by and large, it is, yet it is not to say that this is an irreversible process and will not evolve in future. One lives, one learns.

The FDI flows are non-debt-creating and the returns paid on them are 'more positively correlated with changes in a country's ability to service those payments than are interest payments on its external debt'.[76] An examination of the relative importance of FDI in total liabilities of countries that have encountered debt servicing difficulties in the recent years adds support to the hypothesis that adjustment to economic disturbances is easier for LDCs that have a large proportion of FDI in total external liabilities. For 28 LDCs that rescheduled their external debt during 1983, the stock of FDI accounted for an average of only 14 per cent of their total external liabilities at the end of 1983. This compares with an average of 24 per cent during the same period for those 49 LDCs that did not reschedule debt.

6 Resource Flows to and from the Multilateral Financial Institutions

INTRODUCTION

For the purpose of this study multilateral financial institutions (MFIs) are being defined as those institutions which include developing as well as the developed countries in their membership. These institutions have played a pivotal and growing role in the flow of financial resources to LDCs. Looking at the external financial receipts of LDCs one notices that LDCs received 9.2 per cent of their total resources through these institutions in 1970, 13.7 per cent in 1980, and 7.6 per cent in 1983. Approximately 90 per cent of the financial resources received by the MFIs came from the industrial market economies. Many of the MFIs which are now one of the important channels of providing concessional financial resources to LDCs were created in the decade of 1958–67. Prior to this the MFIs were limited essentially to the UN and its specialised agencies and the Bretton Woods institutions. The newly created institutions were of two kinds: First, two major funds were created in the framework of the existing institutions with a view to consolidating multilateral operations. These were the International Development Association (IDA) (1960) administered by the World Bank, and the UN Development Programme (1965), forged out of the Expanded Programme of Technical Assistance and the Special Fund. Second, this was also the decade marked by the establishment of three principal regional banks; namely, the Inter-American Development Bank (IDB) (1959), the African Development Bank (AfDB) (1963) and the Asian Development Bank (ADB) (1966).

Although the institutions of the World Bank group and the three regional develoment banks were established over a period of twenty years, they were almost identically designed to make loans from the capital provided by the member countries and through borrowings in

179

the capital market. The basic goal of all of them was to stimulate economic growth in LDCs. Over the years the World Bank group and the development banks have proved to be adaptable institutions, which are constantly learning and evolving, where a constant dialogue goes on on policy dynamics. Their policies have been responsive to the changing perceptions of the needs of LDCs, and their own role in meeting those needs. Their flexibility to adapt, which the Pearson Commission Report referred to as their 'encouraging capacity for evolutionary change', added to their reputation as a leading authority on economic development.[1] Apart from learning by doing, there was a good deal of cross-fertilisation among these financial institutions – for example, the World Bank's greater reliance on social priorities after the establishment of the IDA, the IDB's move to emulate ADB through inclusion of the non-regional members, and the ADB's increased attention to the role of concessionary lending in its operations, somewhat identical to that of the IDA.

The role of the MFIs is not limited merely to providing financial resources and technical assistance. They try to be financial catalysts and policy advisers. They have succeeded in institution building and human capital formation in several developing countries. The dependence of low income countries on MFIs is significantly high, besides their assistance is not procurement-tied. Their economic justification rests upon their ability to play an efficacious role in situations which would not interest the private investors and require government intervention. Many of such projects have high long-term social returns. The MFI lending helps correct market imperfections – internal or external – which retard developing economies, and facilitate projects which yield positive externalities. An important observation in this context is that the activities of the MFIs are seldom a substitute for the private enterprise. An analysis of the World Bank and Asian Development Bank projects revealed that the economic rates of return on these projects are relatively high, 15 to 20 per cent on average.[2] This proves that the MFIs are sound institutions and are making a positive contribution to the cause of economic development. But the record is mixed on their ability to influence economic policies in developing countries.[3]

CONTRIBUTIONS TO MULTILATERAL INSTITUTIONS

Table 6.1 sets out the net disbursements of the industrial market economies to various multilateral institutions:

TABLE 6.1   *Contributions to multilateral institutions, 1956–83 (in millions of $)*

Year	Net disbursement	Percentage of ODA	In constant $ (1975 = 100)
1956	219	6.8	422
1957	385	9.5	385
1958	357	8.3	659
1959	345	8.1	637
1960	655	13.5	1 206
1961	811	13.5	1 499
1962	691	11.3	1 275
1963	411	6.7	761
1964	441	7.5	815
1965	498	7.9	902
1966	341	5.2	597
1967	718	10.1	1 255
1968	682	9.5	1 164
1969	1 007	13.8	1 654
1970	1 124	16.6	1 781
1971	1 338	17.5	2 052
1972	1 917	22.5	2 815
1973	2 268	24.2	2 945
1974	3 060	27.0	3 344
1975	3 772	27.8	3 772
1976	4 161	30.4	3 978
1977	4 934	31.4	4 336
1978	6 333	31.7	5 187
1979	5 272	23.1	3 823
1980	7 581	27.8	4 735
1981	5 786	22.6	n.a.
1982	7 849	28.2	n.a.
1983	7 709	27.9	n.a.

SOURCE   *Development Co-operation Review* (Paris: OECD(, various issues.
N.B. Series deflated by the US wholesale prices using IMF tape data.

The above data indicate that contributions made to MFIs remained at a low level during the first decade (1956–66), while they were buoyant between 1967 and 1978. The latter was the year when they were at their peak in real terms. Between 1966 and 1967 the net contributions to MFIs doubled, while between 1967 and 1978 they increased ninefold in nominal terms and almost sixfold in real terms. After 1978 there was a roller-coaster trend in nominal terms, but the contributions declined in real terms. The apparent sharp rise in 1982, an increase of 28 per cent over 1981, is deceptive. It is entirely due to a bunching of the deposit of notes in funding the sixth replenishment of the IDA – that is, it was simply a catching up on repayments which under normal circumstances should have been made in 1981. During the period when contributions to MFIs grew at a steep rate, all the institutions participated in their expansion, though with different rates. The volume of the UN activities more than trebled, net disbursement by the World Bank group expanded five times and those of regional development banks expanded almost ninefold. Conspicuous in this expansion were the IDA replenishments and their rapid expansions. With the growth in volume the sectors of activity diversified and the role of MFIs as economic assistance agencies steadily grew.

One should not, however, be lulled into thinking that this steep growth occurred without problems. One big problem vexing donors during this period was the proliferation of MFIs. In the ten years between 1958 and 1968 ten financial agencies and several UN agencies were born. In a space of six months during 1968 three sub-regional banks were established – namely, the Andean Development Corporation, the East African Development Bank and the Caribbean Bank. Admittedly these institutions met specific regional needs, but for the donors it meant a problem of allocation and division of work.

All the donors participated in contributing to the MFIs, between 1965 and 1975, as a percentage of their GNP, their contributions trebled. They rose from 0.03 to 0.10 per cent. In 1980 they were 0.09 per cent, and stayed at the same level in 1983. The share of multilateral contributions in ODA rose steadily, reaching a peak in 1978 at 31.7 per cent. The Pearson Commission had recommended that the donors provide 20 per cent of the total ODA by 1975 for the multilateral aid programmes. Table 6.1 shows that this target was surpassed in 1972.

The latest picture emerges as follows: the bilateral flows in general have hit a plateau and the proportion going to the MFI has not kept the level reached during the mid-1970s (refer to Table 6.1). Several large MFIs are suffering from resource constraints. In the present climate, it seems that financial resources to the MFIs are going to be increasingly scarce.

With a rise in the number of financial institutions the field of activity expanded. These institutions started financing in social sectors like health, education and housing, where the rate of return cannot be directly assessed. In general the UNDP concentrated on financing pre-investment projects, while the IBRD, and to a lesser extent the regional development banks, assumed responsibility for the developmental projects and economic planning.

Since the beginning of the 1960s the resources received by the MFIs far exceeded those disbursed by them to LDCs. However, by 1975 this difference between the inflows and outflows was substantially reduced, to about 15 per cent of the inflows. With a better liquidity position these institutions felt themselves well equipped to develop the key sectors of LDCs and to bring in the required structural changes in their economies. For example, the World Bank slowly built up a formidable battery of experts in the field of agriculture and allied activities. The share of bank loans to this sector increased from 14 per cent in 1956–7 to 28 per cent in 1975–6; this includes IDA credits. On the whole around 30 per cent of the multilateral assistance was devoted to this sector in 1975, which is about three times the proportion of the bilateral assistance to agriculture.

DONORS' POLICY PREFERENCES REGARDING THE MULTILATERAL INSTITUTIONS

The following policy areas of the MFIs have interested the donors: sectoral concentration and geographical distribution. The complementary roles of the MFIs and bilateral assistance has also attracted a good deal of attention. The resource position of the MFIs has played a crucial role in determining their efficacy and effectiveness, both qualitatively and quantitatively. The credibility of an institution's advisory role is directly related to its professional quality, yet its effectiveness in this respect is partly determined by – and reinforced by – the extent of its ability to enter into supporting financial commitments, for example, the IMF. Severe resource constraints are a disincentive to the innovation and creativity of an institution; they would make it overly cautious and risk-averse, two qualities which most adversely affect the development orientation of the institution.

Considered in a time sequence, the MFIs have concentrated on the following sectors: physical infrastructure, especially power and transportation, which are two traditional activities for the deployment of external resources, followed by agriculture and the social sectors. The MFIs were the first to emphasise the farm sector, whereas the bilateral programmes concentrated on the social sectors. Besides, among the UN agencies, the largest recipient of extra-budgetary voluntary contribution is the Food and Agriculture Organisation. The reason is that donors who allocate below average for agriculture, but are convinced about its significance, prefer to channel their resources to this sector through the MFIs.

It has been amply demonstrated that the latest trend in geographical distribution of bilateral assistance is towards the LLDCs and other low-income LDCs.[4] It is generally understood by the donors that access by this group of countries to financial resources on soft-terms is important, and most donors provide funds relatively easily when they are meant for the low-income LDCs, therefore with the result that some of the MFIs now heavily concentrate upon this country-group. The story of the UN agencies is slightly different because, by their mandate, they are under pressure to maintain a wide geographical spread and avoid giving priority status to any country-group. The net disbursements to this country-group in 1978–9 were as follows:

	%
IDA	91.1
AfDB	94.3
ADB	92.3
IDB	4.9
UNDP	46.2

This implies that the resource flows to the LLDCs and other low-income LDCs would be affected almost in the same proportion as the contributions to MFIs.

Apart from implementing their own projects the MFIs have come to acquire a much wider function as leaders in the field of allocation policy formulation. Advice rendered by institutions like the World Bank – and to an extent the regional development banks and the UNDP – is heeded by the donors, it carries weight and usually goes far.

INTERACTIONS BETWEEN THE MULTILATERAL INSTITUTIONS AND DONORS

Although their attitudes have varied widely, the industrial market economies have rendered a general support to the MFIs, largely because there was a uniformity of views that a certain share of assistance should be channelled through them. The clear advantages were: insulation from the political and commercial concern of the individual donors and the growing utility of the MFIs as a repository of accumulated knowledge and experience on development economics. The second one of these was, perhaps, an unintended gain. The established programmes of large donors essentially remained bilateral, but the newer donors, like the Scandinavian countries, who did not have links with any particular recipient, allocated a high proportion through the MFIs. This enabled them to expand their programmes rapidly, by making use of the professional machinery that was already in smooth operation.

In the second section of this chapter (pages 180 through 183) we have seen that, between 1967 and 1978, the contributions to the MFIs went up ninefold in nominal terms and sixfold in real terms. The reasons for this were both institution-specific and general. The most significant institutional-specific factor was the creation of IDA, which the donors thought was best placed to channel the required quantum of financial resources to low-income and LDCs. These countries were beginning to come to the fore in donors' concern. Also the quantum and pattern of contributions to each of the regional banks exhibited the differing geographical priorities of the donors' programmes.

Since the control of the MFIs is based on the weighted voting by members, the donors are sure that the institutions would be accountable for the way in which the resources are utilised and that they will have some influence over them. Second, the regular replenishments also helped brisk growth of the MFIs and the donors' feeling of a certain measure of reassurance about their *modus operandi*. The replenishments were far from smooth, but they did draw donors' attention to the relevant questions and the resources needed to sustain a desired lending programme.

That multiplicity of funds and multilateral institutions can lead to duplication and so waste has been the age-old worry of the donors. As the institutions proliferated in the 1970s there was a fissiparous trend in financing the UN funds, which led to diminution in the scope of the UNDP. It is observed that the donors whose contributions were small percentages of their GNP concentrated their resources on the World Bank and the large financial institutions. On the other hand, those with high ODA/GNP ratios preferred the UNDP and other UN agencies. Yet there is no clear pattern in donors' institutional affinity, except for a slight tendency for the UNDP to be favoured by Belgium, France, the

Netherlands and the UK. However, the four Scandinavian countries clearly leaned in the past towards the UNDP; they accounted for a large – about a third – proportion of total contributions to it.

The question, however, arises if these funds are additive. As already mentioned, several of them were created in a short space of time, e.g. IFAD, WEP, UNHCR and other UN funds. Perhaps LDCs had visualised that more funds would multiply resources, which is disputed by the donors, who maintain that the primary decisions relate to the annual volume of the ODA, out of which bilateral and multilateral allocations are made. Apart from the additivity, there are other issues which the LDCs and the donors approach with differing considerations in mind. For instance, in the operations of the MFIs, LDCs and the industrial countries display a differing order of sectoral priority. The former lay more emphasis on the importance of industrialisation and transfer of technology, while the latter give greater weight to agriculture, and now to energy. Besides, the LDCs have been keen for a greater share of voting rights and of senior management positions in the MFIs. They also seek minimum of conditionality. The records of the 1970s show a marked preference by the industrial market economies for retention of conditionality and some accountability of these institutions to the major contributors. Of the senior management positions LDCs presently have a reasonable share.

INTERNATIONAL BANK FOR RECONSTRUCTION AND DEVELOPMENT

The International Bank for Reconstruction and Development (IBRD), popularly known as the World Bank, is the single largest source of development funds.[5] It was the first international organisation created with the basic objective of making world-wide loans available to governments and, under government guarantee, to private enterprises in the member states. Its scale of operations have expanded fast. Its high importance is not due to the volume of its operations, but because of the fact that it is a dynamic organisation with a reputation for considerable competence. It has an institutional style, a spirit, rivalled by few other international or bilateral economic assistance organisations.

It organised country consortia, advisory groups and negotiated with governments and multilateral agencies, and in the process played a combined role of an analyst, promoter and co-ordinator, and then innovator of development policies. It has left its imprint over a broad range of developmental issues and sectors. Its research capabilities are highly respected even in the academic circles. The Bank's image as a first-rate professional organization looms large in front of LDCs. Besides, since they share in its management, it appears less of an alien to them than many bilateral agencies. On the other hand, the donors prefer it because the weighted voting gives them considerable control over its operations.[6] So much for the bright side of the image.

There are some who aruge that the Bank has come to acquire eminence by default. It has moved into the vacuum created by flagging bilateral assistance and the unpreparedness of other multilateral institutions. It is questioned whether it is genuinely well cast for the assignment, since all it offers are loans at interest rates high enough to repay the borrowing costs in the international capital market, and leave a slim margin for its running. Despite its neatly articulated view on development it is overly concerned with the banking aspect of its operations. It is thought that the Bank's preoccupation with the rate of return on investment would eventually make it less responsive to the objective of eradication of mass poverty. Also, it tends to induce a capital intensive bias into the technology transferred to LDCs, which may be unwholesome.[7]

The Purpose of the Bank

The Articles of Agreement of the IBRD were signed by twenty-eight governments on 28 December 1945 and the Bank's doors were opened for business on 25 June 1964. According to the Articles of Agreement its principal task is to assist in two separate and distinct fields: the reconstruction of the developed members, which were war-ravaged, and the development of LDCs. The Articles of Agreement required the Bank to give 'equitable consideration to projects for development and projects for reconstruction alike', but it was decided at Bretton Woods that the initial emphasis would necessarily have to be on the urgent problem of reconstruction. The first loans of the Bank, made in 1947, totalling $497 million, were in the nature of emergency assistance to four Western European countries to prevent a threatened interruption in the flow of essential imports.[8] However, since 1948 the Bank placed almost its entire emphasis on LDCs.

The foundation of IBRD was laid on conservative lines, and inevitably so given the dominance at Bretton Woods of the countries that were to pool in the financial resources, and the need to have an institution which would inspire confidence in the face of the unhappy financial record of the immediate past. This conservatism, some believe, has been the source of the commercial success of the Bank. On the other hand, it has been the source of sustained dissatisfaction to Bank's critics and some LDCs.[9] For the purpose of this study we shall look into the Bank's operations divided into two periods: 1947–60 and 1961–84.

An example of the Bank's conservative approach is its much publicised one-to-one gearing ratio, which means that it may lend the equivalent of its capital reserves. This constraint is imposed by the Articles of Agreement of the Bank. It should be noted that commercial banking institutions lend fifteen to twenty times their capital base. The Bank is a large borrower in the capital market, in fact, it was the biggest borrower in the bond markets for the fourth consecutive year in 1984. The other side of the coin is that a higher gearing ratio may increase the cost of raising funds in the capital market, and affect its AAA rating adversely.

The First Period: 1947–60

During its first five years the Bank was not much of a supplier of capital, neither for reconstruction nor for development. Why a low-key start? It was because under its Articles of Agreement, the Bank was expected to finance only productive projects for which other financing was not available on reasonable terms. Surveying the field during its formative years the management had come to the conclusion that private capital would naturally be attracted for the development of export industries, e.g. tin, rubber, jute, etc. Also light manufacturing, such as textiles, which are generally in the private sector and need small doses of capital, would be taken care of by the local private enterprises. The Bank management was averse to financing government-owned industries. Although it was formed to take calculated risks, which would be unusual for an ordinary bank, yet the history of many pre-war industrial loans led the Bank to follow lending policies modelled on the best practices of private investment banking.[10] Let us first see the quantitative dimension of the loan operations during the first period before commenting on them.

Between 1947 and 1960 the Bank's lending operations increased two and a half times, but this was not a steady year-to-year expansion; rather it proceeded from one level to another. The first two years were

TABLE 6.2 *Lending operations of the World Bank, 1967–60*

	Number	Amount (in millions of $)
1947	1	250
1948	5	263
1949	10	137
1950	12	166
1951	21	297
1952	19	299
1953	10	179
1954	26	324
1955	20	410
1956	26	396
1957	20	388
1958	34	711
1959	30	703
1960	31	659

SOURCE E. S. Mason and P. E. Asher, *The World Bank Since Bretton Woods* (Washington, DC: The Brookings Institution, 1973) p. 192.

dominated by commitments and loans to Europe. Then, after a temporary decline in disbursements, it loaned at an annual rate of $300 million to $400 million until the fiscal year 1957. During the remaining three years of this period it rose to around $700 million. The Bank lending during this period was limited by the creditworthiness of the potential borrowers and projects, and by the rate with which viable projects could be brought forward – not by liquidity shortage. The Bank was set up to finance productive projects rather than to make programme lending, and to finance only the foreign exchange cost of those projects, and to secure a guarantee of repayment from the government of the country in which the project was to be located, and to finance only those activities for which other finance was not believed to be available. These considerations made the Bank operate under a rigid structure. Also, these requirements practically made the Bank concentrate on power plants, railroads, highway network, and similar overheads. It was the availability of finance for such undertakings that stimulated philosophising about the crucial role of economic infrastructure in the development process, rather than the reverse.[11]

During this period the geographical distribution of Bank lending appears anomalous for a development institution. The large LDCs were ignored, and one of the Bank's largest borrowers was a developed country, Japan. Also, lending operations were not done keeping in mind the uneven distribution of bilateral flows during this period, which were heavily influenced by the former colonial interests of the metropolitan powers.

The Bank's charter allowed it to charge an interest rate high enough to cover its cost of borrowing in the capital market, as well as the Bank's operating expenses and yield a moderate amount of reserves against contingencies. The Bank also charged a commission of 1 per cent a year on the outstanding amounts. By comparison with the market interest rates, the combined interest and other charges made by the Bank – from 3 to 4.75 per cent – were favourable to the borrowers.[12] The membership at the end of the period reached sixty-eight countries.

Two Questions: One Answer

There are two tendencies to be noted in the Bank lending policies of this period: first, its conservativeness and, second, the fact that loaning operations were limited to project loans. A vexing question arises, why? Were there cogent reasons leading the Bank to adopt such a posture? Or was it simply inexperienced, and irrational in its prudery? The answer is that during this period, particularly during the first decade of operation, the Bank was heavily dependent on the US capital market for raising liquidity. Therefore, it needed to generate an aura of confidence and financial acumen among the major financial houses of Wall Street. At this time the US financial community was rather sceptical of foreign lending, particularly to the Latin American countries because of their high rate of default in the 1920s and 1930s. Paradoxically these were the only LDCs which had been independent long enough to try to borrow on their own credit. Thus, to reassure the financiers and for institutional building, the first administration of the Bank was obliged to demonstrate a conservative stance.

To this end, much was made of the creditworthiness of the country soliciting loans. Countries which were in default of the past debts, or which expropriated foreign property without just compensation were considered ineligible. Much of this applied to the Latin American countries, who during this period were denied the use of Bank resources. For the same reason there existed a tendency to emphasise project lending, which was easy to supervise and monitor. The notion of more general programme lending appeared ridiculously unacceptable.

The Second Period: 1961–84

The institutional personality of the Bank started undergoing a transformation during this period. As we have already seen, during the preceding period it was a conservative institution, a little too concerned about the reaction of the financial centres and its AAA rating. A commentator has called the Bank of this period 'the conservative club of Boston Brahmins'. The establishment of the IDA was perhaps the beginning of this change. It dawned on the perceptive people in leadership positions that development was a more complex process than visualised before. One such person was George Woods,[13] under whose leadership the Bank began to change the complexion of its operations and increased lending to agriculture and education sectors, and embarked upon programmed lending to India and Pakistan. Also, the terms of lending were made more flexible by extending the grace periods and maturities, and more of local costs were financed. It extended more help to poor member countries in project preparation.[14]

McNamara was to assume the reins after Woods' departure; he not only accelerated the trend set in motion by Woods, but imprinted his own thinking and personality over the institution. It was revealing to learn from a man of his background that to "limit our attention to expanding GNP ... can only lead to greater political, social and economic disequilibrium. However important an increase in GNP may be as a necessary condition of development, it is not a sufficient condition."[15] He lent strong support to the agricultural sector, as a means of relieving poverty, and eliminating unemployment and malnutrition. In general he took a wider view of things and was concerned about the distribution of income in LDCs; he advocated 'institutional reforms to redistribute economic power are critically required in many developing countries – land reform, corporate reform, credit and banking reform and many others. Continuation of the existing land-tenure patterns, tax laws and banking regulations will simply ensure that the present distribution of assets and income will be perpetuated. The Bank will support reforms in these areas with technical and financial assistance'.[16] The Bank underwent profound changes and gave up its ideological hostility to public ownership of national development banks and manufacturing enterprises. Hitherto the Bank had functioned as an institution which mostly financed infrastructure; it gradually turned into a multilateral development institution, dedicated to both financing and influencing the direction of socioeconomic changes in LDCs.

The same period witnessed the decline of bilateral resource flows, due in part to disillusionment in the industrial market economies with the skimpy results of aid, as well as for reasons detailed in Chapter 4. In this period of institutional change within the donor community, the role of the Bank grew substantially. The vision of the development process, as we have seen, varied with the personality of the Bank's president, by the Bank's relationship with its creditors and by the perception of reality by its, by now, highly beefed-up staff.

Until the late 1960s the funds for the Bank's regular loans had traditionally been obtained almost wholly in the American market of Wall Street, but in the following decade the base broadened and it started utilising all the major financial markets of the world. The Bank periodically sent economic missions to LDCs, which played an important part in formulating the lending policy towards that particular LDC. These missions expanded in number and in the scope of coverage. They also provided the basic economic intelligence needed to determine the Bank's strategy in terms of the volume of lending operations, and the sectors and areas to which attention should be diverted in accordance with the economic and social priorities. They also helped show the LDC its growth points. Another objective of these missions was to form an opinion regarding the 'country performance'. Soon the Bank became something it was not in the past – that is, the foremost world centre for authoritative studies of key developmental issues. This did not make it necessarily right or wise, but it did mean that its voice carried weight, and over time came to be valued by LDCs and the donors alike. These economic studies are made available to the Executive Directors of the Bank, to assist them in their considerations of individual lending operations. They are also made use of by the UN and regional organisations, and at times commercially published.[17]

The Bank's concern about the ability of an LDC to repay leads its interest into the general financial state of the LDC. In order to consummate the project successfully the Bank invariably attaches conditions to its project loans; for example, it has a streamlined procedure regarding the method of putting out the contracts to ensure competitive bidding, in order to control the use of funds to avoid waste. It is also concerned with the pricing policies and management methods.

The practice of subsidising various activities in LDCs inspires the Bank's ire because it distorts the optimal allocation of resources. In some cases the Bank's interests have gone into areas which the LDCs consider as sensitive; for instance, fiscal and monetary policies. The Bank has had things to say about the control of inflation, curbing the balance-of-payments deficits, etc. On its own, perhaps the Bank would not have enough influence to change these, but if these opinions are shared with other institutions like the IMF or bilateral donors, pressure can be mounted on the LDC to sway the policies.

Apart from the tangible assistance, LDCs benefit from advice on economic management, and economic and sectoral assessments. Development constraints are identified and a groundwork is made for project preparation. The advice is, generally, on neoclassical lines, meaning thereby, on the external side, it emphasises the need for open international trading, realistic exchange rates and the use of world market prices to reflect the real opportunity costs. On the domestic side the emphasis is placed on appropriate resource allocation, realistic pricing policies, cost recovery and maintenance of sensible fiscal and monetary policies.[18] The Bank is sure that this is where the economic nirvana of LDCs lies, therefore it has been persuading them that competitive exchange rates help growth, that positive real interest rates are good for savings accumulation and so investment, that food prices should not be pushed down to please the urban population at the expense of the farmers.

The steeply rising yearly lending in the 1960s and the 1970s can be seen in Table 6.3. Between 1961 and 1970 the lending operations increased by two and a half times in nominal terms. They more than doubled in real terms. This rise was far from monotonic, because there were years of fall in lending as well as dramatic spurts. However, since 1969, operations have grown steadily, and at a steep rate, although 1972 and 1973 were lean years, when there was a virtual stagnation in nominal terms and a fall in real terms. Except for these, the lending operations soared briskly. During the recession period, after 1979, the lending operations maintained a high rate of growth in nominal terms, and in real terms they maintained their level. A detailed quantitative picture is presented in Table 6.3:

The net transfer of funds, however, was considerably less than that shown by the gross figures above. Net transfer means gross disbursement minus the service payments. Net transfer was $62 million in 1965. It was minus $59 million in 1970, $620 million in 1975, $1 380 million in 1980 and $2 414 million in 1983.

TABLE 6.3   *Lending operations of the World Bank, 1961–84 (amounts in millions of $)*

Year	Operations approved	Loan amount	Percentage change over last year	Loan amount in constant $ (1975 = 100)	Disbursement	Member
1961	27	610	−8	1 128	398	68
1962	29	882	45	1 627	485	75
1963	28	449	−49	831	620	85
1964	37	810	80	1 497	559	102
1965	39	1 023	26	1 853	606	102
1966	37	839	−18	1 469	668	103
1967	46	777	−7	1 358	790	106
1968	44	847	22	1 445	772	107
1969	82	1 399	65	2 297	762	110
1970	69	1 580	13	2 503	754	113
1971	78	1 921	22	2 946	915	116
1972	72	1 966	2	2 887	1 182	117
1973	73	2 051	4	2 664	1 180	122
1974	105	3 218	57	3 516	1 533	124
1975	122	4 320	34	4 320	1 995	125
1976	141	4 977	15	4 758	2 470	127
1977	161	5 759	16	5 188	2 636	129
1978	137	6 098	6	5 094	2 787	132
1979	142	6 989	15	5 188	3 602	134
1980	144	7 644	9	4 976	4 363	135
1981	140	8 809	15	5 259	5 063	139
1982	150	10 330	17	NA	6 326	142
1983	136	11 138	10	NA	6 817	144
1984	129	11 949	10	NA	4 232	146

SOURCE   *Annual Report, World Bank* (various issues).
N.B. For deflating the nominal series of loan amount the US wholesale price deflator has been used, which in turn has been taken from the IMF data tape.

During the 1960s the largest borrowers were the Latin American LDCs and the south European countries. Oil- and mineral-rich countries were another group which had a large capacity to service debt despite low per capita income. Also, there was a smaller group of countries whose per capita income was low enough to qualify them for the IDA assistance, but which was also judged to have a limited capacity to service debt on World Bank terms, e.g. India, the largest single borrower from the World Bank group.[19] During this period the operational philosophy of the World Bank was that creation of viable capacity was its *raison d'être*. Therefore, subsequently, the effects of investment on human capabilities and attitudes became important. This enlarged consideration of relations between investment and development greatly complicated the process of project selection and appraisal.[20]

In the early 1970s, the Bank became more and more concerned about the issues of employment and income distribution, so it started emphasising rural development. The Bank's projects were intended to raise the productivity of small farmers, as a way of both reducing absolute poverty and increasing total agricultural output. It also expanded its operations in the fields of population planning, tourism and other special purpose projects, which was a break from the conventional modes of lending. Ethically, politically and socially population was a sensitive issue; in addition there was a complicated technical aspect. Yet if LDCs do not draw reins, population growth would impede their economic development. In many LDCs the harmful effects were already obvious. To spread this awareness the Population Project department was established, which designed its first project for Jamaica in 1970. Tourism was a major source of foreign exchange earnings for some LDCs; it could do so for many others. Since it is a labour-intensive activity its development could potentially mitigate the unemployment problem. Besides, tourism is known to have the highest multiplier effect. LDCs needed assistance in drawing up co-ordinated development plans, for both infrastructure and superstructure facilities. The first project undertaken by the Bank in this field was for a tourism master-plan for the island of Bali in 1970.[21] The Bank stepped up its activities related to inter-sectoral projects which involved lending in a number of different areas, e.g. integrated water and agricultural development, urban and regional projects and developing multi-country intersectoral projects.[22] Two more fields, *inter alia*, were added later in a big way: energy lending, which amounted to 26 per cent of the lending in 1982, and structural adjustment lending, which accounted for 9 per cent of lending in 1982.[23]

Table 6.2 shows that during 1982 and 1983 the number of operations approved by the bank declined, so did the growth rate in loans. Bank lending at $11.9 billion in 1984 was slightly less than early plans envisaged. The Bank was constrained by the difficulties faced by borrowing LDCs. Besides, the 'requirements of prudent financial management'[24] limited the number of operations that could meet the planned target. Notable is the fact that disbursements slid substantially back, to the level of 1980. Brazil, India and Indonesia were the largest borrowers in 1984. A further drop in loan commitments as well as disbursements is on the cards for 1985; this decline is again attributed by the Bank to economic stress in many LDCs which leaves them unable to provide counterpart funds for projects the Bank has approved. Besides, the Bank's own tests of creditworthiness of prospective borrowers forces the postponement of loan commitments.

The practice of reviewing periodically the financial terms was continued. The main determinant of the interest rate still remained the rate at which the Bank was able to borrow on the international financial market. Another factor influencing the lending rates is the return that the Bank gets on its own liquid assets. All loans continued to be made at the same interest rate; the country to which the loan is made, or the project for which it is made, did not make a difference during this period. However, the repayment period and the grace period did take into account the economic position of the borrower or the nature of the project or both. By and large, variation on project grounds was both more common and more systematic than variation with respect to countries. Likewise the grace period in which the interest, but not amortisation payments, is due is decided in relation to the expected lapse of time between the date of commitment and the time at which the project concerned will come into operation, and begin to yield substantial net benefits.[25] Thus, in education loans a ten-year grace period is common, while loans for roads typically have a shorter period of four to seven years.

The Bank does not absorb exchange risks on the currencies it borrows. Under its latest lending policy it is to receive interest on its loans at a fixed spread above its cost of borrowing. Its bonds represent the highest quality debt securities available in the capital market. This is the outcome of following conservative financial discipline, like keeping its debt equity ratio (or gearing ratio) to 1:1.

During the early 1970s the Bank's borrowing cost, weighted by amount of maturity, averaged 7.28 per cent. The lending rate continued at $7\frac{1}{4}$ per cent during this period.[26] In the fiscal year 1981 the average interest rate was 7.5 per cent. Early during 1982 a front-end fee of 1.5 per cent was introduced on new loan commitments. This measure was designed to forestall any potential decline in the Bank's income over the medium-term, primarily as a result of volatility in the movements in interest rates and exchange rates. It was, however, decided that this change will be reviewed every quarter.[27] The gross revenues of the Bank, generated primarily from its loans and investments, reached a total of $3 400 million in the fiscal year 1982, up 12 per cent from the previous year. As a matter of fact, gross revenues have risen steadily during the whole of the 1970s. The net income for the fiscal year 1983 went up by 50 per cent again, and in 1984 it reached a record $1.3 billion, the highest ever. Judged by the statements in the press, the Bank was a trifle uncomfortably self-conscious by such high profits. It reflects an increase in return on the Bank's investment of its liquid assets, as well as lower borrowing costs on the world capital markets. By declaring a profit the Bank is able to maintain a high rating on world bond markets. It argues that over the long haul this is more beneficial to its borrowers than a cut in its own interest margin at a time when the profits are high.[28] The Bank's total assets place it among the forty largest banks in the world. Measured by profits it is one of the largest banking organisations, with an annual borrowing programme of $11 billion. It is also the largest non-governmental borrower of fund in the world.[29] It uses all the capital markets of the world, adding to its financial efficiency. As indicated, in 1984 the Bank was the largest borrower in the international bond markets for the fourth consecutive year. It continuously seeks to diversify currency exposure and lower borrowing costs by reducing reliance on debt issues in dollars. In the early 1980s the Bank decided gradually to expand Japan's role in providing it with funds. During 1983 the Japanese bank syndicates lent a record amount to the World Bank.

The probability of an expansion of the capital stock of the Bank has been a topical issue in the financial press. But at the end of 1984 the Bank had only used 63 per cent of its total lending capacity: $38.1 billion against a possible $60.8 billion.[30] Therefore a change in the financial structure seems unlikely in the foreseeable future.

The Programme Lending Debate

Whether the Bank lending to LDCs has to be confined to project lending has been an issue of keen debate during the second half of the 1960s, both inside and outside the Bank. The Articles of Agreement provide that: 'loans made or guaranteed by the Bank shall, except in special circumstances, be made for the purpose of specific projects of reconstruction and development'.[31] Initially the Bank had a prejudice against programme lending;[32] it may partly be due to a lack of confidence in the economic management ability of LDCs. Project management creates assets, but who knows about programme lending? How does one trace it in the system?

First, this is myopic thinking, because ultimately financial resources are fungible and no one needs to nurse the illusion that the donor has control over end-use; they can and are easily transferred from project to project, depending upon the borrowing government's priority. Second, in this line of argument there is a confusion about what is productive. If a plant is not working to capacity, then it makes much more economic sense to provide programme lending to replenish the inputs, instead of insisting on project lending for installing more capacity. This, for sure, is misplaced emphasis on concreteness.[33] This apart, a lot of LDCs constantly worry not about the gross inflows of foreign assistance but about the net transfers. Most of the controversy about programme lending disappears if one focuses on the concept of transfer of resources, and treats project and programme lending as alternative ways of arranging such a transfer.

In early 1971 the executive directors of the Bank went into this issue. Although several of them expressed misgivings, President McNamara supported expanded use of this technique of lending. His arguments were based on the quantitative gap theory of development finance.[34] In his memorandum he argued that 'the exceptional circumstances' in which programme lending was permissible should be broadened if: (1) 'A borrowing country presents a development programme with supporting economic and financial policies, which are hedged to provide a satisfactory basis for external assistance in a given amount; (2) The needed transfer of resources from external lenders in support of the development programme cannot be achieved effectively and expeditiously by the financing of investment projects . . .; (3) Other external lenders are not prepared to fill this gap by non-project lending.'[35] In 1971 it was concluded by the executive directors that it was appropriate for the Bank to make programme loans available, subject to the above-mentioned criteria.

INTERNATIONAL DEVELOPMENT ASSOCIATION

Introduction

The genesis of the idea of an International Development Association (IDA) goes back to a resolution submitted by the American Senator Monroney to the US Senate in late 1957. His resolution expressed a desire to support international development by means of multilateral resources based on sound economic principles, rather than by bilateral loans and grants.[36] The US Senate was favourably disposed towards his idea. President Eisenhower introduced the idea to the World Bank's board of governors at the annual meeting held in Washington in 1959, he emphasised that assistance to LDCs would result in a stronger and more stable free world.

The Bank, from its experiences of the 1950s, had learnt that economic development is a complex meta-process, and it was constantly learning from its experience. It noticed that a narrow definition of credit-worthiness, eliminated the neediest LDCs from being candidates for Bank loans. Numerous projects existed in the poorer LDCs which could not be financed by the existing financial machinery, despite their soundness. The creation of IDA was, in part, aimed at circumventing this issue. It is a soft loan fund which is administered by the Bank. Soft loans mean those repayable over a longer term, and at low or no interest. An interesting fact is that prior to the birth of the IDA the Bank was averse to the notion of soft loans, maintaining that the impediment to the increased flow of finance to LDCs was lack of adequately prepared projects, not the dearth of liquidity. It also maintained that extention of assistance for health, education, sanitation and other purposes indispensable for development, should not be a part of the Bank's functions.

The creation of the IDA in September 1960 was, in at least three ways, an important landmark. It made poverty a major concern of the world's richest countries. At an international level it institutionalised the giving of concessional finance to promote economic development. And it strengthened the efforts to establish a multilateral system of world trade and payments.[37] It is the world's largest single source of concessional multilateral developmental finance. Credits are given for sound economic projects which measure up to the rigorous standards of IBRD loans. The lending policies of the IDA and the IBRD are identical, both institutions lend only for projects or programmes which have high priority for the borrowing LDC and which have satisfactory prospects of being carried out and operated successfully. The two institutions apply the same methods and standards in determining what conditions need to be established to achieve the desired ends. Bearing in mind the severely limited debt-servicing capacity of the low-income countries, the IDA provides funds on unique terms.

The Sources of Funds

The IDA has three sources of funds: its initial capital subscriptions, replenishments and special contributions. Also, since 1964, the IBRD has transferred some of its income annually to the IDA. The contributions made by donors take the form of non-interest-bearing notes. The number of donors has grown, initially there were seventeen industrial economies subscribing to the IDA, in 1983 this number was thirty-three, and it included nine LDCs. The replenishments made the IDA dependent on donors, and this dependency became increasingly clear with each request for replenishment. It depended overwhelmingly on the American share, which has to be voted by an increasingly reluctant Congress. The times have changed and the US attitude has become a chronic problem. It has been the largest contributor and has been conscious of the balance-of-payments effects of its contributions; though its contributions amounted to around 40 per cent of the total for the first three IDA replenishments, and around 30 per cent for the next three, the IDA-financed procurements in the US only accounted for 20 per cent of the total.[38]

Since 1965 the IDA has been replenished six times, each time by enough to boost the real value of its annual commitments. The objective of increasing the real value of IDA's finance has always been widely shared, but accelerating inflation has meant that the real increase has been less than what was intended. Besides, the size of each increase has often become a subject of intensive bargaining; yet no formula for deciding it has emerged.

For IDA-6 the donors agreed to contribute the same proportion (0.046 per cent) of their GDP as they had provided in the previous

TABLE 6.4　*Replenishment of IDA resources (in millions of $)*

	Current $	Constant $ (1981 = 100)
Initial (1961–4)	757	3 128
IDA–1 (1965–8)	745	2 844
IDA–2 (1969–71)	1 271	3 466
IDA–3 (1972–4)	2 441	4 495
IDA–4 (1975–7)	4 501	6 200
IDA–5 (1978–80)	7 732	8 688
IDA–6 (1981–3)	12 000	11 204

SOURCE　IDA, *In Retrospect* (World Bank, 1982) p. 5.

replenishment, thus tying the real growth in IDA to the expected real growth in GDP. The replenishment process has never been easy, being dogged by the problem of burden-sharing among the principal donors, and by delays in payments by the US.

Debate is currently going on about the size of IDA-7, which will depend largely on the US, because other donors, particularly West Germany, do not want the US share to fall below 25 per cent – having been 42 per cent when the IDA started in 1960. The Reagan Administration is proposing an annual $750 million, for three years, which would produce a total of $9 billion. Other donors preferred the IDA-7 to be between $12 billion and $16 billion, or the same as the IDA-6 in real terms. The White House is sceptical about Congress accepting it. After protracted and agonising negotiations the size of the IDA-7 was finally limited to $9 billion, an amount felt to be inadequate in view of the pressing needs of the low-income LDCs.

Eligibility Criteria

In the early years it was decided that the IDA funds should be lent on the basis of the country-characteristics, rather than on the basis of the project or sector. It was also decided that the standards of the IDA projects should be the same as those of the IBRD. Three principal criteria have been evolved:
- The recipient's poverty, measured by per capita income.
- The recipient's limited creditworthiness for borrowing from the conventional sources.
- The recipient's economic performance, including its ability to make effective use of resources and the availability to suitable projects.

Since the outset it was decided that the IDA should not lend to countries having a per capita income of $250 in 1964. In real terms the ceiling has remained at that level, although inflation adjustments have raised it to $730 in 1980. An important purpose of the ceiling is that when the GNP or the creditworthiness of an LDC improves it automatically graduates from the IDA to other forms of lending. A limited capacity to service debt in foreign currency has always been an important criterion of eligibility. The IDA credits are to supplement, not substitute for finance from the conventional sources. The Articles of Agreement also require it to pay 'due attention to considerations of economy, efficiency and competitive internal trade and without regard to political or other non-economic influences or considerations'. Measuring performance, though inexact, has been assisted by quantitative indicators such as the savings rate and GNP growth, as well as by quantitative assessment of the administrative and economic management, and the extent to which economic growth is broad-based.[39]

Lending Terms

The standardised credit terms are as follows: a fifty-year maturity, including a ten-year grace period. In each year of the second ten years of the loan, one per cent of the principal is repayable, and 3 per cent in each year of the remaining thirty years. An annual service charge in convertible currencies of 0.75 per cent is made to meet the administrative cost. All credits are repayable in convertible currency.[40] There is a commitment charge of 0.75 per cent on the undisbursed amount of the Bank loans, the IDA did not charge anything on this count until 1982, but thereafter started charging a commitment fee of 0.5 per cent a year. Thus, the terms have changed little since 1960. The commitment fee was slapped on to bring the income into line with its administrative expenses. Basically the terms were designed to be as close as feasible to the economic equivalent of grants, while retaining the form of repayable loans. With this set of repayment terms the grant element of an IDA credit line comes to 86 per cent. The dynamics of debt is such that to maintain a given level of net transfer, gross lending must grow faster than the interest rate. An outlet like the IDA comes in handy in keeping the net transfer of the World Bank group at a high level. Net transfers from the IDA are almost always way above that of the IBRD. When the IDA terms were being decided the debate about whether aid provided as grant is better than that provided as loan was still hot. The intellectual debate was subsequently settled in favour of the grants,[41] yet the IDA persisted with loans largely on pragmatic grounds. Some donors find loans politically more acceptable and convenient. Also it was believed that loans, even when they are highly concessional, are taken more seriously by the recipients, because at the end of it there are repayment obligations.

Lending Operations

The variable determining the volume of lending was the size of contributions agreed upon by the donors. Between 1961 and 1968 IDA's annual commitments fluctuated between $100 million and $360 million, and averaged $299 million a year. They then increased to an annual average of $525 million in 1969–71 and rose more than sixfold to $3.8 billion in 1980. There is a money illusion here; a large part of this growth reflects inflation.[42] The IDA credits, as they should, essentially go to low-income countries. On a cumulative basis 81 per cent of the IDA's commitments went to countries that in 1980 had a per capita income of $410 or less; 98 per cent went to countries with income of $730 or less. In keeping with its character its list of client LDCs has undergone a change since its inception. Some 56 LDCs were added to the list of recipients after the initial subscription period, while 27 have 'graduated' from the IDA on the grounds that their prospective levels of development and creditworthiness justified a reasonable amount of debt on commercial terms. During the period of the IDA's initial subscription (1961–4) 22 LDCs received credit; of these only 8 were still eligible in 1982. In all, 78 LDCs have at one time or another received IDA credits.

If there are any focal points of lending, they are two of the poorest regions of the world, South Asia and Sub-Saharan Africa. Countries in South Asia received 59 per cent of the total commitments between 1961 and 1982. India, IDA's largest single borrower, obtained 39 per cent of the total. While the share of credit to South Asia fell to 55 per cent in the early 1970s, largely to accommodate new borrowers in other regions, it rose again to 60 per cent in the second half of the decade. This rise reflects increased lending to countries other than India, as well as the absence of the other South Asian graduates. The share of lending to African countries doubled from 10 per cent in the early 1960s to 20 per cent in the second half of the decade, as former colonies became independent and joined the IDA. During the 1970s this share has remained at about 25 per cent. Latin America accounted for 5 per cent of credits during 1961–70, but thereafter this proportion fell to 2 per cent. With the exception of Haiti all Latin American borrowers from the IDA have become graduates.

The volume of IDA lending during the first decade did not show much rise, or rose slowly and uncertainly; it remained largely unchanged in real terms during this period. It, however, rose 11 per cent a year in the 1970s. The reason for this increase was largely the increase in the number of donors, which expanded from 18 in IDA–1 to 33 in IDA–6. During the twenty-two years of its operations, the IDA approved 1 302 credits amounting to $26.7 billion to 78 countries. Disbursements of these credits totalled $14.7 billion.

The IBRD and the IDA complement each other in their lending. Countries in the lowest income group, which received 83 per cent of the

TABLE 6.5 Resource flows from IDA, 1961–82

Fiscal year	Number of credits	Number of countries receiving credits	Current dollars (millions)			1982 dollars (millions)	
			Commitments	Disbursements	Net transfer	Commitments	Disbursements
1961	4	4	101.0	–	–	452.9	–
1962	18	8	134.1	12.2	12.2	596.0	45.3
1963	17	9	260.1	56.2	56.1	1 140.8	209.7
1964	18	8	283.2	124.1	123.4	1 236.7	457.9
1965	20	11	309.1	222.2	220.4	1 338.1	802.2
1966	14	8	284.1	266.9	263.3	1 208.9	939.8
1967	18	13	353.6	342.1	336.7	1 437.4	1 187.8
1968	18	14	106.6	318.8	310.7	399.3	1 185.1
1969	38	28	385.0	255.8	245.5	1 287.6	943.9
1970	56	33	605.7	143.3	131.1	1 786.7	479.3
1971	52	34	584.1	235.0	221.5	1 493.9	723.1
1972	74	38	999.8	260.6	243.2	2 216.9	730.0
1973	89	43	1 357.0	492.9	460.7	2 660.8	1 156.8
1974	77	41	1 095.4	711.1	678.4	1 952.6	1 347.0
1975	80	39	1 576.2	1 026.3	984.7	2 567.1	1 699.3
1976	75	39	1 655.3	1 252.4	1 200.6	2 441.4	2 036.4
1977	80	36	1 307.5	1 298.2	1 232.2	1 762.1	1 946.3
1978	107	42	2 313.0	1 061.8	983.9	2 927.8	1 344.1
1979	113	43	3 021.5	1 222.2	1 137.6	3 644.8	1 384.1
1980	114	40	3 837.5	1 411.1	1 309.7	4 395.8	1 451.7
1981	116	40	3 482.1	1 878.0	1 760.8	3 728.2	2 025.9
1982	104	42	2 686.3	2 067.1	1 924.9	2 686.3	2 067.1
Total	1 302	78*	26 738.2	14 658.4	13 837.6	43 362.1	24 162.8

IDA commitments in 1977–82, obtained only 8 per cent of the IBRD lending. Conversely, countries in the high-income group which received 66 per cent of the IBRD loans got only 1 per cent from the IDA. The lending pattern of the IDA has changed over time in response to the needs of its clients and the changes in development thinking. Accelerating growth was the main objective, and it was assumed that once the economy's basic infrastructure was in place, growth would follow. Therefore the IDA concentrated largely on investments ranging from railways and roads to ports and power plants. It was also assumed that poverty would be reduced and income disparities narrowed in the wake of industrialisation. Both sets of assumptions proved too simplistic.[43] Early efforts at industrialisation failed to generate sufficient employment and resulted in a neglect of agriculture. As food production fell and payments imbalances mounted, it became clear that agricultural production was indeed a key priority. In response, the IDA increased its agricultural lending, which rose from 23 per cent of total commitments in 1961–70 to 32 per cent in 1971–6, and further to 42 per cent in 1977–82. In the beginning, basic infrastructure was the top priority. Soon this sector started receiving less; its share fell from 41 per cent of the total in 1961–70 to 30 per cent in 1977–82. Yet another sector to fall out of favour was transport. It accounted for 30 per cent of the total during the first period and 10 per cent during the second. With rising oil prices, investments in the energy sector were considered more worthwhile. Such projects acquired high priority in many IDA countries. This sector received only 6 per cent in the first period, while its share increased to 16 per cent in the second.

The IDA approved credit worth $3 575 million in fiscal 1984, which is a small improvement over the previous year when this amount was $3341 million. Disbursements totalled $2 545 million in fiscal 1984, compared with $2 596 million the preceding year. This implies that the lending operations did not increse during these two years, yet a significant improvement over the 1982 performance was clearly visible. China became eligible to borrow from the IDA in 1984 and borrowed $424 million for five projects. However, with $1 001 million for nine projects, India was again the largest borrower.

INTERNATIONAL FINANCE CORPORATION

Introduction

The seeds of the idea of an organisation of this kind were laid by the IBRD, the reason was the financial limitation imposed by the charter of the Bank against financing private enterprises in LDCs without government guarantee. The Bank found that this limitation could not be circumvented without the creation of a separate institution. The contemporary American Administration was favourably disposed towards the idea of having such a parallel agency.[40] What the US felt was important because they were expected to foot a major part of the capitalisation bill.

The year of birth of the International Finance Corporation (IFC) is 1956 (July). It was founded with the primary purpose of promoting and financing private enterprises in the LDCs; that is, it is the private-sector arm of the Bank. It is empowered by its charter to invest in private enterprises without the guarantee of the host government. A business venture needs two kinds of capital: working capital and the long-term capital, or the fixed capital. The IFC furnishes both; its investments act as a catalyst which encourage local and foreign investors to commit the majority of the funds needed to get the project on stream.

The Rationale

Some economists hold that the role of private investment in the economic growth process is more important than that of public investment. From their perspective many of the essential ingredients for an effective performance in the industrial sector can usually be obtained, and sometimes can only be obtained, in the private sector.[45] The dynamics of private sector was, indeed, recognised by LDCs, but there were many barriers to its effective and efficacious growth. In addition to the usual local handicaps, the obstacles in the flow of external private capital to this sector were slow to go.[46] Why the inflows of private capital were reduced to a trickle in certain periods has already been dealt with in the appropriate section (see pp. 166–76). Expressions like 'economic imperialism' occurred frequently to the leaders of LDCs. This tendency delayed the dismantling of many unnecessary restrictions on foreign investment.[47] Theories – or dogmas – apart, private capital could not be expected to flow to LDCs on a substantial scale until basic economic, social and administrative conditions were welcoming.

The significance of private capital for economic development was well realised in international circles and discussed in fora like the UN. It was generally perceived that the impediment in the flow of private capital could be removed by means of an international organisation established for this specific purpose.

Financial Operations

At the outset it needs to be clarified that the IFC is not a lending institution but an investing and development institution which finances productive private enterprises. Unlike the World Bank it deals exclusively with the private business, to the total exclusion of government undertakings. The IFC does not seek or accept government guarantees of repayment as does the Bank. All that the IFC charter requires is that the project, to be established or expanded, be productive and profitable, and contribute to the economic development of the LDC.[48] Initially the IFC invested only in enterprises which had a predominantly industrial character, e.g. manufacturing, processing, mining. However, there are no barriers to investing in agriculture and commercial undertakings. It does not, however, finance public utilities, like electric power stations, transportation or real-estate development. The selection of projects is based on two yardsticks: (1) a socio-economic rate of return – meaning thereby how well the enterprise will serve its nation's developmental goals; and (2) a financial rate of return – that is, its ability to turn a profit and attract investment. The annual investments of the IFC over the years have been listed in Table 6.6.

During the first three years the average investments of the IFC were small; they averaged less than $1 million. This accumulated projects in 1960, and the investment was more than the first three years combined. Another year of large commitments was 1962. This was the year when the IFC was allowed to invest directly in the equities of clients by a charter amendment. Additionally the IFC made its first commitments to the Development Finance Corporations of various LDCs. Therefore, between 1963 and 1966 the cumulative total doubled again. During the first ten years a relatively small number of industries recieved IFC assistance. They were basic industries like iron and steel, pulp and paper, and construction material. Why? Because the contemporary development gurus thought that these industries were necessary to achieve higher productivity levels. The IFC provided indirect assistance to these industries, through the Development Finance Corporations of LDCs. During this period much of the IFC investments were concentrated in Latin America, two-thirds of which were concentrated in only four countries: Brazil, Chile, Colombia and Mexico.[49]

Between 1968 and 1969 the investments of the IFC doubled again, and they stayed at a plateau for the next three years. Sharp increases were again observed between 1973 and 1974, and until 1977 this level was, by and large, maintained. After 1977 an era of expansion began,

TABLE 6.6   *Financial operations of the IFC,*
1957–82

Year	Annual investment	No. of commitments (in millions of $)
1957	4	4
1958	6	7
1959	10	7
1960	22	13
1961	6	9
1962	21	9
1963	18	11
1964	21	18
1965	26	15
1966	36	21
1967	49	na
1968	50	na
1969	93	na
1970	112	na
1971	101	na
1972	116	na
1973	144	na
1974	238	na
1975	232	na
1976	236	na
1977	259	34
1978	338	41
1979	425	48
1980	681	55
1981	811	56
1982	612	65

SOURCE   *Annual Reports* of the *IFC* (various years).

and investments recorded sharp increases. This was because, in 1977, a sixfold increase in capital – from $110 million to $650 million – was approved. Once the money was subscribed the Corporation began aggressively pursuing and promoting project finance in its role, both as an equity investor and lender. It began focusing on private enterprises in smaller and poorer LDCs.[50]

The prolonged recession, which bottomed out in 1983, kept many private sector investors from undertaking large industrial projects in the developing countries. Therefore in 1984 much of the demand was for consolidating and improving the productivity of the existing industrial facilities, 34 out of 62 investment projects were to expand, modernise or restructure existing industries.

The investment philosophy of the Corporation was somewhat conservative in the 1960s. Diversification was later achieved, but too much emphasis was given to the same set of industries, almost at the neglect of the tertiary sector. Again Latin America attracted a lot of the attention of the Corporation, while Africa and Asia were neglected. One possible explanation can be that the Latin American LDCs could not provide the government guarantee needed for the World Bank loan, while the Asian and African LDCs could. Therefore the Latin American resorted more frequently to IFC assistance.

During the 1970s the IFC concentrated promotional efforts in smaller and poorer LDCs, particularly in Africa where the projects tended to be smaller. As the Corporation continued to expand, manufacturing attracted a good deal of investment, but investment in agribusiness and the financial institutions of LDCs rose by a steeper rate. Service sectors, like tourism, were also assisted. As for the geographical distribution, the dominance of the western hemisphere continued, but not to the extent as in the past. In 1982 32 per cent of the total investment was made in Latin America and the Caribbean. The dollar volume of investment was lower in 1982, than the preceding year. This was attributed to a lack of large projects for financing.[51]

As its operations grew, the Corporation became increasingly profitable. Net income in both 1980 and 1981 was about $20 million on total investments of $1.4 billion and $1.6 billion, respectively. The Corporation is justly proud of the fact that (up to 1982) in over twenty-six years it has had to write off only about 4 per cent of its equity investment and about 0.6 per cent of its loan portfolio.[52] In all, over 650 projects were financed by 1982.

In June 1984 the Corporation resolved for another increase in the capital base. The member countries have agreed to expand the capital to $1 300 million. This capital increase is to support a five year (1985–9) programme drawn up by the Corporation. The programme would pursue the high priority development projects in developing countries, the areas of special interest are agriculture and agro-industries. Modern food processing plants and oil and gas explorations will be the focus of increased promotion and investment. This programme would particularly augment the Corporation's activities in Africa, with sub-Saharan countries getting special attention. During the five years the Corporation plans to invest $7 billion in projects worth over $30 billion in co-operation with private investors. This would exceed the amount lent over its entire 28-year history.

The IFC is considering some new and imaginative methods of mobilising finance such as a regional fund for east Asia. The Corporation is already credited with pioneering the idea of a closed-end trust in Korea, called the Korea Fund.

The *Modus Operandi*

Although during the first five years the Corporation was prohibited from making investments in the capital stock of the enterprises, yet its investments were not fixed-interest debt obligations. Some feature of both, debt and equity, were present. During this period the Corporation called its investments 'venture capital', which means that the owners are able and willing to bear substantial risk in anticipation of the expected gains. The IBRD does not provide any such loans; it only offers fixed interest loans. The participation of the IFC has taken the following forms: (1) a right to convert the loan or some part of it into capital; or (2) a right to some additional income related to earnings; or (3) a combination of both. The last of the three is the most frequent.

As noted, in 1961 the board of Governors changed the charter of the IFC to enable it to invest in the capital stock. It was authorised to do so because it was observed that this prohibition against equity participating was seriously hampering the potential operations of the Corporations. This amendment assisted in investing in the development finance corporations in LDCs and the portfolio of investments widened. There are no upper or lower limits on the size of investment, but prudence dictates that they should remain in the medium range, because large investments would limit the spread of funds and too small investments would be uneconomical in relation to the administrative costs.[53] The Corporations role is that of a catalyst for other investors, rather than having a formative presence on its own. The IFC usually takes a 15 per cent share in any project it invests in. The terms of repayment and interest rate are a matter of negotiation between the borrower and the IFC, and are kept confidential. There are no standard norms; they vary with the enterprise as well as with the economic and money-market conditions in the host country. The IFC does charge 1 per cent commitment fee over the undisbursed amounts; its maturity can range from five to fifteen years.

Inasmuch as the rapid growth in the investment of the IFC is a recent phenomenon, therefore, much of its portfolio has not matured. Of the 333 companies in the portfolio, seventy were added between 1979 and 1981.[54] A number of these projects are still under construction, and the loans of these companies are still within their grace periods. In most cases they are just beginning to provide the IFC with a return on its equity investment. A quick glance at the investment trend reveals that the IFC came into its own in the late 1970s. Its financial operations moved in the form of a slow crescendo. It is interesting that the IFC was able to move into high gear during the period when the international economic climate was a daunting one, afflicted with stagflation, and stagnating world trade and while the uncertainties on the financial markets were aggravated by all-time high interest rates.

ASIAN DEVELOPMENT BANK

Organisation

After three years of preparatory meetings under the aegis of the Economic Commission for Asia and the Far East (ECAFE), the Asian Development Bank (ADB) came into existence in August 1966. Unlike the other two regional development banks, the ADB was not created to promote regional integration or social reforms. The ADB is a product of ECAFE's economic seminars, so, rather than political or diplomatic, it took on a techno-economic image. Since its inception the ADB was less assimilative of international tensions and was wider in outlook. This line of thinking allowed the Bank to open its membership to all countries with an interest in the area. Thirty-one nations, including nineteen from the region, signed the organisational charter in Manila in December 1965. Since then two European and seven Asian states have joined the Bank, bringing the number of forty in 1973. The present number is forty-five (end-1982).

Once again, the US initiative played a meaningful role in the creation of the ADB. It bears repeating that the IDA and the IFC were the outcome of the US support and initial endeavours. Inb case of the ADB US role stemmed partly from the growth of its involvement in Vietnam and South-East Asia during the mid-1960s. In 1965 the US President proposed 'a greatly expanded co-operative effort for development' in

South-East Asia, pledging a '$1 billion American investment in this effort when it is under way'.[55] This decision of the US turned out to be a major determinative factor in assuring the non-regional character of the Bank. The Bank is owned by its 45 member countries, including 17 developing member countries which together hold 63 per cent of its shares. The biggest shareholders are Japan and the United States, each one of them owns 16.4 per cent. These two countries dominate the voting strength with 13.6 per cent of votes each. The developing member countries control 42.2 per cent of the votes.

In creating a regional bank of this nature, it is important not to lose the regional character in trying to gain access to external resources. Japan played an active role because it was interested in increasing the purchasing power of the region and developing new trade partners. They did not, however, want to be over-extended as Asia's main source of development finance. The American involvement fitted in this scheme, it contributed to the international character of the institution and the Japanese hegemony became an impossiblity. So non-political is the institution, that Switzerland, which did not join other international economic institutions of more political character, readily joined the ADB. The developed member countries have a say in the operating style, which is close to that of the IBRD. It even has a parallel with the IDA in its operations, called the 'Special Fund', which gives long-maturity, long grace period loans at zero rate of interest to member countries.

Evolution

The beginning of the ADB was more purposeful than the other two regional banks. Since it was a clearly thought out and well-established organisation it got off to a good start. There was little scepticism about its success, because of the general awareness in the financial centres that the return on investments in Asia was higher. In its loan operations the Bank concentrated on building up a stock of projects which conformed to 'sound banking principles'.[56] It also provided assistance in project preparation to the member LDCs who had difficulty in identifying and preparing proposals.

By this time virtually anybody concerned with economic development in Asia had woken up to the need of the development of agriculture sector. The two monsoon failures in India, in 1965 and 1966, further focused the attention on this sector. Mr Watanabe, the President, proposed a special fund for agricultural development and instituted an Asian Agricultural Survey.[57] This sector soon became an area of special interest for the bank.

Lending Operations

In its loan operations the bank takes a solid, stolid and conservative stance; little wonder the Swiss joined in readily. It finances the foreign exchange cost of the project. In a small number of cases it has financed the indirect foreign exchange costs as well. The anxiety of the Bank to be financially viable is demonstrated by the fact that it took the Bank an enormous amount of time and endless rounds of debate to decide the size of its Special Fund. Eventually it was kept at a low level, keeping in mind how the non-regional members would react to it if it were made too large. The economic consideration involved was, the larger the size, the lesser would be the yield on the resources lent to member countries. The lending operations of the Bank since its inception have been as shown in Table 6.7.

TABLE 6.7   *Lending operations of the ADB, 1967–84 (amounts in millions of $)*

Year	Ordinary loans No.	Ordinary loans Amount	Special fund loans No.	Special fund loans Amount	Total	Percentage change over last year	At constant price (1975 = 100)
1967	–		–		–	–	–
1968	7	42	–	–	42	–	72
1969	14	76	6	22	98	133	161
1970	22	212	10	34	246	151	390
1971	16	203	12	51	254	3	390
1972	16	222	16	94	316	24	464
1973	30	303	24	118	421	33	547
1974	21	375	19	173	548	30	599
1975	27	494	14	166	660	20	660
1976	21	540	16	236	776	17	724
1977	24	615	21	272	887	14	799
1978	31	778	22	381	1 159	31	968
1979	29	835	29	416	1 251	7	929
1980	29	959	30	477	1 436	15	935
1981	30	1 147	27	531	1 678	17	n.a.
1982	32	1 185	25	546	1 731	3	n.a.
1983	–	1 189	–	704	1 893	9	n.a.
1984	–	1 150	–	684	2 234	18	n.a.

SOURCE   *Annual Reports of the ADB* (various issues).

N.B. In order to deflate the nominal series the wholesale series of US prices, has been used, which has been taken from the IMF tape data.

In nominal terms the volume of loans have grown impressively, particularly since 1972 through 1978. Two more impressive growth years were 1980 and 1981. For all appearances the Bank has taken an aggressive stance in its lending operations since 1978. Also, there has been a liberalisation in loaning policies and a more flexible approach has been adopted. In real terms as well the volume of figures have not been unimpressive till 1978; after that they levelled off. The slow pace in 1982 reflects the fact that the world-wide recessionary pressure started telling on the Bank. Second, for several large joint-financing ventures partners were not available.

The loans approved by the Bank and the special fund in 1984 totalled $2234 million, 18 per cent more than in 1983. The sharp recent increases are attributed to the brisker pace of economic growth in the member LDCs. Masao Fujioka, the current president, has set a lending target of $13 billion for the five years ending in 1987. Concern has been expressed over the fast expansion of loaning operations, this simmering concern over the Fujioka strategy came to a boil at the board of governors' meeting in April 1984. The US was the most vocal critic and threatened to stop budgeting for replenishment.

In view of the importance of agriculture and rural development in regional socioeconomic growth, particularly in the low-income member LDCs, the agriculture and agro-industries sector continued to receive high priority. The second major sectoral focus now is on the development of energy sector, particularly on the increased utilisation of indigenous energy sources. Lending to these two sectors has increased in recent years, both in absolute terms as well as in terms of the share of the total lending. A third area which has attracted a great deal of finance has been the development of social infrastructure, such as potable water, urban development, health care and education. In a ministerial meeting held in 1981 it was reassessed and reasserted that the ADB should continue to give high priority to agriculture and the development of energy resources in the region.[58]

The ADB loans are made on fixed interest rates which are kept under constant review. In determining the interest rates the Bank computes its borrowing costs in the previous twelve months and estimates its borrowing costs for the coming twelve months, takes an average and adds 40 basic points to cover operating expenditures. The Bank does not see any need to adopt floating rates. The charter forbids the Bank to incur exchange risks, so it spreads the risk among all borrowers by using a device called the exchange risk pooling system, whereby loan accounts are adjusted for movements in the dollar's value. The Bank regularly borrows in the capital market and prudently tries to minimise its carrying cost and maximise its yield. The rate of return on its investments has been higher than its borrowing costs. In 1983, its average cost of new borrowings was 8.54 per cent while its average return on investment was 10.35 per cent, leaving the Bank a healthy spread of 1.81 per cent.[59] Borrowings are done in eight different currencies, the favourites are the low-coupon currencies, such as, yen, Swiss francs and Deutschmark. Largest amount of funds are raised in yen, the dollar takes the fourth place after Deutschmark and Swiss francs. A consistent policy has been gradually developed which aims at maintaining a presence in all the main capital markets, diversifying the sources of capital, and especially taking advantage of favourable market conditions.

AFRICAN DEVELOPMENT BANK

Organisation

A panel of experts was convened in 1961 to study the feasibility of establishing the African Development Bank (AfDB). Next year the Economic Commission for Africa constituted a committee of nine African states to make necessary arrangements for its establishment, the Bank was established in August 1963. Unlike the ADB, the African Development Bank (AfDB) got off to a poor start. First, there was a long-drawn-out delay over the choice of its headquarters; there were disputes, sometimes bitter, over the staffing pattern; and numerous other preparatory administrative snags. It was because of these reasons that its rate of progress was also slow, and the non-regional countries were reluctant to render support because the AfDB gave an impression that it was still feeling its way. That said, one should be circumspect of such a comparison, because the ADB started with almost five times as many resources. Apart from this luxuriant base the participation of developed countries gave it professional acuity and a feeling of general security. Other bottlenecks of the African environment were: shortage of skilled personnel, especially of financial and economic administrators, and the difficulty of identifying a role for the new institution.[60] This was exacerbated by the fact that, in the post-colonial era, several international organisations were keen to expand their activities in Africa, creating a climate of competition rather than co-operation.

Evolution

It was natural to expect the Bank not to do remarkably well in its operations. While moving slowly it kept mulling over criteria like the search for projects which could contribute to regional integration. It was firmly believed that the Bank's first few projects should be conspicuously bankable to be able to attract the attention of developed countries. The Bank found it difficult to locate projects to link the African countries. In course of time, it adopted the World Bank's practice that projects with good economic return should be given preference. Since the Bank was operating within stringent financial limits and tended to look for revenue-earning projects having quick financial return, its operations slowed which created dissatisfaction among the members. While the AfDB was having its share of problems in identifying sound projects, the IBRD set up two regional offices in Abidjan and Nairobi to intensify its project hunt. This, again, deterred the Bank.

Lending Operations

Since the resources were meagre, the Bank's operations started gingerly. Also there was a considerable amount of irresolution regarding the choice of projects. The loan figures since its inception are presented in Table 6.8.

The low volume of operations is obvious from the above statistics. In the year 1980 the loan figures of the AfDB were one-third that of the ADB. Until 1974 the rate of growth in nominal terms had been small, though it picked up after 1977, both in real as well as nominal terms. The African Development Fund was established in November 1972; its operations commenced in August 1973 while the first credits were disbursed in 1974.

Lending favoured the low-income member countries. The twenty-nine countries having per capita income below \$280 (in 1976 dollars) received 63.4 per cent of the total loans in 1979 and 65.1 per cent in 1980.[61] The cumulative loans approved between 1967 and 1980 show the following sectorial distribution: public utilities, which include telecommunication, energy, water-supply and sewerage, received 34 per cent, the transport sector was the next most important, receiving 25 per cent, industries and the development banks received 24 per cent and agriculture 16 per cent. Agriculture was not accorded high priority by the AfDB.[62]

TABLE 6.8   *Lending operations of the ADB, 1967–82 (amounts in millions of $)*

Year	Ordinary loans No.	Ordinary loans Amount	Special fund loans No.	Special fund loans Amount	Total	Percentage change over last year	At constant price (1975 = 100)
1967	1	2	–	–	2	–	3.5
1968	2	3	–	–	3	50	5
1969	5	8	–	–	8	167	13
1970	7	11	–	–	11	38	17
1971	12	25	–	–	25	127	38
1972	17	27	–	–	27	8	40
1973	13	43	–	–	43	59	56
1974	25	89	17	47	136	216	149
1975	28	104	23	93	197	45	197
1976	25	97	18	80	177	– 10	169
1977	31	154	24	142	356	102	320
1978	36	206	31	186	392	10	327
1979	35	274	30	228	501	28	372
1980	28	297	34	273	570	14	371
1981	35	323	36	311	634	11	NA
1982	33	399	42	358	757	19	NA

SOURCE   *Annual Reports of the ADB* (various issues).
N.B. In order to deflate the nominal series the wholesale series of the US dollar, has been used, which has been taken from the IMF data tapes

The officially commissioned biography of the Bank, published on its twentieth anniversary,[63] identified four areas for future activity:

(1) Improvement in the Bank's management and financial performance;
(2) To help raise the absorptive capacity of the member states;
(3) To allocate resources in such a manner as to make a maximum impact on development of the member state and, in so doing, be result oriented;
(4) To increase the mobilisation of capital.

Thus, the Bank needs qualitative improvement along with quantitative expansion. Of the two, the latter appears more difficult at this point of time. The reason is that the recession has dampened the eagerness of the non-regional members to maintain the growth of contributions to the Bank as well as the ability of the regional developing members to pay in extra capital.

INTER-AMERICAN DEVELOPMENT BANK

Organisation

The Inter-American Development Bank (IDB) has an operational record some six years longer than that of either of the other two regional banks. Prima facie, the factor that differentiates the IDB from its sister institutions is the greater volume of resources at its disposal. Financial constraints, in addition to limiting the scale of operations, have a qualitative effect on the policy. The IDB, in contrast to the AfDB, succeeded in attracting additional resources as it needed them. The agreement establishing the IDB was drawn up in Washington in April 1959, and entered into force the following December. The Latin Americans were interested in the establishment of a regional development bank for several reasons. One was the expansion of economic integration and trade within the region. The IDB was created almost simultaneously with the Latin American Free Trade Association (1960). Second, the Latin Americans thought that having a bank of their own would give them more control over the management of bilateral economic assistance programmes in the region. Third, it was their belief that a new institution would increase the flow of financial resources into the region and improve access to the sources of external capital so vital for attaining their developmental goals.[64] However, the single most important factor was the discontent of the Latin American states with the operating style and the requirements of the World Bank. They found the standards of project appraisal a little too rigorous, and so a little too frustrating. Besides, they had come to realise that, as the newly independent African and Asian states entered the international arena, the claims of the relatively less needy Latin American states to the World Bank funds would tend to be less effective.[65] Perhaps the principal strand in the thinking was to have an institution specialising in Latin American development which would place greater emphasis on innovative social and economic programming than had occurred in the IBRD, with its orthodox banking approach. Also, there was an implicit desire for access to development loans on easier terms than those of the World Bank. Until the creation of the IDA the World Bank was opposed to the idea of concessional lending out of fear of potential damage to its standing in the international capital market. Frequently the Latin American states felt that potential and needy borrowers failed to obtain funds because they were too poor and ill-prepared to draw up an acceptable proposal.

Evolution

In the evolutionary phase bank policy was influenced by two perceived needs: the need to build up an operational record as rapidly as possible, and the need to construct that record in a manner which would clearly distinguish the Bank from other institutions operating in Latin America, and most conspicuously from the World Bank. It was aided in the first respect by the willingness of the US aid administration to feed it with proposals some appraisal of which has already taken place. The Bank started with a rapid rate of commitment, which drew adverse comments from professional observers, that the standards of project were insufficiently rigorous. To an extent this was true. The IDB chose to emphasise its speed, boldness and desire to please. Most other international financial institutions chose to emphasise their prudence, high technical standards and unwillingness to compromise. The Bank adopted a policy to a wide scatter of small loans rather than concentration on a few substantial projects. This policy was followed fairly consistently, though it added considerably to the burden of administration.[66]

The brisk pace of commitment of the IDB had an impact on the operations of the other international institutions operating in Latin America, particularly the World Bank. The two institutions had operated on roughly similar scales. If one adds to that the very favourable composition of the IDB resources, a large proportion of which were available on highly concessional terms from the Fund for Special Operations, the IDB could claim to be the leading financial institution for Latin America. This was one of the objectives of the IDB.

Like the other two regional banks the IDB had a Fund for Special Operations, which was established as a source of loans to be extended on terms and conditions adapted to meeting special circumstances which might arise in specific countries or with regard to specific projects. To meet these purposes it originally had relatively limited assets. However, with the much greater resources provided in recent years, its lending operations have extended significantly. These loans are extended on terms as favourable as possible to the fund.[67] The rate of interest charged varies from $2\frac{1}{4}$ per cent to 4 per cent per annum, according to the nature of the project. In addition, a service charge of 0.75 per cent is applied in some cases. The Bank's emphasis on agriculture is reflected in the loans extended from the fund.

Lending Operations

The constantly rising trend of the Bank's lending was possible because of the continual additions to its financial resources, which the Bank received from its member countries, non-member countries and from the capital markets of the world. The Bank continued to issue bonds in the international capital market to raise capital.[68] From the point of view of the transport infrastructure Latin America was an underdeveloped region in the 1960s. Since its transportation system was basically developed for the exploitation and export of mineral resources, its development was lop-sided. Even in 1970 there were glaring deficiencies in the continent's highway and railway network. The Bank's policy during the 1960s was to support those infrastructure projects which had a favourable cost–benefit ratio.[69] Initially the Bank's primary focus of financing was on import-substitution, but it was soon discovered that the industries created thus were not adept at competing with the sophisticated transnational corporations. In the light of this experience the lending policy was moderated. In the early 1970s the Bank took to encouraging larger enterprises which could achieve higher levels of efficiency in all forms of industrial organisation: managerial, financial, technical and marketing.[70] In terms of volume the operations of the IDB over the years were as listed in Table 6.9.

To be sure, there have been fluctuations, but the commitments have increased both in nominal and real terms. Growth, however, has been steadier after 1972; 1978 can be called a lean year. In 1971 the commitments grew by only 1 per cent in nominal terms, and fell by $21 million in real terms. The President of the IDB, A. Ortiz Mena, regretted in his address the financial bottleneck which led to such slow growth of the Bank in nominal terms, and a fall in real terms. The programmed targets for 1971, therefore, were not achieved.[71] Again 1981 was a year of poor performance when the nominal growth was so low that it was not able to keep with inflation, therefore in real terms the commitments fell by $15 million. Although in 1981 the Bank registered a new high in borrowing from the international capital markets.[72]

The downturn in the economic performance of Latin America was deeper and more widespread in 1983 than in 1982, and many of these economies were reeling under a stringent austerity programme imposed by the IMF. Even in this milieu the IDB kept expanding its financial commitments and, for the first time, topped the $3 billion yearly lending mark in 1983. Its cumulative lending rose to $25 billion.

TABLE 6.9   *Lending operations of the IDB, 1963–83 (in millions of $)*

Year	Amount	Percentage change over the last year	At constant prices (1975 = 100)
1963	259	–	480
1964	299	11	553
1965	373	25	676
1966	396	6	694
1967	496	25	867
1968	431	– 13	734
1969	632	47	1 038
1970	644	2	1 021
1971	652	1	1 000
1972	807	24	1 185
1973	884	10	1 148
1974	1 111	26	1 214
1975	1 375	24	1 375
1976	1 528	11	1 461
1977	1 809	18	1 630
1978	1 870	3	1 562
1979	2 051	10	1 523
1980	2 309	13	1 503
1981	2 493	8	1 488
1982	2 744	10	NA
1983	3 045	10	NA

SOURCE   *Annual Reports, IDB* (Washington, DC: various issues).
N.B. In order to deflate the nominal series the wholesale series of the US dollar has been used, which in turn has been taken from the IMF data tapes.

The Bank began to draw the attention of a good number of industrial countries, who were its non-regional members. Canada was one of the first non-regional members, after the US. Others joined hands later. These countries contributed to the bank resources in two ways: the capital, which is used to make loans on concessional terms through the Fund for Special Operations; second, the non-regional members augmented the human resources by providing professionals who were not locally available.[73]

At the end of 1983 the IDB's resources were augmented substantially. Its authorised capital stock was increased by $15.7 billion. The IDB enjoys a high credit rating in the capital market and is a regular borrower. It borrows exclusively through long-term, fixed-rate instruments, rejecting the World Bank's lead of borrowing and lending at floating interest rates. To facilitate its lending at fixed rates the Bank sets the price of its loans at the time of their disbursement rather than at the time of their approval. The currencies favoured by the Bank for its borrowings are the dollar, yen, Swiss-franc and Deutschmark. The dollar borrowings have fallen over the years because of the high US interest rates, yet they still dominate the portfolio. Bonds in each of the other three currencies favoured by the Bank have almost evenly made good the ground lost by dollars.[74]

MULTILATERAL DEVELOPMENT BANKS

With the passage of time the operations of the multilateral development banks grew, and the volume of financial resources contributed to them by the donors and by them to the LDCs became larger. With this they started attracting more and more attention, and there was some scepticism about their operations among the anti-aid lobbies in the donor countries. The result was that these institutions started coming under harsh scrutiny. The Reagan Administration asked the US Treasury to undertake an evaluation of the policies and operations of the multilateral development banks. The resulting study focused on the World Bank group, the ADB, the AfDB and the IDB.[75] The main finding of the study was that the multilateral development banks' value lies primarily in their cost-effective contribution to the LDCs' economic growth and stability. The economic justification for these institutions, in its view, rests particularly on their capacity 'to play an effective role in situations which require government intervention to provide economic benefits that private investors would or could not generate'. The study emphasises the importance of the multilateral development banks' assistance to the poorer countries who 'tend to be significantly dependent' on these institutions.

It study concludes that the multilateral development banks have generally been effective, citing average rates of return of 15 to 20 per cent as an evidence of the 'positive contributions to economic development'. It also concludes that these institutions are a useful complement to bilateral programmes and possess special capabilities in stimulating efficient long-term economic growth. Private capital could not substitute entirely for the multilateral financial institutions' assistance, because poorer countries lack access to private capital markets and because these institutions also give substantial technical assistance and policy advice.

The study finds evidence for two major criticisms: First, an indication that in some instances there was an over-emphasis on loan quantity as opposed to quality, which may have eroded their influence over policy. Second, the study recommended a more effective graduation/maturation policy to focus scarce resources on the poorer LDCs.

INTERNATIONAL MONETARY FUND

The International Monetary Fund (the Fund or IMF) is a source and creator of international liquidity. It is a reserve depository for the members, its resources are of a revolving character. The Fund embodies the quintessential elements of international co-operation, that is, 'from each member according to its ability [quota subscriptions and loans] and to each member according to its need [balance of payments].'[76] It is now at the centre of the world financial and banking system, and has come to have a great deal of clout despite having limited liquid resources. Among the large transnational banks the image of the Fund is no longer that of a remote and irrelevant arcana. Today, what the Fund decides and negotiates with debtor LDCs, is important for the balance sheet of many, if not all, money-centre banks.

THE CONDITIONALITY TUSSLE

In the recent past there has been some friction between the IMF and LDCs. On occasions it even took unseemly and distasteful proportions. The Fund's view is that monetary and fiscal stability constitutes a necessary precondition for economic growth. A preoccupation with the domestic monetary stability and a belief in the efficacy of internal adjustment as a means of ensuring it, can result in a conflict with the objective of development. This is the essence of the theme adopted by the critics of the Fund. In their opinion the IMF puts too much emphasis on internal adjustment as a means of obtaining BOP equilibrium at the cost of development. Indeed, in many cases monetary restrictions designed to temper inflation succeed only at the cost of growth. Critics argue that the BOP problems which LDCs encounter are more of a structural nature rather than monetary. If LDCs export goods which have low price and income elasticities, and import goods for which the LDCs own elasticities are high, then it is likely that economic growth with a low rate will be consistent with BOP equilibrium. In this situation the BOP options are clear: One is to adjust imports to match exogenously determined export earnings by altering the rate of growth and the level of the GNP. The other is to change the structure of the BOP, including the structure of production, in such a way that an acceptable rate of development is maintained, which is also consistent with the BOP equilibrium.[77] The Fund prescribes the first approach, the LDCs prefer the second; the situation is ready for confrontation.

The origins of the word 'conditionality' are obscure. It does not appear in the original Articles of Agreement or in the First or Second Amendments of the Fund. It may have emerged as a result of the debate on global liquidity in the 1960s, because of the necessity to distinguish between the unconditional asset that was being discussed and the drawing rights that were not unconditional.[78] The conditionality arises when a government requests financial support from the IMF in the form of upper-tranche credit or from the Extended Fund facility. In order to secure the Fund approval of such a request a government will have to specify the stabilisation programme in support of which the credits are needed.[79] Subsequently accommodating responses were made by the IMF. New loan conditionality facilities for LDCs were instituted in the form of the Compensatory Financing Facilities in 1963 and the Buffer Stock Facility in 1969.

Something in the nature of the definition appears in the *Annual Report of the Fund for 1965*: 'the credit tranches ... which are made available on condition that the drawing country maintains or adopts policies calculated to correct in due time the payments deficits in question, constitutes "conditional" liquidity'.[80] To sum up, conditionality refers to the policies that the Fund wishes to see a member follow in order that it can use the Fund's resources in accordance with the purpose and provisions of the Articles.[81]

Financial Assistance Policies

A member's ability to use the Fund's resources was measured in terms of the member's quota and the total holdings of its currency by the Fund. A member is expected not to request a purchase unless it has a need as described by the Articles. The need is one that arises because of the member's BOP or its reserve position or developments in its reserves, as understood by the Fund. The currencies that a member may purchase are selected by the Fund. A service charge of $\frac{1}{2}$ to 1 per cent of the amount of the purchase is to be paid by the member. The rate increases by $\frac{1}{2}$ per cent each year until it reaches 6 per cent per annum in the fifth year. The Fund expects a member to repurchase as its balance of payments and/or reserve positions improve. Heavy indebtedness of several LDCs has already pushed the Fund into becoming a *de facto* development finance institution, more so because its assistance is made available on the basis of a mutually agreed adjustment and development programme.[82]

The evolution of borrowing policies of the Fund can be compared to a row of windows through each of which the Fund makes resources available under a discrete policy. The various windows are as follows:

* First credit tranche
* Upper credit tranche
* Compensatory financing facilities for export fluctuations – CFF (1963), amended 1979 and 1983–4
* Buffer stock financing facilities (1969), amended 1979 and 1984
* Oil facility 1974
* Oil facility 1975
* Extended fund facility (1974), amended 1979 and 1981
* Supplementary financing facility
* Trust funds
* Policy on enlarged access (1981), amended 1984.

Under one of the above policies the conditionality is proscribed; for all others it is prescribed, but it can vary in rigor or in the speed with which adjustment is expected. Some policies are permanent, others are temporary. Some policies are financed with the Fund's ordinary resources, but particular transactions under these policies may be financed in whole or in part with resources borrowed by the Fund. Some policies deal with a member's need for assistance because of its difficult BOP and reserve situation without distinguishing the origin of the difficulty, while other policies are intended to deal with specific difficulties. Some policies take account of the fact that a member's problem may be largely beyond its control; other policies do not make this distinction. Other distinctions can be made, but this sufficiently demonstrates that the Fund has been flexible in evolving policies on the use of its resources.[83]

Of late the Fund is beginning to favour a broadly-based and longer-term macroeconomic policy approach in case of LDCs. Why? It has learnt from the past experience, and seen the general failure of precise macroeconomic targeting. It goes to suggest that the Fund is becoming increasingly sceptical of the scope of economic fine-tuning in the LDCs. While the new guidelines on conditionality permit a significant alteration in the economic management, their effect will depend crucially on how they are interpreted while implementing. Yet, monetary stability still seems to be viewed as a prerequisite for economic development. In a speech delivered by the managing director in 1980, he maintained that: 'sound adjustment menas, above all, implementation of fiscal and monetary policies designed to avoid overconsumption in relation to available resources and to prevent waste or mismanagement of these resources'.[84] Nothing could be more sagacious and prudent. In the same speech he goes on to say that the adjustment programmes do not represent comprehensive solutions for the difficulties now confronted by some LDCs. Such remarks make it plain that the shift in conditionality from demand management to supply management is generally overdrawn by the critics. The Fund remains basically committed to what it sees as sound domestic financial policy. If there has been a change in emphasis it seems to be that the Fund now recognises that sound financial policy may not be sufficient to ensure economic growth, and that the short-term costs of some of the policies may have concentrated too much on the sole objective of bringing about a short-run improvement in the BOP.[85]

LDC Drawings on the Fund

First the Latin American LDCs and those exporting primary commodities, and then the newly independent ex-colonies in Africa and Asia, began to request drawings on the IMF after their own reserves were spent. The Korean War boom in raw material prices collapsed, and the LDCs found themselves short of funds for implementing their development programmes. The Fund, noting that in their pursuit of development these countries were using exchange controls, multiple exchange rates, and other restrictions which were frowned upon by the Fund's articles, used these requests as an opportunity to press these countries to liberalise their trade and payments. This was because by this time (1950s) the Fund had come upon its ideology of development, which was in harmony with its philosophy of economic liberalism.[86] The drawings of the LDCs on the Fund over the years were as documented in Table 6.10.

The above series originates in 1952. During the 1940s and the early 1950s the Fund assisted the LDCs in a small way, though, as may be visualised, the Fund policies were not designed for this specific purpose. The Fund's world view was essentially static during this period, and little consideration was given to the dynamic potential for assisting economic development.[87]

The drawings of the LDCs during the early 1950s were either negative or of relatively insignificant amounts. The *Annual Reports* of the IMF during the early 1950s confirm that the Fund had little specific interest in the travails of the LDCs. In the late 1950s and through 1960s the Fund's attitude towards LDCs shifted significantly. This apparent shift, the tangible aspect of which was the introduction of a number of innovations explicitly intended to help alleviate the monetary implications of the economic problems faced by the LDCs, may be put down to a number of factors: first, the deterioration in the terms of trade of the primary producing LDCs; second, a growing awareness of the instability of the export proceeds of the LDCs; third, increasing representation of the LDCs in international agencies; and finally, the appointment of Per Jacobsson in place of Ivar Rooth as the managing director of the Fund, bringing to this position more imaginative leadership and a more flexible outlook.[88]

This change in attitude led to several innovations: first, the increase in the size of the quotas; second, a considerable shift in the direction in which the Fund made its resources available – away from the industrial countries and towards LDCs; third, after some initial resistance, in 1963 the Fund reached a decision to compensate members against shortfalls in export receipts. This facility, although officially open to all members alike, was of the greatest benefit to primary product exporting countries. Initially the compensation was available only on relatively restrictive terms, but in 1966 amendments were introduced which made the Compensatory Financing Facility more attractive. A fourth change was made in 1969; the Fund took action to assist members who faced BOP difficulties as a result of their participation in the international buffer-stock schemes. This facility was, again, of direct help to LDCs.

TABLE 6.10   *Net drawings of non-oil developing countries (in millions of $)*

1952	− 29
1953	− 7
1954	15
1955	− 56
1956	63
1957	375
1958	47
1959	4
1960	87
1961	401
1962	49
1963	122
1964	− 52
(in millions of SDR)	
1965	487
1966	556
1967	370
1968	588
1969	329
1970	236
1971	424
1972	792
1973	315
1974	1 701
1975	1 959
1976	3 835
1977	1 035
1978	1 211
1979	1 770
1980	3 753
1981	7 082
1982	8 133
1983	13 213
1984	8 009

SOURCE   *International Financial Statistics* (Washington, DC: IMF) various volumes.

Thus, by the second half of the 1960s, the Fund had modified its role substantially to the advantage of the LDCs. This is visible in the drawings of the LDCs during this period. For the first time these drawings were not paltry amounts.

The 1970s represent the period of an active relationship between the Fund and the LDCs, for two reasons: the breakdown of the Bretton Woods system, and the two rounds of the oil price hike. The collapse of the Bretton Woods system resulted in the establishment of the Committee on Reform of the International Monetary System and Issues. This so-called Committee of Twenty was given the task of advising and reporting on all aspects of the international monetary reform. The membership of the committee was such that the interest of the LDCs (nine members) was well represented. The committee and its reports were a significant landmark in the evolution of a relationship between the Fund and the LDCs. For the first time the LDCs were able to participate fully in the remaking of the international monetary system. The momentum generated by the Committee of Twenty has to some extent been maintained subsequently. At both the 1974 and 1975 annual meetings of the Fund, *a*, if not *the*, dominant theme was the economic situation of the LDCs. There was a wide-ranging discussion about ways in which economic growth in LDCs could be protected from the effects of inflation and recession.

Further suggestions made by the Committee of Twenty resulted in the establishment of the oil facility, designed to assist the members in withstanding the impact of the increase in oil prices, and the extended financing facility, designed to provide longer-term assistance to members having BOP problems. Because of these facilities and the needs of the LDCs the drawings of the LDCs were at a much higher level between 1972 and 1979, as compared to those in the 1960s.

Further benefits to the LDCs came from the trust funds which provided highly concessionary resources to assist the low-income LDCs in meeting their BOP needs. Between 1979 and 1980 the drawings by the LDCs, by way of various facilities, doubled. Between 1980 and 1981 they doubled again, and recorded a rise in 1982 of a substantial order. In 1983 there was a dramatic rise and the drawings reached their all time high mark. This was due to the Fund operations related to the rescue of debt-ridden Latin American LDCs. These facts and the drawings figures bring out four phases of relationship between the Fund and LDCs: the first period was in the 1940s and the early 1950s, which was a period when the two sides virtually ignored each other. The second period was the late 1950s and the 1960s, when the relationship started formulating, though the drawings stayed at a low level. The third period was between 1972 and 1979 when the relationship became mature and the drawings rose to a substantial level. The fourth period was after 1979, when the relationship between the Fund and LDCs was one of intimacy; the drawings rose by leaps and bounds as seen in Table 6.9.

LDC drawings peaked in 1983; they fell by 43 per cent the next year. The 1984 figure was still the third highest in the Fund's history. New commitments under standby and extended arrangements also eased substantially in 1984. All the 1984 drawings were by LDCs, the dominant share (87.7 per cent) of which was subject to relatively strong economic policy conditions designed to support economic adjustment programmes. Translated, it means that the dominant share was under high conditionality.

THE NEW-FOUND POWER

As a result of the changing economic and financial circumstances, the Fund has developed from an institution constrained by the polices of its birth into a powerful organisation. In order to know how the Fund developed its power, we shall have to examine some of the recent events. During the 1970s the Latin American LDCs over-borrowed or were over-lent, both statements are equally valid. A large part of their capital market debt was on short-term, which had a baneful effect on its maturity-structure. They soon started having serious debt service problems. To keep these countries from going under, co-financing plans were jointly made by the Fund and the commercial banks, and a symbiotic relationship was established between the two. The banks also needed the Fund to enforce financial discipline on the recalcitrant debtors. The rescue operation developed by the Fund and the banks earned high marks in the cases of Mexico and Brazil. It works on the following lines: when the LDC calls on the Fund for a standby credit, the Fund puts together an economic adjustment programme, or conditionality. Once the LDC in question agrees, the loan is released and in lock-step the banks release their part of the additional credits. Such financial rescue packages had to be prepared for several LDCs, which has immensely increased the importance of the Fund and it has become the linchpin of the international financial system.

UNITED NATIONS DEVELOPMENT PROGRAMME

Genesis

The United Nations Development Programme (UNDP) came into being on 1 January 1966.[89] It was established through the merger of the UN Special Fund and the UN Extended Programme for Technical Assistance. It is not a lending or investing organisation. It has been founded as an international trust fund for development. Its work encompasses virtually every aspect of economic and social development under a large number of resolutions from the UN General Assembly. Since its creation it has come to be the nodal point of multilateral aid as given by the UN family.[90] The member governments of the UN, both developed and developing, contribute financial resources through voluntary contributions. The member states also establish policy guidelines and country and inter-country resource allocations through a rotating service of a forty-eight-nation Governing Council. Both developing and industrial countries are represented on this council. In short the UNDP is a channel for international technical and financial co-operation.[91] The UNDP has a different world vision, from its plateau one glimpses unfamiliar fields. It extends its frontier by deliberate effort, to cover the world's surface. Though it is bound by the inherited conceptions of national sovereignty, it makes an attempt, though a limited one, to consider the globe not so much in terms of national boundaries and man-made impediments as in terms of fields and forests, rivers and mines, sea-coast and desert.[92] The UNDP considers itself a 'truly global partnership'.[93]

Functions and Objectives

In the absence of formally approved guidelines, the draft Article 1 of the statute of the UNDP might be used as a basis for arriving at an agreed definition of the purposes and general principles governing it. The draft article states: 'The purpose of the UNDP shall be, in accordance with the principles and policies laid down by the General Assembly and the Economic and Social Council, to organize universal international co-operation and to assist the developing countries in their effort to accelerate their economic and social development by providing systematic and sustained assistance geared to their national development plans and objectives, including their pre-investment needs.'

Two things are clear from the above: first, the purposes are very broad and the definition of the purposes is in terms of the objectives of its activities, not in terms of the instruments that it may or may not adopt to attain those objectives.[94] Since the UNDP works through the other organisations in the UN system the resources financed by the UNDP go into almost every conceivable kind of activity linked with development. Four agencies in the past accounted for at least three-fourths of the total expenditure. They were: the UN, ILO, FAO and UNESCO.

The Two Cycles

Since 1972 the UNDP has started dividing its activities in terms of five-year cycles. The first cycle ran between the years 1972–6, while the second one between 1977–81. The third one is currently under way. The voluntary contributions received by the UNDP, from the developed and developing countries alike, during the first two cycles totalled $5 billion, of which $1 795 million was contributed in the first cycle and $3 175 million in the second. While total voluntary contributions during the first cycle somewhat exceeded on average the annual 9.6 per cent growth target set by the Governing Council for this period. The voluntary contributions for the second cycle fell marginally short of the expanded growth target, based on annual increases of 14 per cent. The other sources of income, however, rose substantially during the second cycle to help offset the shortfall. Most notably, the cost-sharing contributions to projects and programmes, made by LDCs themselves and the third party donors, advanced sharply.

In real terms the project expenditure of the UNDP has doubled while in nominal terms it soared six-fold. There is no clear trend, though some of the earlier years were the years of good growth; that is, between 1966 and 1972. The period between 1978 and 1980 was also of high growth, both in nominal and real terms.

On a regional basis, the project expenditure showed a distinct shift toward lower-income countries in Africa and Asia over the two cycles. The shift reflects major reallocation of resources towards countries most in need, this has been an outstanding characteristic of the second cycle. The same line of thinking also influenced the planning for the third cycle. The data given in Table 6.12 vividly show this shift.

In accordance with the same line of thinking, the share of the low

TABLE 6.11 *Project expenditure under various UNDP programmes, 1966–81*

Year	Amount in millions of $	Percentage change over last year	Amount (in constant $) (1975–100)
1966	125	–	219
1967	143	14	250
1968	166	16	283
1969	190	14	312
1970	210	11	333
1971	261	24	400
1972 First Cycle	277	6	407
1973	275	– 1	357
1974	295	7	322
1975	426	44	426
1976	400	– 6	382
1977 Second Cycle	338	– 16	305
1978	436	29	364
1979	548	26	407
1980	678	24	441
1981	732	8	437

SOURCE UNDP, *Performance, Policy and Prospects*, DP/L. 277 (New York: UN) and DP/1982/6/Add. 1.

N.B. For deflating the nominal series the US wholesale price index has been used, which was taken from the IMF data tapes.

TABLE 6.12 *Allocations of resources under various UNDP programmes*

	LDCs below $500 GNP per capita	LDCs above $500 GNP per capita	Inter-country projects
	%	%	%
First cycle	42	43	15
Second cycle	53	29	18
Third cycle (*ex ante*)	61	17	22

SOURCE DP/1982/6/Add. 1 (New York: UNDP).

income LDCs has gone on increasing from 42 per cent in the first cycle, to 53 per cent in the second and the target for the third cycle is 61 per cent of the total resources. Against this background of progressive reallocation for the needy countries, the countries in Africa and Asia and the Pacific gained a large share of expenditure, while countries in Latin America, Europe and the Middle East showed a decline.

The share of the UNDP expenditure going to such sectors as industry, transport and communications, human settlements and infrastructure support for development efforts increased on average in the second cycle as compared to the first. On the other hand, the share of expenditure going to sectors like agriculture, population, health and education declined marginally. The increase in expenditure for the industrial and human settlements sector is in line with the needs as determined by the LDCs themselves.

One of the newest areas of concentration for the UNDP is the renewable sources of energy in the LDCs. During 1981 the UNDP was helping to underwrite some 386 energy projects at a cost of over $127 million. Also it undertook special appeals for the support of the Special Measures Fund for the LDCs which were adversely affected by exogenous circumstances beyond their control.

THE THIRD CYCLE AND THE DECLINE OF THE UNDP

In principle the UNDP has operated as the central funding source for technical co-operation provided by UN Agencies. However, its share of total funding, and hence the weight that it carries in its attempt to fulfil a co-ordinating role, have stagnated in real terms over most of the 1970s. In the past few years, this decline was due to the fact that the growth rate in the resources of the UNDP has not been brisk enough, whereas the other UN technical co-operation programmes have grown rapidly. Therefore the UNDP has lagged behind.[95] Weaknesses have begun to emerge on the financial scene of the UNDP; while main programme expenditure rose by 8 per cent in 1981, voluntary contributions pledged by governments decreased. This development was counter to the traditions of the UNDP. Total pledges in 1981 amounted to $673 million, a 6 per cent reduction from the 1980 level of $716 million. Thus 1981 was a disappointing year for the UNDP as its target was not achieved. The statistics in Table 6.13 show the estimates of annual project expenditure during the third cycle, which began in 1982. The project targets were established by the Governing Council. The same

TABLE 6.13   *UNDP targets and voluntary contributions (in millions of $)*

Year	Project targets	Voluntary contributions
1982	750	697
1983	858	746
1984	983	800
1985	1 124	858
1986	1 287	921

SOURCE   *Promises to Keep* (New York: UNDP, 1981).

table also shows the estimated voluntary contributions which the governments, based on current trends, are expected to make available each year as resources for carrying out the assignments.

The contrast between the two sets of figures needs no commentary. The preliminary results of the 1983 Pledging Conference, held in New York on 8–9 November 1982, confirmed the decline in the voluntary contributions to the UNDP. The UNDP administrator stated that he has no option but to advise Programme recipients immediately of the need to reduce their planning estimates for the UNDP-funded technical co-operation projects to 55 per cent of agreed indicative planning figures. These countries had already been operating on the basis of a reduction to 80 per cent of the indicative planning figures for the third cycle period (1982–6). Across-the-board cuts have been unavoidable; they are being applied to all the categories of funding and include regional, inter-regional, inter-country and global programmes.[96]

Notes and References

1 TRANSNATIONAL FLOW OF LONG-TERM RESOURCES – A HISTORICAL PERSPECTIVE

1. Emperor Hammurabi (2067–2025 BC) made Babylon the capital of a large empire stretching from the Persian Gulf northward and westward, through the Tigris valley and Assyria to the Syrian coast of the Mediterranean. The ruins of Babylon still exist 88 km from the present-day Baghdad.
2. F. A. Lees and M. Eng, *International Financial Markets* (New York: Praeger Publishers, 1975).
3. For example, according to the latest available (1983) statistics, per capita income of Switzerland is $17 430, which makes it the richest industrialised country in the world. It is, however, generally forgotten that 100 to 150 years ago, the situation was different. Shortly after the destruction and turmoil of the Napoleonic Wars (1815) the Czar, Alexander I, of Russia, one of the victors of the Corsican war, sent 100 000 silver roubles to Switzerland to relieve the plight of the starving population. Switzerland was something of a Chad of that epoch. Since then, despite its lack of natural resources, rugged terrain and harsh climate, the poor developing country of the early nineteenth century has become a modern affluent nation.
4. *The New Encyclopaedia Britannica*, vol. 7, p. 767, gives an interesting account of the founding of the family empire and its influence on the policies of these rulers.
5. M. Postan, *Medieval Trade and Finance* (Cambridge University Press, 1973).
6. R. de Roover, *The Medici Bank* (New York: New York University Press, 1948). Also see Y. S. Park and J. Zwick, *International Banking in Theory and Practice* (Reading, Massachusetts: Addison-Wesley Publishing Company, 1984) particularly chapter 1.
7. G. Liska, *The New Statecraft* (Chicago: University of Chicago Press, 1960) p. 38.
8. I. M. D. Little and J. M. Clifford, *International Aid* (London: Allen & Unwin, 1965).
9. H. Feis, *Foreign Aid and Foreign Policy* (New York: St Martin's Press, 1968).
10. C. Lewis, *America's Stake in International Investment* (Washington, DC: The Brookings Institution, 1938).

11. A. K. Cairncross, *Home and Foreign Investment, 1870–1910* (Cambridge: Cambridge University Press, 1953).

12. D. C. North, 'The United States Balance of Payments, 1790–1860', in *Trends in the American Economy in the Nineteenth Century* (Princeton, NJ: Princeton University Press, 1960) p. 623.

13. P. Hartland, 'Canadian Balance of Payments since 1868', in *Trends in the American Economy in the Nineteenth Century* (Princeton, NJ: Princeton University Press, 1960) p. 735.

14. H. Hughes, 'Debt and Development: The Role of Foreign Capital in Economic Growth', *World Development*, vol. 7 (Feb 1969) pp. 95–112.

15. J. H. Dunning, 'Capital Movement in the Twentieth Century', *Lloyds Bank Review*, Apr 1964.

16. W. Arthur Lewis, *The Evolution of Economic Order* (Princeton, NJ: Princeton University Press, 1978).

17. H. W. Singer and J. A. Ansari, *Rich and Poor Countries* (London: George Allen & Unwin, 1977) p. 34.

18. F. A. Lees and M. Eng, *International Financial Markets* (New York: Praeger Publishers, 1975).

19. D. Avramovic, *et al.*, *Economic Growth and External Debt*, (Baltimore, Md: Johns Hopkins University Press, 1964).

20. *Annual Report of the Executive Directors* (Washington DC: IMF, 30 Apr 1977) p. 21.

21. A. I. Bloomfield, *Monetary Policy under the International Gold Standards: 1880–1914* (New York: Federal Reserve Bank of New York, 1959) p. 55.

22. H. Feis, *Foreign Aid and Foreign Policy* (New York: St Martin's Press, 1963) p. 33.

23. Ibid. pp. 34–40.

24. *International Capital Movements during the Inter-War Period* (New York: UN, Department of Economic Affairs, Oct 1947).

25. Ibid. p. 28.

26. W. Arthur Lewis, *Growth and Fluctuations, 1870–1913* (Boston and Sydney: Allen & Unwin, 1978) p. 225.

27. *International Capital Movements during the Inter-War Period* (New York: UN, Department of Economic Affairs, 1949).

28. Ibid.

29. *International Capital Movements in the Inter-War Period* (New York: United Nations, 1949 reprint) pp. 12–14.

30. Ibid.

31. R. Mikesell, *US Private and Government Investment Abroad* (Eugene, Ore.: University of Oregon Press, 1962).

32. *World Debt Tables 1* (Washington, DC: World Bank, 2 Sep 1977) p. 210.

33. Ibid. p. 39. See also Marcells De Cesco's article 'The International Debt Problem in the Interwar Period', *Banca Nazionale Del Lavoro Quarterly Review*, March 1985, pp. 45–64.

34. Based on estimates by J. H. Dunning in 'Capital Movements in the Twentieth Century', in *International Investments*, ed. J. H. Dunning (Harmondsworth, Middx: Penguin Books, 1972) p. 63.

35. Ibid. p. 64.

36. *International Capital Markets during the Inter-War Period*, op. cit.

37. A. S. J. Baster, *American Economic Review* (1937) p. 294.
38. C. Lewis, *America's Stake in International Investment*, op. cit.
39. J. H. Dunning (ed.) *International Investments* (Harmondsworth, Middx: Penguin Books, 1972) p. 141.
40. H. Feis, *Europe the World's Banker, 1870–1914* (New Haven, Conn.: Yale University Press, 1930).
41. Ibid.
42. I. M. D. Little and J. M. Clifford, *International Aid* (London: George Allen & Unwin, 1965) p. 30.
43. Ibid. pp. 31–3.
44. *Britain and Developing Countries* (London: British Information Services, The Central Office of Information, July 1968).
45. The source of these statistics is Feis's classic book, see note 40.
46. *Report of the US Alien Property Custodian* (Washington, DC: Feb 15 1919).
47. C. Lewis, *America's Stake in International Investment* (Washington, DC: The Brookings Institution, 1938) p. 370.
48. Ibid. p. 375.
49. Ibid. p. 412.
50. J. T. Madden *et al.*, *America's Experience as a Creditor Nation* (New York: Institute of International Finance, 1937) p. 144.

2　INFLOW OF FINANCIAL RESOURCES AND ECONOMIC GROWTH

1. S. Robinson, 'Sources of Growth in Less Developed Countries: A Cross-section Study', *Quarterly Journal of Economics* (Aug 1971), pp. 391–408.
2. At the outset it is imperative to clarify what the term 'grant element' means. It reflects the financial terms of a transaction: interest rate, maturity and grace period. It is a measure of the concessionality (or softness) of the loan. The extent of the benefit depends on the difference between the interest on aid and commercial market rate, and the length of time for which the funds are available to the borrower. To calculate this benefit, the present value of the market rate of interest is ascertained for each repayment. The excess of the loan's face value over the sum of these present values, expressed as a percentage of the face value is the 'grant element' of the loan. Conveniently, the market rate is taken as 10 per cent. Thus the grant element is nil for a loan carrying an interest rate of 10 per cent, it is 100 per cent for a grant, and it will lie between these two limits for a soft loan. Generally speaking, a loan will not convey a grant element of over 25 per cent if its maturity is less than ten years unless its interest rate is well below 5 per cent.
3. R. F. Mikesell, *The Economics of Foreign Aid* (Chicago: Aldine Publishing Co. 1968), p. 220.
4. H. W. Singer, *American Economic Review* (May 1950), pp. 473–85.
5. P. B. Simpson, 'Foreign Investment and National Economic Advantage: A Theoretical Analysis', in Raymond F. Mikesell (ed.) *US Private and Goverment Investment Abroad* (Eugene, Ore: University of Oregon Press, 1962), p. 504.

6. G. C. Abbott, 'Economic Aid as a Unilateral Transfer of Resources', *Journal of Political Economy* (Nov–Dec 1970), pp. 1213–27.
7. M. Kalecki and I. Sachs, 'Forms of Foreign Aid: An Economic Analysis', *Social Science Information*, vol. 5, no. 1 (Mar 1966), pp. 21–44.
8. Y. Onitsuka, 'International Capital Movements and the Pattern of Economic Growth', *The American Economic Review* (Mar 1974), pp. 24–36.
9. A. Amano, 'International Capital Movements and Economic Growth', *Kyklos*, vol. xviii–1965–fasc. 4, pp. 639–99.
10. P. N. Rosenstein-Roden, 'Notes on the Theory of the Big Push: Economic Development of Latin America', *Proceedings of a Conference of the International Economic Association* (New York: St Martin's Press, 1961).
11. P. N. Rosenstein-Roden, 'International Aid for Underdeveloped Countries', *Review of Economics and Statistics,* **43** (2) (1961), 107–38.
12. *Quantitative Models as an Aid to Development Assistance Policy* (Paris: Organisation for Economic Co-operation and Development, 1967) p. 21.
13. J. H. Adler, *Absorptive Capacity – The Concept and Its Determinants* (Washington, DC: The Brookings Institution, 1965).
14. H. B. Chenery, and A. MacEvan, 'Optimal Pattern of Growth and Aid: The Case of Pakistan', in *Structural Change and Development Policy*, ed. H. B. Chenery (New York, London: Oxford University Press, 1979) p. 371.
15. An intricate model has been developed by D. Lal in 'When is Foreign Borrowing Desirable?' *Bulletin of Oxford University Institute of Statistics*, (Aug 1971) pp. 197–206.
16. D. Lal, 'The Evaluation of Capital Inflow', *Industry and Development*, no. 1 (1978) 2–19.
17. H. B. Chenery, and A. Strout, 'Foreign Assistance and Economic Development', *The American Economic Review* (Sep 1966) pp. 679–733.
18. G. F. Papanek, 'The Effect of Aid and Other Resource Transfer on Saving and Growth in Less Developed Countries', *Economic Journal*, vol. 82 (Sep 1972) 943–50.
19. K. B. Griffin and J. L. Enos, 'Foreign Assistance: Objectives and Consequences', *Economic Development and Cultural Change* (Apr 1970).
20. G. F. Papanek, 'Aid, Foreign Private Investment, Savings and Growth in Less Developed Countries', *Journal of Political Economy*, vol. 81 (Jan–Feb 1973).
21. P. M. Sommers and D. B. Suits, 'A Cross-Section Model of Economic Growth', *Review of Economics and Statistics* (May 1971) 121–8.
22. H. B. Chenery, H. Elkington and C. Sims, 'A Uniform Analysis of Development Patterns', *Economic Development Reports*, no. 148 (Centre for International Affairs, Harvard University, July 1970).
23. K. B. Griffin and J. L. Enos, 'Foreign Assistance: Objectives and Consequences', *Economic Development and Cultural Change* (Apr 1970) op. cit.
24. H. B. Chenery, 'Trade, Aid and Economic Development', in *International Development* (1965) ed. S. H. Robock and L. M. Soloman (New York: Oceana Publications, p. 187).
25. B. F. Massell, 'Exports, Capital Imports and Economic Growth', *Kyklos*, vol. xvii–1964–fasc. 4, pp. 627–35.
26. H. W. Singer, 'The Distribution of Gains Between Investing and Borrowing Countries', *The American Review* (May 1950), pp. 473–85.

27. K. B. Griffin, 'Foreign Capital, Domestic Savings and Economic Development', *Bulletin of Oxford University Institute of Statistics* (May 1970), pp. 99–112.
28. Ibid.
29. A. Rahman, 'Foreign Capital and Domestic Savings: A Test of Haavelomo's Hypothesis with Cross-section Data', *Review of Economics and Statistics* (Feb 1968).
30. See note 17.
31. K. L. Gupta, 'Foreign Capital and Domestic Savings: A Test of Haavelomo's Hypothesis with Cross-section Data: A Comment', *Review of Economics and Statistics* (May 1970).
32. L. Laudau, 'Differences in Saving Ratios among Latin American Countries', in *Studies in Development Planning*, ed. H. B. Chenery (Cambridge, Mass: Harvard University Press, 1969).
33. H. B. Chenery and P. Eckstein, 'Development Alternatives for Latin America', *Journal of Political Economy* (Supplement to July–Aug 1970) pp. 996–1006.
34. T. E. Weisskopf, 'The Impact of Foreign Capital Inflows on Domestic Savings in Underdeveloped Countries', *The Journal of International Economics*, 2 (1972) 24–38.
35. The national accounts relationship equates investment with the sum of domestic and foreign savings, implying thereby that savings equal investment minus foreign inflows.
36. G. F. Papanek, 'The Effect of Aid and Other Resource Transfer on Saving and Growth in Less Developed Countries', *Economic Journal*, vol. 82 (Sep 1972) op. cit. pp. 943–50.
37. A. S. Manne, 'Key Sectors of the Mexican Economy, 1960–1970', in *Studies in Process Analysis*, ed. A. S. Manne and H. M. Markowitz (New York: John Wiley & Sons, 1963).
38. R. I. McKinnon, 'Foreign Exchange Constraint in Economic Development', *Economic Journal* (June 1964) pp. 388–409.
39. A. Sengupta, 'Foreign Capital Requirement for Economic Development', *Oxford Economic Papers* (Nov 1967) pp. 38–55.
40. H. Feis, *Europe the World's Banker, 1870–1914* (New Haven, Conn.: Yale University).
41. Ibid.
42. I. M. D. Little and J. M. Clifford, *International Aid* (London: George Allen & Unwin, 1965) p. 30.
43. Ibid. pp. 31–3.
44. *Britain and Developing Countries* (London: British Information Services, The Central Office of Information, July 1968).
45. The source of these statistics is Feis's classic book, see note 40.
46. *Report of the US Alien Property Custodian* (Washington, DC Feb 15 1919).
47. C. Lewis, *America's Stake in International Investment* (Washington, D.C.: The Brookings Institution, 1938) p. 370.
48. Ibid. p. 375.
49. Ibid. p. 412.

3 DEVELOPING COUNTRIES IN THE INTERNATIONAL
  ECONOMY – PROGRESS AND INTERACTION

1. Only six OPEC countries are capital surplus, namely, Iraq, Kuwait, Libya, Qatar, Saudi Arabia and the UAE.
2. From the speech of A. W. Clausen, President of the World Bank, delivered at the International Monetary Conference, Vancouver, Canada, 25 May 1982.
3. The World Bank, *World Development Report, 1978* (Washington, DC: World Bank, 1979).
4. D. Morawetz, *Twenty-five Years of Economic Development 1950–75* (Baltimore and London: Johns Hopkins University Press, 1977) pp. 11–13.
5. Ibid. pp. 14–15.
6. UN, *Trade and Development Report, 1981* (New York: United Nations Conference on Trade and Development, 1981) p. 34.
7. D. Morawetz, op. cit., pp. 15–22.
8. *Trade and Development Report, 1981*, op. cit., p. 34.
9. Euromoney, *World Economic Performance, 1973–83* (Oct 1983) pp. 274–83.
10. P. Bairoch, *The Economic Development of the Third World since 1900* (London: Methuen, 1975) pp. 30–40.
11. *World Agriculture: The Last Quarter Century* (Rome: FAO, 1970) pp. 5–10.
12. Bairoch, *The Economic Development of the Third World since 1900*, op. cit. pp. 43–4.
13. P. Bairoch, 'Le Mythe de la Croissance Économique Rapide au XIX Siècle', in *Revue de l'Institut de Sociologie*, no. 2 (1962).
14. P. Bairoch, 'Le Mythe . . .', op. cit. pp. 63–8 (1962).
15. *World Industry since 1960: Progress and Prospects* (Vienna: UNIDO, 1979), pp. 34–6.
16. L. G. Reynolds, 'The Spread of Economic Growth to the Third World: 1950–1980', *Journal of Economic Literature* (Sep 1983) pp. 941–80.
17. *World Industry in 1980* (Vienna: UNIDO), pp. 31–5.
18. L. M. Dominguez, *International Trade, Industrialization and Economic Growth* (Washington, DC: Pan-American Union, 1954).
19. A. Maizels, *Industrial Countries and World Trade* (London: Cambridge University Press, 1963).
20. *Trends in International Trade*, A Report by a Panel of Experts (Geneva: General Agreement on Tariffs and Trade, 1958), pp. 39–47.
21. R. Blackhurst, N. Martin and J. Tumlir, *Adjustment, Trade and Growth in Developed and Developing Countries* (Geneva: General Agreement on Tariffs and Trade, 1978) pp. 7–10.
22. *International Trade 1980/81* (Geneva: General Agreement on Tariffs and Trade, 1981) pp. 16–17.
23. Ibid. p. 18. *International Trade, 1981/82*, table A–24 (Geneva: General Agreement on Tariffs and Trade, 1982.
24. D. B. Keesing, 'World Trade and Output of Manufactures: Structural

Trends and Developing Countries' Exports', *World Bank Staff Working Paper No. 316* (Jan 1979), pp. 22–9.

25. *Commodity Trade and Price Trends*, A World Bank publication (Baltimore and London: Johns Hopkins University Press, 1981) p. 3.

26. R. N. Cooper and R. Z. Lawrence, 'The 1972–75 Commodity Boom', *Brookings Papers on Economic Activity*, 3 (Washington, DC: The Brookings Institution, 1975) pp. 672–3.

27. C. A. Enoch and M. Panić, 'Commodity Prices in the 1970s', *Bank of England Quarterly Bulletin* (Mar 1981) pp. 42–3.

28. D. G. Newbery and J. E. Stiglitz, *The Theory of Commodity Price Stabilization* (Oxford: Clarendon Press, 1981), p. 14.

29. 'Price Trends in Agricultural Commodities, 1960–81', *Commodity Review and Outlook* (Rome: FAO, 1982).

30. See Raul Prebisch, 'Commercial Policy in the Developing Countries', *The American Economic Review* (May 1959).

31. A. H. Sarris, P. C. Abbott and L. Taylor, 'Grain Reserves, Emergency Relief and Food Aid', in W. R. Cline (ed.) *Policy Alternatives for a New International Economic Order* (New York: Praeger, for the Overseas Development Council), 1982, p. 168.

32. According to the GATT computations, the highest import-weighted nominal tariff in any major product was 25 per cent for clothing.

33. I. Walter, 'Non-Tariff Barriers and the Export Performance of Developing Economies', *American Economic Review* (May 1971).

34. S. Golt, *Developing Countries in the GATT System*, Trade Policy Research Centre (London: Thames Essay No. 13, 1978) p. 11.

35. Final statement by the delegation during the Multilateral Trade Negotiations, statement made by Dr P. Tomić, on behalf of the developing countries (GATT, Document no. MTN/P/5, p. 36).

36. O. Long, Director-General, GATT (GATT Press Release No. 1199, 9 Nov 1977, p. 3).

37. Based on personal conversation with Jan Tumlir, Director, Economic Research Division, GATT. See also, 'Western Protectionism Alarms Trade Officials', by A. Kraus, *International Herald-Tribune*, 25 Jan 1982. He puts this figure at 50 per cent.

38. *International Trade 1980/1* (Geneva: GATT) p. 11.

39. *World Industry since 1960: Progress & Prospects* (Vienna: UNIDO, 1979) p. 18.

40. W. M. Corden, *The Revival of Protectionism*, Occasional Paper no. 14, (New York: Group of Thirty, 1984), p. 13.

41. *The Resurgence of Protectionism in the Industrial Countries* (ECLA: E/CEPAL/1055), p. 5.

42. 'New Protectionism and Attempts at Liberalization in Agricultural Trade', *Commodity Review and Outlook: 1979–80* (Rome: FAO), pp. 109–21.

43. Colombia is on the border-line of becoming a NIC, and India has an industrial sector larger than any developing country other than Brazil and Mexico.

44. W. Hong, and L. B. Krause, *Trade and Growth of Advanced Developing Countries in the Pacific Basin* (Seoul: Korea Development Institute, 1981) p. 36.

45. *The Impact of Newly Industrializing Countries* (Paris: OECD, 1979) p. 6.
46. E. K. Y. Chen, *Hyper-growth in Asian Economies* (London: Macmillan Press, 1979) pp. 11–34.
47. R. Blackhurst, N. Martin and J. Tumlir, *Adjustment, Trade and Growth in Developed and Developing Countries* (Geneva: GATT, Sep 1978) p. 14.
48. B. Balassa, 'Adjustment of External Shocks in Developing Economies', *World Bank Staff Working Paper No. 472* (July 1983).
49. A. M. Soloman, 'Towards a More Resilient International Financial System', *Federal Reserve Bank of New York, Quarterly Review*, New York, Autumn 1983, pp. 1–5. See also A. W. Clausen, *International Trade and Global Economic Growth: A Critical Relationship*, address before the Economic Club of Detroit, 23 May 1984, published by the World Bank, Washington, DC, 1984.

4 THE STRUCTURE AND VOLUME OF BILATERAL RESOURCE FLOWS

1. Much to my chagrin I find a superabundance of the expression 'aid' in the literature for the nominal value of direct and indirect flow of financial resources from the governments of the industrial market economies to LDCs. One of the sources of this misnomer is journalists, who find it handy to use a short, but misleading, expression instead of an accurate, but unwieldy, one – that is, flow of long-term financial resources to developing countries and multilateral agencies. The term 'aid' should not be used loosely in professional writing.
2. The semantics of external resource inflows are of interest in themselves, but not to the present study; the suppliers of financial resources are often referred to as 'donors' even if their assistance is in the form of loans.
3. Cf. Chapter 2, note 2.
4. M. Blackwell, 'Aid Flows: the Role of the DAC', *Finance and Development* (Mar 1984), pp. 42–3.
5. In this work the terms 'aid' or 'assistance' refer strictly to flows which qualify as Official Development Assistance (ODA) according to the DAC definition – that is, grants and loans undertaken by the official sector with (1) promotion of economic development and welfare as the main objective; and (2) having concessional financial terms; meaning thereby in case of a loan, the grant element should be at least 25 per cent. In this work the term 'aid' has not been used loosely; wherever it has been used it complies with the given definition.
6. K. Griffin, 'Economic Development in a Changing World', *World Development*, 9 (Mar 1981) 221–6.
7. An interesting example is that of American aid to Israel, almost one-quarter of all US aid goes to Israel every year. It amounts to $2.7 billion per year – or between $3 500 to $4 000 a year for a family of five in Israel, which is more than what the unemployed get in Detroit.
8. L. Dudley and C. Montmarquette, 'A Model of Supply of Bilateral Foreign Aid', *American Economic Review* (Mar 1976), pp. 132–42.

9. M. L. Weiner and R. Della-Chiesa, 'International Movements or Public Long-term Capital and Grants, 1946–1950', *IMF Staff Papers* (Sep 1954) pp. 113–78.
10. Ibid., p. 163.
11. J. Barnérias, 'International Movement of Public Long-term Capital and Grants, 1951–1952', *IMF Staff Papers* (Feb 1965) pp. 108–27.
12. C. Avramovic and R. Gulhati, *Debt Servicing Capacity and Postwar Growth in International Indebtedness* (Baltimore, Md: Johns Hopkins University Press, 1958, p. 34).
13. Economic Commission for Latin America, *Economic Survey, 1954*.
14. These statistical data come from Avramovic and Gulhati, *Debt Servicing Capacity and Postwar Growth in International Indebtedness,* op. cit., which is one of the few sources available for this period.
15. *International Trade* (Geneva: GATT, 1952).
16. *The World Economic Survey* (New York: UN, 1955).
17. F. X. Colocao, *Economic and Political Considerations and the Flow of Official Resources to Developing Countries* (Paris: Development Centre, OECD, 1973).
18. *The Flow of Financial Resources to Less-developed Countries 1956–1963* (Paris: OECD, 1964), p. 36.
19. *World Economic Survey 1958* (New York: UN, 1959) p. 180.
20. One can mention the war in Vietnam, the US dock strike, the threat of a steel strike, the Japanese dock strike.
21. The source of these data is: *Commodity Trade and Price Trends*, 1978 ed. Report No. EC–166/78 (World Bank, Aug 1978).
22. *Partner in Development*, Pearson Commission Report (London: Pall Mall Pion, 1969), pp. 3–4.
23. *Development Co-operation Review: 1974* (Paris: OECD, 1975) p. 14.
24. Published in June 1969.
25. *Development Co-operation Review: 1973* (Paris: OECD, 1974) p. 13.
26. Ibid. p. 14.
27. The first set of the DAC recommendations in this regard was put forth in July 1965.
28. Two notable studies are: M. J. Harper and K. Kunze, 'The Slowdown in Productivity Growth: Analysis of Some Contributing Factors', *Brookings Papers on Economic Activity*, 2 (1979) 387–421, and J. A. Rasch, 'Energy Resources and Potential GNP', *Federal Reserve Bank of St. Louis Review* (June 1977).
29. The first time it happened was in 1958.
30. The source of these data is: *Commodity Trade and Price Trends*, 1978 ed., Report No. EC–166/78 (Washington, DC: World Bank, Aug 1978).
31. Source of these data is: *World Economic Outlook: 1982* (Washington, DC: IMF, 1983) appx B, table 1, p. 158.
32. R. Dornbusch, *Open Economy Macroeconomics* (New York: Basic Books, 1980), p. 19.
33. Published in February 1980.
34. LDCs with per capita income between $266 and $1 075 in 1975.
35. Cf. Chapter 2.
36. ODA as proportion of the GNP.

37. Of January 1974.
38. *Annual Report* (Washington, DC: IMF, 1975) p. 2.
39. R. M. Solow, 'The Economics of Resources or the Resources of Economics', *American Economic Review, Papers and Proceedings* (May 1974) p. 2.
40. I. F. I. Shihata, *OPEC as a Donor Group, the OPEC Fund for International Development* (Vienna, 1980).
41. I. F. I. Shihata and R. Marbo, 'The OPEC Aid Record', *World Development*, vol. 1979, pp. 161–73 (London: Pergamon Press).
42. Z. Iqbal, 'Arab Concessional Assistance 1975–81', *Finance and Development* (June 1983) pp. 31–3.
43. M. J. William, 'The Aid Programs of the OPEC Countries', *Foreign Affairs* (Jan 1976) pp. 308–24.
44. P. Hallwood and S. Sinclair, *Oil, Debt and Development* (London: Allen & Unwin, 1981).
45. The OPEC members do not concede that higher prices of oil *per se* constitute a case for concessional aid. A Nigerian suggestion to sell oil to the African states at a reduced price was rejected in February 1975 as being contrary to OPEC rules.
46. I. F. I. Shihata and R. Marbo, 'The OPEC Aid Record', op. cit.
47. Ibid.
48. *Annual Report, Organization of the Petroleum Exporting Countries, 1981* (Vienna, 1982) p. 102.
49. *Annual Report, Organization of the Petroleum Exporting Countries, 1982* (Vienna 1937) pp. 56–67.
50. Z. Iqbal, 'Arab Concessional Assistance 1975–81', op. cit.
51. *Annual Report, Organization of the Petroleum Exporting Countries, 1982* (Vienna, 1983). p. 18. Several oil producers are having difficulty selling their ware, so they are offering various financial concessions to entice the potential buyers. See also OPEC, 'Austerity As a Way of Life', *The Economist*, 13 April 1985, pp. 70–1.
52. P. Hallwood and S. Sinclair, *Oil, Debt and Development*, op. cit. pp. 96–9. See also the address given by Dr Awni Shakir Al-Ani, Assistant Director-General of the OPEC Fund for International Development, published in *The OPEC Bulletin*, July 1983, Vienna, pp. 5–9.
53. The expressions Centrally Planned Economies (CPEs) and Non-Market Economies (NMEs) would be interchangeably used. The following countries are covered in this study: Bulgaria, Czechoslovakia, the German Democratic Republic, Hungary, Poland, Romania and the USSR.
54. UNCTAD Secretariat calculations, published in Document No. TD/B/505/Supp. 1.
55. D. Nayyar, (ed.) *Economic Relations Between Socialist Countries and the Third World* (London: Macmillan Press, 1977), pp. 4–5.
56. *World Economic Survey, 1975* (New York: UN, 1976) part I.
57. V. Vassilev, *Policy in the Soviet Bloc on Aid to Developing Countries* (Paris: Development Centre Studies, OECD, 1969).
58. L. Transky, *US and USSR Aid to Developing Countries* (New York, Washington, London: Praeger Publishers, 1967) pp. 5–10.
59. A. Noman, 'Pakistan and Socialist Countries: Politics, Trade and Aid', in

Economic Relations Between Socialist Countries and the Third World, op. cit.
60. R. Porter, 'East, West and South: The Role of Centrally Planned Economies in the International Economy', *Harvard Institute of Economic Research, Paper No. 630* (Cambridge, Mass.: Harvard University Press, 1978).
61. K. Billerbeck, *Soviet Bloc Foreign Aid to the Underdeveloped Countries* (Hamburg: Weltwirtschafts Archiv, 1960).
62. Unlike most recent studies Billerbeck dates the initiation a year earlier.
63. It is easy to see the propaganda line. During this period the Soviet Union did not give any grants, even to its own bloc members.
64. Based on personal correspondence with the author.
65. A. McAuley, and D. Makto, 'Soviet Foreign Aid', *Bulletin of the Oxford University Institute of Economics and Statistics* (Nov 1966) pp. 261–71.
66. V. Vassilev, *Policy in the Soviet Bloc on Aid to Developing Countries*, op. cit. p. 77.
67. L. Transky, *US and USSR Aid to Developing Countries*, op. cit. pp. 27–30.
68. *Flow of Resources to Developing Countries* (Paris: OECD, 1973) p. 415.
69. *Ekonomicheskie otnosheniia sotsialisticheskikh gosudarstv so stranami Afriki* (Moscow: USSR Academy of Sciences, 1973). Quoted in the *World Economic Survey* (New York: UN, 1974) part I, p. 177.

5 INTERNATIONAL CAPITAL MARKET AND THE DEVELOPING COUNTRIES

1. 'International Banking', *The Economist* survey (9 Mar 1984).
2. *World Development Report, 1981* (Washington DC: World Bank, 1982) p. 56.
3. C. S. Hardy, 'Commercial Bank Lending to Developing Countries: Supply Constraints', *World Development* (Feb 1979) pp. 189–98. According to this source international earnings accounted for 95 per cent of the increase in total earnings of thirteen largest US banks during 1970–5 period. As a group these banks derived almost 50 per cent – in one case 80 per cent – of their earnings from their overseas operations.
4. 'International Banking', loc. cit.
5. F. Lees and M. Eng, *International Markets* (New York: London Praeger Publishers, 1975) pp. 5–8.
6. E. E. Hagen, *The Economics of Development* (Homewood, Ill.: Irwin, 1980) p. 126.
7. Both the assumptions were to be proved wrong.
8. I. S. Friedman, *The Emerging Role of Private Banks in the Developing World* (Citicorp, 1977) pp. 6–7.
9. *The Euromarket, Money and Capital Market without National Borders* (Zurich: Union Bank of Switzerland, Jan 1983) p. 4.
10. R. Z. Aliber, 'The Integration of Offshore and Domestic Banking Systems', *Journal of Monetary Economics*, 6 (1980) 509–26.
11. A. E. Fleming and S. K. Howson, 'Conditions in the Syndicated Medium-

term Eurocredit Market', *Bank of England Quarterly Bulletin* (Sep 1980) p. 311.

12. *Borrowings in International Capital Markets*, EC-181/811 (Washington, DC: World Bank, 1981).

13. E. L. Mercaldo, 'Are the Euromarkets too Competitive?', *Euromoney* (Oct 1981) pp. 264–7.

14. P. Engstrom, *Credit Substitution in Eurocurrency Markets by Developing Countries* (Washington, DC: IMF, Department Memoranda Series, DM/74/82, Aug 1974).

15. C. S. Hardy, 'Commercial Bank Lending to Developing Countries: Supply Constraints', op. cit.

16. *International Capital Markets* (Washington, DC: IMF, July 1982).

17. 'Private Bank Lending to Developing Countries', *World Bank Staff Working Paper* no. 482 (1981).

18. D. Delamaide, 'Who is Pulling Out of Country Lending?', *Euromoney* (Sep 1983) pp. 269–71.

19. 'Arab Banking', *Institutional Investor* (Aug 1981) pp. 77–95.

20. Ibid.

21. R. Z. Aliber, *Stabilizing World Monetary Arrangements* (London: Trade Policy Research Centre, 1980).

22. *The Economist* (11 Dec 1982).

23. C. Johnson, 'Banks Will Go On Lending to LDCs', *The Banker* (Nov 1981) pp. 27–30.

24. See the interview of Robert Hunter, Senior Vice-President, Chase Manhattan Bank, *Euromoney* (Aug 1983) p. 38.

25. *How Bankers See the World Financial Market* (New York: Group of Thirty, 1982).

26. Ibid.

27. D. Lascelles, 'Resolutely Keeping Pace With That Brave New World', *The Financial Times*, 7 May 1985.

28. F. A. Lees and M. Eng, 'Developing Country Access to the International Capital Market', *Colombia Journal of World Business* (Fall 1979) pp. 71–84.

29. A clarification, the term 'external bond' means foreign and internal bonds combined.

30. *Development Co-operation, 1969 Review* (Paris: OECD) pp. 56–7.

31. R. G. Hawkins, W. L. Ness and Il SaKong, *Improving the Access of Developing Countries to the US Capital Market* (New York: Center for Study of Financial Institutions, Graduate School of Business Administration, New York University, 1975) p. 22.

32. Ibid.

33. *Development Co-operation, 1976 Review* (Paris: OECD, 1977) p. 71.

34. According to the IMF data, the deficits on current account of the non-oil LDCs were $86.8 billion in 1982 and $68.0 billion in 1983.

35. *Financial Market Trends* (Paris: OECD, Sep 1981).

36. Ibid. p. 104.

37. *The Export Credit Financing Systems* (Paris: OECD, 1982).

38. *Export Credits and Development Financing* (New York: UN, 1966) ST/ECA/95.

39. *International Trade, 1967* (Geneva: GATT, 1968).
40. N. McKitterick and B. J. Middleton, *The Banker of the Rich and the Banker of the Poor* (Washington, DC: Overseas Development Council, 1972) pp. 29–32.
41. This was done by a team led by A. F. Mohammed, and was entitled 'The Use of Commercial Credits by Developing Countries for Financing Imports of Capital Goods', *IMF Staff Papers* (Mar 1970).
42. *Export Credit and Development Financing* (New York: UN, 1966) ST/ECA/95.
43. *The Flow of Financial Resources to Less Developed Countries, 1956–1963* (Paris: OECD, 1964).
44. A. F. Mohammed, 'The Use of Commercial Credits by Developing Countries for Financing Imports of Capital Goods', op. cit.
45. *Development Co-operation, 1976 Review* (Paris: OECD, 1977) pp. 72–5.
46. *Financial Times*, 13 May 1985.
47. A. C. Cizauskas, 'The Changing Nature of Export Credit Finance and Its Implication to Developing Countries', *World Bank Staff Working Paper No. 409* (July 1980).
48. R. Taylor, 'A Case for Export Credit Subsidies', *The Banker*, Feb. 1984, pp. 29–38.
49. 'Failure by OECD to Set Export Credit Rates', *Financial Times* 28 Apr 1983.
50. M. Blomström and H. Persson, 'Foreign Investment and Spillover Efficiency in an Underdeveloped Economy: Evidence from the Mexican Manufacturing Industry', *World Development* **11**, 6 (1983) 493–501.
51. Two notable works are: G. C. Haufbauer and J. Adler, 'Overseas Manufacturing Investment and the Balance of Payments', *Tax Policy Research Paper No. 1* (Washington, DC: US Treasury Department, 1968); and W. B. Reddaway *et al.*, 'Effects of UK Direct Overseas Investment', *DAE Occasional Paper No. 15* (Cambridge: Cambridge University Press, 1967). In both the works the results are unfavourable to the investment outflows from the developed countries.
52. H. C. Bos, M. Sanders and C. Sechhi, *Private Foreign Investment in Developing Countries* (Boston, Mass.: D. Riedel Publishing Co., 1974) p. 7.
53. See Chapter 2.
54. H. C. Bos *et al., Private Foreign Investment . . .*, op. cit.
55. H. W. Singer, 'The Distribution of Gains Between Investing and Borrowing Countries', *American Economic Review* (1950) pp. 473–85.
56. G. D. A. MacDoughall, 'The Benefits and Cost of Private Investment from Abroad: A Theoretical Approach', *Bulletin of the Oxford University Institute of Statistics* (Aug 1960).
57. T. Balogh and P. P. Streeten, 'Domestic vs Foreign Investment', *Bulletin of the Oxford University Institute of Statistics* (Aug 1960).
58. M. C. Kemp, 'Foreign Investment and National Advantage', *Economic Record* (Mar 1962).
59. P. Ady, *Private Foreign Investment and the Developing Countries* (New York, London: Praeger Publishers, 1975) pp. 3–5.
60. C. Stoneman, 'Foreign Capital and Economic Growth', *World Development* (Jan 1975) pp. 11–26.

61. D. Avramovic and R. Gulhati, 'Debt Servicing Capacity and Postwar Growth', in *International Indebtedness* (Baltimore, Md: Johns Hopkins University Press, June 1958).
62. *The International Flow of Private Capital 1946–1954* (New York: UN, Department of Economic Affairs, 1954) II. D.1.
63. *The International Flow of Private Capital 1956–1958* (New York: UN, Department of Economic Affairs, 1959) II.D.2.
64. S. Lall and P. Streeten, *Foreign Investment, Transnationals and Developing Countries* (London: Macmillan Press, 1977).
65. *The International Flow of Private Capital 1956–1958*, see also note 60 above, op. cit.
66. J. H. Dunning, *International Investment* (Harmondsworth, Middx: Penguin Books, 1972) pp. 64–5.
67. *The Growth and Speed of Multinational Companies* (London: The Economic Intelligence Unit, QER Series, no. 5, 1968) pp. 30–2.
68. *Development Assistance, 1971 Review* (Paris: OECD, 1972) pp. 86–8.
69. J. C. Sachdev, 'Foreign Investment Policies of Developing Host Nations and Multinationals: Interactions and Accommodations', *Management International Review*, 18 (1978) 33–43.
70. J. E. Sachs, 'The Current Account and Macroeconomic Adjustment in the 1970s', *Brookings Papers on Economic Activity*, 1 (Washington, DC: The Brookings Institution, 1981) pp. 201–82.
71. D. Goldsbrough, 'Foreign Direct Investment in Developing Countries: Trends, Policy Issues and Prospects', *Finance and Development*, Mar 1985, pp. 31–34.
72. J. Kühn, 'Developing Countries Rethink Their Approach to Foreign Investment', *Intereconomics*, Nov/Dec 1984, pp. 280–92.
73. *Foreign Direct Investment 1973–87* (New York: Group of Thirty, 1984).
74. W. Olle, 'New Forms of Foreign Direct Investment in Developing Countries', *Intereconomics*, July/Aug 1983, pp. 191–8.
75. Ibid., p. 192.
76. *Foreign Private Investment in Developing Countries*, Occasional Paper No. 33 (Washington, DC: IMF, 1985), p. 13.

6 RESOURCE FLOWS TO AND FROM THE MULTILATERAL FINANCIAL INSTITUTIONS

1. *Partners in Development* (Commission on International Development. Chairman: Lester B. Pearson) (New York: Praeger Publishers, 1974) p. 128.
2. *United States Participation in the Multilateral Development Banks in the 1980s* (Washington, DC: Department of Treasury, Feb 1982) pp. 2–4.
3. Ibid., p. 55.
4. Cf. Chapter 4.
5. According to the 1983 *Annual Report* the World Bank lent $10 330 million, which is the highest amount loaned by any donor, bilateral or multilateral.
6. Cf. the fourth section of his chapter, 'Interactions between the multilateral institutions and donors'.

7. W. Baer, 'The World Bank Group and the Process of Socio-economic Development in the Third World', *World Development* (June 1974) pp. 1–10.
8. *The World Bank Policies and Operations* (Washington, DC: IBRD, June 1957).
9. H. G. Johnson, *The World Economy at the Crossroad* (Oxford: Clarendon Press, 1965) p. 71.
10. E. R. Black, 'Financing Economic Development', *United Nations Review*, vol. 8, no. 2, 1972 p. 20.
11. E. S. Mason and R. E. Asher, *The World Bank Since Bretton Woods* (Washington, DC: The Brookings Institution, 1973) pp. 150–95.
12. Ibid.
13. President of the IBRD between 1963 and 1965.
14. R. S. McNamara, *One Hundred Countries, Two Billion People* (New York: Praeger Publishers, 1973) p. 55.
15. Quoted by E. Reid in *Strengthening the World Bank* (Chicago, Ill.: The Adlai Stevenson Institute, 1973) p. 20.
16. McNamara, op. cit. p. 115.
17. *Policies and Operations: The World Bank Group* (Washington, DC: IBRD, 1974) pp. 41–3.
18. *The Economist* (16 Apr 1983) p. 14. See also *The Economist*, 3 Dec 1983, p. 20.
19. The expression 'World Bank group' includes the IDA and the IFC.
20. E. S. Mason and R. E. Asher, op. cit. pp. 201–6.
21. *Annual Report 1970, World Bank*, pp. 23–4.
22. Ibid. p. 26.
23. *Annual Report 1982, World Bank*, p. 12.
24. *Annual Report 1984, World Bank*, p. 15.
25. P. D. Henderson, 'Terms and Flexibility of Bank Lending', in J. P. Lewis and I. Kapur (eds) *The World Bank Group, Multinational Aid and the 1970s* (Lexington, Mass: Lexington Books, 1973).
26. *Annual Report 1973, World Bank*, p. 71.
27. *Annual Report 1982, World Bank*, pp. 52–3.
28. *Financial Times* (3 Mar 1983) p. 4.
29. J. C. Whitehead, 'Sowing the Seeds of Prosperity', *Euromoney* (Oct 1983) p. 243.
30. *Financial Times*, 4 April 1985.
31. Article III, section 4, clause vii.
32. Programme lending is a technique based on the macroeconomic gap analysis. With the help of the Chenery–Strout model it is determined what are the financial needs of an LDC to maintain a certain rate of growth. On the one hand, statistical projections are made for imports, exports, debt service, investment and other variables in the borrowing LDC. On the other hand, macroeconomic projections are made for the borrower's capital requirements. Then the sources of finance and their volume are quantified; these sources are: trade, private investment, export credits, and bilateral and multilateral assistance. In the end the 'gap' between the two, that is, need and availability of financial resources is determined, it is calculated how much of this gap can be filled by the Bank.

33. M. Haq, 'Transfer of Resources', in J. P. Lewis and I. Kapur (eds) op. cit.
34. Cf. note 28.
35. Quoted in *The United States and the Multilateral Development Banks* (Washington, DC: Mar 1974). Committee on Foreign Affairs, Congressional Research Service, Library of Congress.
36. Hearings before a Subcommittee of the Committee on Banking and Currency, US Senate, Eighty-fifth Congress, Second Session, on SR 264, International Development Association (Washington, DC: 1958).
37. IDA, *In Retrospect*, published for the World Bank (New York, London: Oxford University Press, 1982) p.1.
38. W. Baer, 'The World Bank Group and the Process of Socio-economic Development in the Third World', op. cit.
39. IDA, *In Retrospect*, op. cit. pp.23–4.
40. *Special Report to the President and to Congress on the Proposed Replenishment of the Resources of the IDA* (Oct 1973) (Washington, DC: The Committee on Banking and Currency, US Government, 1973).
41. Cf. Chapter 2.
42. IDA, *In Retrospect*, op cit. p.21.
43. Ibid. pp.36–7.
44. Two events which supported the IFC idea were: the Gray Report submitted to President Truman in 1950 and the Rockefeller Report, called *Partners in Progress*, submitted in 1951. Later on, the Treasury Department, Federal Reserve System and the Export Import Bank were to take a negative stance on it.
45. R. L. Garner, President, International Finance Corporation, *Statement at the Tenth Annual Meeting of the Board of Governors of IBRD* (Washington, DC: 1955) p.3.
46. *Annual Report, IFC, 1959* (1960), p.4.
47. U. Kirdar, *The Structure of United Nations Economic Aid to Underdeveloped Countries* (The Hague: Martinus Nijhoff, 1966) pp.176–7.
48. E. R. Black, *Address to the 19th Session of the Economic and Social Council of the United Nations* (IFC, undated) p.6.
49. J. C. Baker, *The International Finance Corporation* (New York: Praeger Publishers, 1968).
50. P. Bayless, 'Merchant Banker of the Third World', *Institutional Investor* (Sep 1982) pp.213–22.
51. *Annual Report of the IFC, 1982*, p.16.
52. P. Bayless, op. cit.
53. *The World Bank, IFC and IDA*, prepared by the Staff of the World Bank, Apr 1962 (Washington, DC: World Bank) pp.99–100.
54. *Annual Report of the IFC, 1982*, p.6. See also International Finance Corporation, *The Banker*, London, March 1985, pp.66–7.
55. L. B. Johnson, *Public Papers of the President of the United States, 1965*, vol. 1, (Washington, DC: US Government Printing Office, 1966) p.397.
56. *Annual Report of the ADB, 1968*.
57. Published in February 1969.
58. ADB, *Quarterly Review* (Apr 1981).
59. N. Peagom, 'Guiding Asia's Growth', *Euromoney* (London: April 1984), pp.S1–S10. See also Gabriel Rosario, 'Is the Asian Development Bank

Lending Too Much?', *The Banker* (London: April 1985), pp. 53–7.
60. J. White, *Regional Development Banks* (London: Overseas Development Institute, 1970) pp. 110–21.
61. *Annual Report of the AfDB* (Abidjan: African Development Bank, 1981) p. 11.
62. Ibid. pp. 33–4.
63. R. K. A. Gardiner and J. Pickett, *The African Development Bank, 1964–1984* (Abidjan, Ivory Coast: African Development Bank, 1984) pp. 161–5.
64. The United States and the Multilateral Development Banks (Washington, DC: Committee on Foreign Affairs, Congressional Research Service, Library of Congress, Mar 1974) pp. 18–19.
65. Ibid. p. 19.
66. J. White, *Regional Development Banks*, op. cit. pp. 164–86.
67. *Annual Report, IDB* (Washington, DC: 1967 Inter-American Development Bank, 1968) p. 61.
68. *Annual Report, IDB* (Washington, DC: 1968 Inter-American Development Bank, 1969) p. 3.
69. J. A. Lynn, *The IDB's First Decade and Perspectives for the Future* (Punta del Este, Uruguay: Inter-American Development Bank, Round Table, Apr 1970) p. 3.
70. A. Ortiz Mena, President, IDB, *Address before the Third Meeting of the United Nations* (Santiago, Chile: 21 Apr 1972).
71. A. Ortiz Mena, President, IDB, *Address at the Thirteenth Meeting of the Board of Governors of the IDB* (Quito, Ecuador: 9 May 1972).
72. *Annual Report, 1981, IDB* (Washington, DC: 1982).
73. *A Partnership in Action, IDB* (Washington, DC: n.d.).
74. *The Wall Street Journal* (New York: 28 Mar 1985).
75. *United States Participation in the Multilateral Development Banks in the 1980s* (Washington, DC: US Treasury, 1982).
76. *The International Monetary Fund: Its Financial Organization and Activities*, Pamphlet Series, No. 42 (IMF, Washington, DC: 1984), p. 77.
77. G. Bird, *The IMF and the Developing Countries* (London: Overseas Development Institute March 1981) pp. 14–15.
78. J. Gold, *Conditionality*, Pamphlet Series, No. 31 (Washington, DC: IMF, 1979) p. 1.
79. T. Killick, *IMF Stabilization Programmes* (London: Overseas Development Institute Working Paper No. 6, Sep 1981).
80. *Annual Report, IMF, 1965*, p. 10.
81. They include measures to control some or all of the following: domestic credit expansion, government expenditure and taxation (related to money supply), foreign indebtedness, prices and wages, trade practices and exchange rate.
82. A. I. MacBean and P. N. Snowden, *International Institutions in Trade and Finance* (London: Allen & Unwin, 1981) pp. 59–60.
83. J. Gold, *Financial Assistance by the International Monetary Fund: Law and Practice*, Pamphlet Series No. 27 (Washington, DC: IMF, 1980) pp. 24–36.
84. J. de Larosière, 'Text of an Address before the Economic and Social Council of the UN; in *IMF Survey* (7 July 1980).
85. G. Bird, *The IMF and the Developing Countries*, op. cit. p. 12.

86. C. Payer, *The Debt Trap: The IMF and the Third World* (Harmondsworth, Middx: Penguin Books, 1974).
87. G. Bird, *The International Monetary System and the Less Developed Countries* (London: Macmillan Press, 1978) p. 17.
88. G. Bird, ibid.
89. It was established by Resolution 2029 (xx), adopted by the UN General Assembly on 22 November 1965, as from 1 January 1966.
90. The following organisations serve as participating and executing agencies of the UNDP: UN, ILO, FAO, UNESCO, WHO, IBRD, ICAO, ITU, WMO, IAEA, UPU, IMCO, UNIDO, UNCTAD, IDB and UNICEF.
91. B. Mores, *UNDP Progress Report 1978* (New York: UN Apr 1979).
92. V. Duchworth-Baker, *Breakthrough to Tomorrow* (New York: UN Centre for Economic and Social Information, 1970) pp. 23–4.
93. *A Report on Growth in the World-wide Work of the UNDP*, II.D.ii (New York: UN 1968) p. 15.
94. A. Robinson, *Future Tasks for UNDP* (London: International Economic Association, 1977) pp. 31–6.
95. *Development Co-operation, 1982 Review* (Paris: OECD, 1983) pp. 79–80.
96. 'Pledges Down – Assistance Plans Cut', *Development in Action* (New York: UNDP, 1983) (Oct–Dec).

Bibliography

I. DOCUMENTAL SOURCES

Asian Development Bank, Annual Report, Manila, The Philippines, Asian Development, various years.

African Development Bank, Annual Report, Adbijan, Ivory Coast, African Development Bank, various issues.

Borrowings in International Capital Markets, EC-181/811, Washington DC, The World Bank, 1981.

Capital Flows and Developing Country Debt, Washington DC, World Bank Staff Working Paper No. 352, World Bank, August 1979.

Commodity Trade and Price Trends, Report No. EC-166/78, Washington, World Bank, August 1978.

Development Assistance, 1968 Review, Paris, OECD, 1969.

Development Assistance, 1969 Review, Paris, OECD, 1970.

Development Assistance, 1970 Review, Paris, OECD, 1971.

Development Assistance, 1971 Review, Paris, OECD, 1972.

Development Assistance Efforts and Policies in 1961, Paris, OECD, 1962.

Development Assistance Efforts and Policies, 1963 Review, Paris, OECD, 1964.

Development Assistance Efforts and Policies, 1964 Review, Paris, OECD, 1965.

Development Assistance Efforts and Policies, 1965 Review, Paris, OECD, 1966.

Development Assistance Efforts and Policies, 1966 Review, Paris, OECD, 1967.

Development Assistance Efforts and Policies, 1967 Review, Paris, OECD, 1968.

Development Co-operation, 1972 Review, Paris, OECD, 1973.

Development Co-operation, 1973 Review, Paris, OECD, 1974.

Development Co-operation, 1974 Review, Paris, OECD, 1975.

Development Co-operation, 1975 Review, Paris, OECD, 1976.

Development Co-operation, 1976 Review, Paris, OECD, 1977.

Development Co-operation, 1977 Review, Paris, OECD, 1978.

Development Co-operation, 1978 Review, Paris, OECD, 1979.

Development Co-operation, 1979 Review, Paris, OECD, 1980.

Development Co-operation, 1980 Review, Paris, OECD, 1981.

Development Co-operation, 1981 Review, Paris, OECD, 1982.

Development Co-operation, 1982 Review, Paris, OECD, 1983.

Development Co-operation, 1983 Review, Paris, OECD, 1984.

External Indebtedness of Developing Countries, Washington DC, International Monetary Fund, June 1981.

Financial Market Trends, Paris, OECD, various issues.

The Flow of Financial Resources to Developing Countries 1965–1963, Paris OECD, 1964.

254

The Flow of Financial Resources to Developing Countries 1973, Paris OECD, 1974.

Inter-American Development Bank, Annual Report, Washington DC, Inter-American Development Bank, various years.

International Capital Markets: Recent Developments and Short-term Prospects, Washington DC, International Monetary Fund, September 1980.

International Financial Statistics, Supplement on Price Statistics, No. 2, Washington DC, International Monetary Fund, 1981.

The International Flow of Private Capital 1946–1952, 1954, II.D.1, New York, United Nations Department of Economic Affairs, 1954.

The International Flow of Private Capital 1956–1958, 1959, II.D.2, New York, United Nations Department of Economic Affairs, 1959.

International Trade, Geneva, General Agreement on Trade and Tariff, various years.

Manual on Statistics Compiled by International Organizations on Countries' External Indebtedness, Basle, Bank of International Settlement, March 1979.

World Development Report 1980, Washington DC, World Bank, 1980.

World Development Report 1981, Washington DC, World Bank, 1981.

World Economic Outlook 1982, Washington DC, International Monetary Fund, 1982.

The World Economic Survey 1955, New York, United Nations, 1956.

The World Economic Survey 1958, New York, United Nations, 1959.

The World Economic Survey 1975, New York, United Nations, 1976.

II. BOOKS

Ady, P. *Private Foreign Investment and the Developing Countries*, New York & London, Praeger Publishers, 1975.

Aliber, R. Z. *Stabilizing World Monetary Arrangements*, London, Trade Policy Research Centre, 1980.

Avramovic, D. and R. Gulhati. *Debt Servicing Capacity and Postwar Growth in International Indebtedness*, Baltimore, Maryland, Johns Hopkins University Press, 1958.

Baker, J. C. *The International Finance Corporation*, New York, Frederic A. Praeger, 1968.

Bird, G. *The IMF and Developing Countries*, London, Overseas Development Institute, Working Paper No. 2, March 1981.

Bird, G. *The International Monetary System and the Less Developed Countries*, London, The Macmillan Press Ltd, 1978.

Bos, H. C., M. Saunders and C. Secchi, *Private Foreign Investment in Developing Countries*, Boston, D. Riedel Publishing Co. 1974.

The Changing Nature of Export Credit Finance and its Implications for Developing Countries, Washington DC, World Bank, World Bank Staff Working Paper No. 409, July 1980.

Colaco, F. X. *Economic and Political Considerations and the Flow of Official Resources to Developing Countries*, Paris, Development Centre, OECD, 1973.

Duchworth-Baker, V. *Breakthrough to Tomorrow*, New York, UN Centre for Economic and Social Information, 1970.

Export Credit and Development Financing, ST/ECA/95, New York, United Nations, 1966.

The Export Credit Financing Systems, Paris, OECD, 1982.

Fred Bergsten, C. *An Analysis of US Foreign Investment Policy and Economic Development*, Washington DC, Agency for International Development, 1976.

Friedman, I.S. *The Emerging Role of Private Banks in the Developing World*, New York, Citicorp, 1977.

Gold, J. *Conditionality*, Washington DC, IMF, IMF Pamphlet Series No. 31, 1979.

Gold, J. *Financial Assistance by the International Monetary Fund: Law and Practice*, Washington DC, IMF, IMF Pamphlet series No. 27, 1980.

The Growth and Spread of Multinational Companies, London, The Economist Intelligence Unit, QER Series No. 5. 1968.

Hagen, E. E. *The Economics of Development*, Homewood, Illinois, Richard D. Irwin Inc. 1980.

Hallwood P. and S. Sinclair, *Oil, Debt and Development*, London, George Allen and Unwin, 1981.

Hawkins, R. G., W. L. Ness and Il SaKong, *Improving the Access of Developing Countries to the US Capital Markets*, New York, Center for Study of Financial Institutions, Graduate Institute of Business Administration, New York University, 1975.

How Bankers See the World Financial Markets, New York, Group of Thirty, 1982.

IDA In Retrospect, New York and London, Published for the World Bank by Oxford University Press, 1982.

International Investment (ed.) J. H. Dunning, London, Penguin Books, 1972.

Johnson, H. G. *The World Economy at the Crossroads*, Oxford, Clarendon Press, 1965.

Killick, T. *IMF Stabilization Programmes*, London, Overseas Development Institute, Working Paper No. 6, 1981.

Kirdar, Ü. *The Structure of United Nations Economic Aid to Underdeveloped Countries*, The Hague, Martinus Nijhoff, 1966.

Lall, S. and P. Streeten. *Foreign Investment, Transnational Corporations and Developing Countries*, London, The Macmillan Press Ltd, 1977.

Lees, F. and M. Eng. *International Markets*, London, Praeger Publishers, 1975.

Lewis, J. P. and I. Kapur. *The World Bank Group, Multilateral Aid in the 1970s*, Lexington, Mass. Lexington Books, 1973.

Lynn, J. A. *The IDB's First Decade and Perspectives for the Future*, Washington DC, Inter-American Development Bank, April 1970.

Mason, E. S. and R. E. Asher. *The World Bank Since Bretton Woods*, Washington DC, The Brookings Institution, 1973.

McKitterick, N. and B. J. Middleton. *The Bankers of the Rich and the Bankers of the Poor*, Washington DC, Overseas Development Council, 1972.

McNamara, R. S. *One Hundred Countries, Two Billion People*, New York, Praeger Publishers, 1973.

Mores, B. *UNDP Progress Report 1978*, New York, United Nations, 1979.

Nayyar, D. *Economic Relations Between Socialist Countries and the Third World*, London, The Macmillan Press Ltd, 1977.

A Partnership in Action, Washington DC, Inter-American Bank, No date.

Partners in Development, Washington DC, Pearson Commission, 1969.

Payer, C. *The Debt Trap: The IMF and the Third World*, Middlesex, England, Penguin Books, 1974.

Porter, R. *East, West and South: the Role of Centrally Planned Economies in the International Economy*, Cambridge, Mass. Harvard Institute of Economic Research, Paper No. 630, Harvard University, 1978.

Private Bank Lendings to Developing Countries, Washington DC, World Bank, World Bank Staff Working Paper No. 482, 1981.

Private Direct Foreign Investment in Developing Countries, Washington DC, World Bank, World Bank Staff Working Paper No. 348, July 1979.

Reid, E. *Strengthening the World Bank*, Chicago, The Adlai Stevenson Institute, 1973.

A Report on Growth in the World-wide Work of the UNDP, 1968.II.D.ii. New York, United Nations, 1968.

Robinson, A. *Future Tasks for UNDP*, London, International Economic Association, 1977.

Shihata, I. F. I. *OPEC As A Donor Group*, Vienna, The OPEC Fund for International Development, 1980.

The United States and the Multilateral Development Banks, Washington DC, Committee on Foreign Affairs, Congressional Research Service, Library of Congress, March 1975.

United States Participation in the Multilateral Development Banks in the 1980s, Washington DC, Department of Treasury, Government of the United States, 1982.

Vassilev, V. *Policy in the Soviet Block on Aid to Developing Countries*, Paris, Development Centre, OECD, 1969.

White, J. *Regional Development Banks*, London, Overseas Development Institute, 1970.

The World Bank, IFC and IDA, Washington DC, Prepared by the IBRD Staff, World Bank, April 1962.

The World Bank Policies and Operations, Washington DC, World Bank, June 1957.

III. ARTICLES

Aliber, R. Z. 'The Integration of Offshore and Domestic Banking Systems', *Journal of Monetary Economics*, No. 6, 1980.

Baer, W. 'The World Bank Group and the Process of Socio-economic Development in the Third World', *World Development*, June 1974.

Balogh, T. and P. P. Streeten. 'Domestic vs Foreign Investment', *Bulletin of the Oxford University Institute of Statistics*, August 1960.

Banerias, J. 'International Movement of Public Long-term Capital and Grants 1951–1952', *IMF Staff Papers*, February 1956.

Bauer, P. and B. Yamey. 'The Political Economy of Foreign Aid', *Lloyds Bank Review*, October 1981.

Einhorn, J. P. 'Co-operation Between Public and Private Lenders to the Third World', *The World Economy*, May 1979.

Fleming, A. E. and S. K. Howson. 'Conditions in the Syndicated Medium-term Euro-credit Market', *Bank of England Quarterly Bulletin*, September 1980.

'A Foot in the Door: A Survey of Banking in the Middle East', *The Economist*, 21 November 1981.

Hardy, C. S. 'Commercial Bank Lending to Developing Countries: Supply Constraints', *World Development*, February 1979.

Harper, M. J. and K. Kunze. 'The Slowdown in Productivity Growth: Analysis of Some Contributing Factors', *Brookings Papers on Economic Activity*, 2, 1979.

Haschek, H. 'What the LDCs Need are Export Credit Schemes', *Euromoney*, September 1980.

'International Direct Investment: A Change in Pattern', *The OECD Observer*, September 1981.

Johnson, C. 'Banks Will Go on Lending to LDCs', *The Banker*, November 1980.

Kemp, M. C. 'Foreign Investment and the National Advantage', *Economic Record*, March 1962.

Killick, T. 'Euromarket Recycling of OPEC Surpluses: Fact or Myth?' *The Banker*, January 1981.

Lees, F. A. and M. Eng 'Developing Country Access to International Financial Markets', *Colombia Journal of World Business*, Fall 1979.

Lewis, J. P. 'Aid Issues: 1981 and Beyond', *The OECD Observer*, November 1981.

McAuley, A. and D. Matko. 'Soviet Foreign Aid', *Bulletin of the Oxford University Institute of Economics and Statistics*, November 1966.

MacDougall, G. D. A. 'The Benefits and Costs of Private Investment from Abroad: A Theoretical Approach', *Bulletin of the Oxford University Institute of Economics and Statistics*, August 1960.

Mercaldo, E. L. 'Are the Euromarkets too Competitive?', *Euromoney*, October 1981.

Mohammes, A. F. 'The Use of Commercial Credits by Developing Countries for Financing Imports of Capital Goods', *IMF Staff Papers*, March 1970.

Sachdev, J. C. 'Foreign Investment Policies of Developing Host Nations and Multinationals: Interactions and Accommodations', *Management International Review*, Vol. 18, 1878.

Shihata, I. F. I. 'The OPEC Aid Record', *World Development*, Vol. 7, 1979.

Singer, H. S. 'The Distribution of Gains Between Investing and Borrowing Countries', *The American Economic Review*, 1950, pp. 473–87.

Solow, R. M. 'The Economics of Resources or the Resources of Economics', *American Economic Review*, Papers and Proceedings, May 1974.

Stoneman, C. 'Foreign Capital and Economic Growth', *World Development*, January 1975.

'Trade Projections and Actual Developments', *Economic Bulletin for Europe*, Vol. 17, No. 2, November 1965.

Wiener, M. L. and R. Della-Chiesa, 'International Movements of Public Long-term Capital and Grants 1946–1950', *IMF Staff Papers*, September 1954.

Williams, M. J. 'The Aid Programs of OPEC Countries', *Foreign Affairs*, January 1976.

IV. UNPUBLISHED MIMEOGRAPHS

Billierbeck, K. 'Soviet Block Foreign Aid to the Underdeveloped Countries', Welt-Wirtschafts Archiv, Hamburg, 1960.

Engstrom, P. 'Credit Substitution in Euro-currency Markets by Developing Countries', IMF Department Memoranda Series, DM/74/82, August 1974.

Hughs, H. 'Industrial Strategies for the 1980s', A paper presented during the seminar on Revised Approaches to Industrialisation in Developing Countries, organised by the Centre for Applied Studies in International Negotiations, Geneva, 4 November, 1982.

Hughs, H. 'Industrialization and Development: A Stocktaking', A paper presented at UNIDO Conference in Vienna, 28–30 June 1976.

Swoboda, A. K. 'International Banking: Its Market and Institutional Structure', A paper presented at Ente Einaudi Conference, at Perugia, Italy, 19–20 September 1981.

Index